NEW

Opportunities

Education for life

Intermediate

Students' Book

Michael Harris
David Mower
Anna Sikorzyńska

PEARSON
Longman

CONTENTS

Exam skills and tasks in the lessons are highlighted in blue

Learning to Learn (p.6–8)

3

		Skills focus	Grammar focus	Skills focus
Module 6 People	**Warm-up** *(p.69)* **Vocabulary:** physical appearance **Listening:** police TV appeal (matching)	**21 Generations** *(p.70–71)* **Vocabulary:** prefixes to make opposites of adjectives (wordbuilding) **Reading:** diary extracts **Reading Strategies:** inferring or 'reading between the lines' **Speaking:** talking about photos; roleplays	**22 People Watching** *(p.72–73)* **Grammar:** modals for speculating (sentence transformations) **Speaking:** speculating about people based on photos	**23 Personality** *(p.74–75)* **Vocabulary:** personality adjectives (1); multi-part verbs (6) **Function:** describing people and speculating **Listening:** radio programme; interviews **Listening Strategies:** true/false questions **Speaking:** describing people
Module 7 Learning	**Warm-up** *(p.81)* **Vocabulary:** preview of key words from the module **Listening:** students talking about learning (matching)	**25 Get Learning!** *(p.82–83)* **Vocabulary:** verbs *get, have, make, take* **Reading:** magazine articles **Reading Strategies:** facts and opinions **Speaking:** describing and talking about a photo; talking about choices	**26 Teachers** *(p.84–85)* **Grammar:** Third Conditional (sentence transformations) **Reading:** magazine article (multiple-choice questions)	**27 Schools** *(p.86–87)* **Vocabulary:** school words; multi-part verbs (7) **Function:** disagreeing and contradicting politely **Pronunciation:** polite disagreement **Listening:** people talking about their old schools; dialogue **Listening Strategies:** multiple-choice questions **Speaking:** contradiction game; talking about school
Module 8 Careers	**Warm-up** *(p.93)* **Vocabulary:** personality adjectives (2); careers **Speaking:** talking about photos	**29 Odd Jobs** *(p.94–95)* **Vocabulary:** collocations; delexicalised verbs *do, make* **Reading:** magazine article **Reading Strategies:** headings and paragraphs (matching) **Speaking:** guessing game	**30 Dangerous Jobs** *(p.96–97)* **Vocabulary:** jobs **Grammar:** reported statements **Speaking:** talking about photos	**31 Getting a job** *(p.98–99)* **Vocabulary:** multi-part verbs (8) **Function:** job interview **Pronunciation:** politeness **Listening:** a job interview; radio documentary **Listening Strategies:** taking notes **Speaking:** roleplays
Module 9 Culture Shock	**Warm-up** *(p.105)* **Vocabulary:** food, famous places, sport **Listening:** describing lifestyles (matching)	**33 Lost in Translation** *(p.106–107)* **Vocabulary:** connotation and translation **Reading:** extracts from Ewa Hoffman's memoirs (true/false questions) **Reading Strategies:** dealing with difficult words **Speaking:** word association game	**34 Living Abroad** *(p.108–109)* **Grammar:** reported questions (sentence transformations) **Speaking:** describing and talking about photos	**35 Mind Your Manners** *(p.110–111)* **Function:** being polite **Pronunciation:** intonation; polite and rude **Vocabulary:** multi-part verbs (9) **Listening:** radio programme; dialogues (matching) **Speaking:** talking about photos; roleplays **Speaking Strategies:** preparing for roleplays
Module 10 Civilisation	**Warm-up** *(p.117)* **Vocabulary:** everyday objects	**37 A Lost City** *(p.118–119)* **Vocabulary:** adjectives (feelings); verbs of movement **Reading:** travel book extracts **Reading Strategies:** word gaps **Speaking:** describing and talking about a photo; information gap	**38 Landmarks** *(p.120–121)* **Grammar:** *wish/should have*	**39 Civilised?** *(p.122–123)* **Vocabulary:** civilisation; multi-part verbs (10) **Function:** giving reasons and examples **Listening:** a TV programme **Speaking:** discussion

Learning to Learn

A Getting Organised

1 Match the module topics in the keywords with the definitions (a–j).

KEY WORDS

Adventure, Stories, Travel, The Media, Advertising, People, Learning, Careers, Culture Shock, Civilisation

a getting knowledge about something or a skill
b jobs or professions you have trained for
c moving from one place to another
d the difficulty you have understanding and adapting to other cultures
e descriptions of events, real or imagined
f men, women and children
g a journey, activity or experience that is strange, exciting and often dangerous
h television, radio and newspapers
i providing information about products and services
j societies and their culture

Choose three modules which you think will be the most interesting.

2 Look through this book and match the descriptions (a–l) with the features below.

Example a = *Comparing Cultures*

a activities focusing on culture
b boxes with important vocabulary
c quotations related to lesson topics
d stories to listen to and read
e monolingual dictionary
f boxes containing strategies
g practice exercises
h boxes with key functions
i list of objectives for each module
j grammar work on difficult areas
k reference section for writing
l articles about English-speaking countries

In this module you will...

FUNCTION FILE

Expressing Opinions

Comparing Cultures

READING STRATEGIES: Prediction

KEY WORDS
cook, diet, dish,

Literature Spot

Review 1

Writing Help

QUOTE ... UNQUOTE

Mini-dictionary

Language Problem Solving

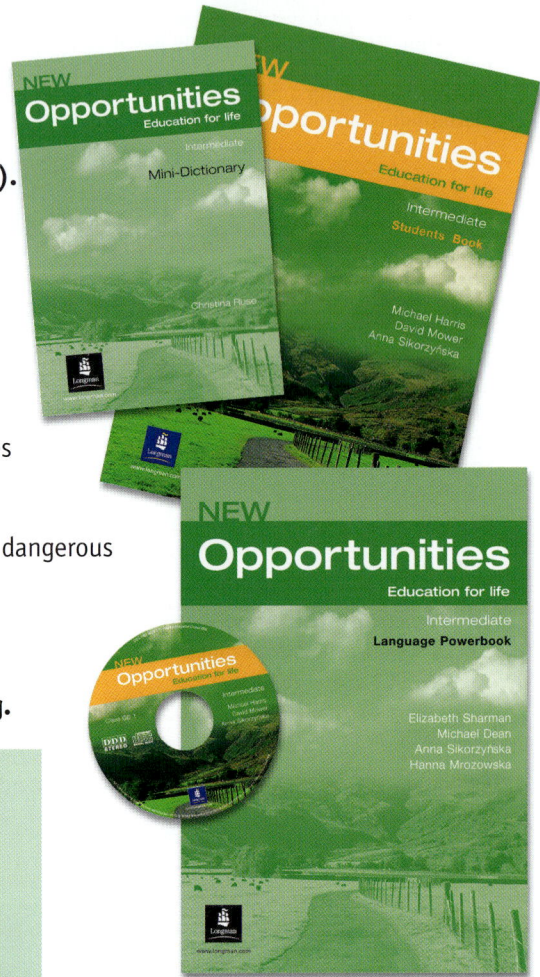

Culture Corner 1

3 What are the best ways of organising vocabulary? Here are some ideas.

- a notebook organised alphabetically or by topic
- small cards for each new word
- topic networks
- tables with groups of words, e.g. shock (*n*), to shock (*v*), shocking/shocked (*adj*)
- lists of useful expressions for different purposes, e.g. expressing opinions

What information are you going to include about new words?

- definitions and example sentences
- translations in your language
- the part of speech of the word, e.g. noun, adjective, verb, etc.
- phonetic symbols, e.g. /θ/

Use these techniques to organise new words from this lesson.

B Word Power

1 English Quiz Try to answer these questions.

1 How many people spoke English in 1000 AD?
  a 2 million   **b** 12 million   **c** 20 million
2 How many people speak it now?
  a 200 million   **b** 500 million
  c a billion
3 What percentage of the world's e-mails are in English?
  a 50%   **b** 80%   **c** 90%
4 How many languages are there in the world?
  a 4,000   **b** 6,500   **c** 9,000

Read the text quickly and check your guesses.

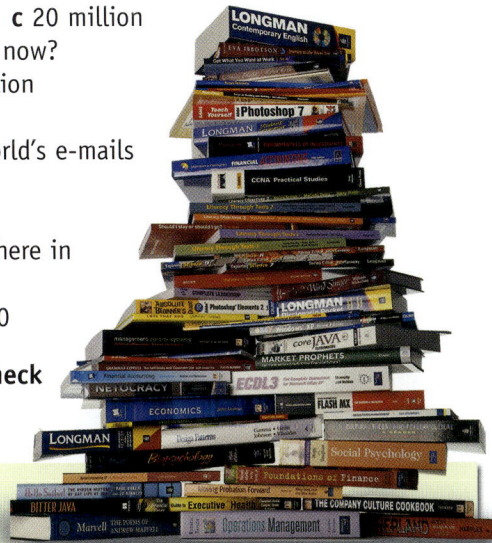

English in the Third Millennium

On the anniversary of Shakespeare's death, Bridget Lewis talks about the future of the English language.

Two thousand years ago English did not exist. A thousand years ago it was a language used by less than two million people. Now it is the most influential language in the world, spoken by more than a billion people on the planet, as their first, second or third language. English
5 currently dominates science, business, the mass media and popular culture. For example, 80% of emails on the Internet are in English. But where will English be at the end of the third millennium?

One view is that English is going to become even more important as a global lingua franca, dominating the world's trade and media while
10 most other languages will become localised or just die out. At present, over half the world's 6,500 languages are in danger of extinction. Another view is that English is already breaking up, as Latin did, into several separate languages. There are already dictionaries of the 'New Englishes', such as Australian English, full of words that a British English
15 speaker would not recognise.

Hopefully, neither of these things will happen. Although different varieties of English will continue to develop around the world, standard English will survive for international communication. In addition, the frightening prospect of a culturally uniform world totally dominated by one language
20 is impossible. Already, other languages are fighting back against the iron grip of English on the Net. Governments around the world are also starting to protect smaller languages and recognise the importance of cultural and linguistic diversity. English will probably stay in control for a long time, at least while the USA remains the top superpower, but it
25 definitely won't become the only language in the world.

2 Read the Strategies.

READING STRATEGIES: Dealing with new words in texts
- Ignore words that you don't need to know to understand the text.
- Try to guess the meaning of important words. Work out the part of speech and use the context to help you guess meanings.
- Use the Mini-dictionary only for important words that you can't guess. Use the part of speech and the context to choose the right word.

Underline all the words in the text that are new for you. Circle those that are very important to understand the text. Then use the Strategies to work out the meaning of these words.

Which words did you have to look up in the Mini-dictionary?

3 Work out the parts of speech of the underlined words below. Can you guess the meanings of the words from the context? Use the Mini-dictionary to help you.

Example
1 = *verb – go round*

Emma left home, **1**rounded the corner on her bike and saw a **2**round metal object on the road. It went **3**round and round in circles making a strange noise. Suddenly, a man came **4**round the corner and fired a **5**round of ammunition at the object before picking it up. Then he looked **6**round and said, 'That's about the tenth alien I've **7**rounded up this week.' He **8**rounded off his speech with a bow and several passersby gave him a **9**round of applause. Emma thought to herself, 'There are some very strange people **10**round here!'

C Doctor Grammar

3 Read the text to get the general idea. Then complete it with the words in the table.

ARTICLES	PREPOSITIONS	QUANTITY EXPRESSIONS
a, the	of, to, from, in	some, all

Example **1** *a*

'My Language' by Haydn Evans

Welsh is **1**_____ Celtic language that is spoken in **2**_____ principality of Wales, with **3**_____ speakers in Patagonia in **4**_____ south **5**_____ Argentina. It is very different **6**_____ English. For example, 'Welcome **7**_____ Wales' is 'Croesu i Cymru' in Welsh. The Celts arrived **8**_____ Europe in **9**_____ fifth century BC. When **10**_____ Anglo-Saxons invaded Britain, the British Celts moved west and northwards. Before **11**_____ sixteenth century, Wales had **12**_____ rich literary tradition and everybody in Wales spoke Welsh. After **13**_____ unification of Wales with England in 1536, Welsh was banned and it declined rapidly. Until the 1960s, Welsh was not taught in schools and English was the only official language. A few years ago, only 500,000 out **14**_____ a population of nearly three million spoke Welsh and **15**_____ people thought that **16**_____ language was dying out. However, now it is growing again: Welsh is used in government, there is **17**_____ Welsh TV station and it is now taught in nearly **18**_____ schools.

---

1 In pairs, use the words below to write as many sentences as possible in five minutes. Sentences must be grammatically correct and must make sense!

Example
Yesterday, Mary left the zoo and took a lot of animals home.

crocodile Mary animals will home goes has was is left zoo the took a watching bigger lot study and to of yesterday tomorrow if than gone

2 Tell your answers to the class. Which of these structures did you use?

Present Simple, Present Continuous, Future forms (x 2), Present Perfect, Past Simple, Past Continuous, Conditionals, Comparison of adjectives, Quantity expressions, Modals of obligation, The passive

4 How well can you use the structures below? Use this scale.

*** I can use this structure with very few problems.
** I have a few problems and I make mistakes.
* I don't understand this structure!

Question forms	Prepositions (e.g. *of, to, from, in*)
Present Simple	Modals of obligation
Present Continuous	The passive (present, past)
Present Perfect	Comparison of adjectives
Future forms	Countables/uncountables
Past Simple	Quantity expressions (e.g. *some, a lot*)
Past Continuous	Articles (*a, an, the*)
Conditionals	

5 Look at the ways of organising grammar notes below.

a tables (e.g. of verb tenses)
b lists (e.g. of irregular verbs)
c time lines (e.g. to contrast tenses)
d examples with translations (e.g. to contrast structures with your language)

Choose one of the grammar areas from Exercise 4 and organise some notes.

6 Write a short composition about your language like the one about Welsh.

1 Adventure

Warm-up

1 **Look at the Key Words. Which activities would you describe as 'adventure'?**

KEY WORDS: Adventure

Explore: a desert, a desert island, another planet, a rainforest
Visit: cities around the world, famous museums, a volcano
Go: canoeing, diving, flying, parachuting, sailing, skiing
Go on: a cruise, a round-the-world trip, a safari, a trek

Add these words to the Key Words.

ancient buildings, climbing, a polar region, a scientific expedition

2 **You will hear four people talking about their 'dreams'. What would they like to do?**

Example
1 *visit the Pyramids*

3 **Listen again. Match the speakers (1–4) with the way they describe their dreams (a–e). There is one extra description.**

a challenging **b** fascinating **c** frightening
d educational **e** exciting

4 **Work in pairs. Is there somewhere you have always wanted to go? Talk about some of your 'dreams'.**

- Where would you like to go?
- What would you like to do?
- What would it be like?

Example
I'd like to go on a safari in South Africa. I've always loved wild animals and I'd love to see them in their natural environment. I think it would be really exciting.

1 Explorers

Captain Scott and his companions

Before you start

1 Look at the photos. Answer the questions for each photo.

1 Where do you think the people are?
2 When and why do you think they went there?
3 How do you think they travelled?
4 How do you think they felt when they got there?

Now read the text quickly and check your guesses.

On 1 June, 1910, Captain Scott left London to begin his Antarctic expedition. He received a telegram from the
5 Norwegian explorer Roald Amundsen: 'I'm going South.' So the race to the South Pole was on!

During the polar summer of 1910–11, both teams organised food
10 stores – they put food in tents along their route in preparation for their expeditions the following year. Then came the darkness of the polar winter. Scott and Amundsen waited for the
15 first signs of spring.

Amundsen was the first to leave on 15 October, 1911. He had teams of dogs pulling his sledges and all his men were on skis. Because of this,
20 he made good progress. Scott left on 1 November and soon had problems. First, his two motor sledges broke down and then his ponies began to have serious difficulty with the snow
25 and the cold. After a while, Scott and his men had to push the sledges themselves.

Amundsen reached the Pole on 14 December and put a Norwegian
30 flag there. Then he prepared for the return journey.

Scott finally arrived at the Pole with four companions on 17 January and found the Norwegian flag.
35 Scott wrote of their disappointment in his diary:

'Well, we lost the race and we must face 800 miles of hard pushing – and goodbye to most of our dreams.'
40 The return journey was one of the worst in the history of exploration. The men were exhausted and were running out of food. The weather conditions were
45 terrible. Scott began to realise their desperate situation: 'We appear very cheerful but what each man feels in his heart, I can only guess. Putting on our shoes in the morning is getting
50 slower and slower.'

The expedition wasn't completely unsuccessful because on their way back, they looked for rocks and fossils as planned. They carried
55 twenty kilos of rocks all the way with them. Later, these rocks proved that in the distant past Antarctica was covered by plants.

However, disaster soon came.
60 One of the men, Edgar Evans, died after a bad fall. The next to die was Captain Oates, who was having difficulty in walking. Scott recorded his death sadly in
65 his diary:

'He said, "I am just going outside and I may be some time." We knew that poor Oates was walking to his death. We tried to stop him but we
70 knew that it was the act of a brave man and an English gentleman. We all hope to meet the end with a similar spirit, and certainly the end is not far.'

Scott and the last two men
75 carried on and got within eleven miles of one of their food stores. But then a storm started and they could not leave their tent. Scott spent his last hours writing. He wrote a letter
80 full of sadness to his wife, Kathleen:

'To my Widow, I could tell you lots about this journey. What stories you would have for the boy ... But what a price to pay.'
85 Scott's diary told the story of their sad end:

'The food is only 11 miles away but I do not think we can hope for any better things now. We are getting
90 weaker and weaker and the end can't be far ... I do not think I can write more.'

The news of Scott's death and disastrous expedition shocked the
95 world. He had failed to win the race to the Pole but the remarkable bravery shown by Captain Scott and his men made them into heroes.

Roald Amundsen

Reading

**2 Read the text more carefully.
Are these statements true (T) or false (F)?**

1 ☐ Scott and Amundsen started their journeys in the polar spring.
2 ☐ Scott's use of motor sledges and ponies was a success.
3 ☐ Amundsen travelled more quickly than Scott.
4 ☐ When they got to the Pole, Scott celebrated.
5 ☐ Captain Oates went out and got lost in a storm.
6 ☐ Scott's last letter was to his wife.

3 Read the Strategies.

READING STRATEGIES: Multiple-choice questions

- Read the questions and the alternative answers (a–c).
- Decide what kind of information you are looking for (e.g. a date, a description).
- Find the part of the text where you think the answer is.
- Read that part carefully and choose an answer – according to the text.
- Remember, you may have to 'read between the lines' – the answer does not always have the same words as one of the alternatives!
- Make sure the other alternatives are not possible answers.

Now choose the best answer (a, b or c) according to the text.

1 Amundsen started for the South Pole on …
a 15 October, 1911. b 1 November, 1911.
c 14 December, 1911.
2 Scott's expedition first had problems because …
a his ponies had difficulties. b the men were hungry. c his motor sledges didn't work.
3 When Scott's expedition arrived at the Pole, the men felt …
a cheerful. b disappointed. c relieved.
4 Scott's men collected rocks and fossils because …
a they had lots of free time. b it was part of their original plan. c they were interested in geology.
5 Scott couldn't get to the food store because …
a he wasn't strong enough. b the weather was too bad. c the tent was too far away.

4 Discuss these questions.

1 Why did Amundsen succeed and Scott fail?
2 What do you think Scott's expedition achieved?
3 Why did Scott and his men become heroes?
4 How did you feel when you read the story?

5 Your Culture What explorers, climbers or travellers do you know in your country? What have they done?

Vocabulary: Wordbuilding

6 Look at the words in *italics*. Are they a noun, verb, adjective or adverb?

1 The Norwegian expedition was *successful*.
2 They *succeeded* in reaching the Pole first.
3 They completed their objective *successfully*.
4 Scott's expedition was not a *success*.

7 Work in pairs. Make adjectives, adverbs and verbs from the nouns below (if possible). Use the Mini-dictionary to help you.

ambition, bravery, death, desperation, difficulty, exhaustion, explorer, organisation, sadness, success

Example
ambitious (adj), ambitiously (adv) – verb not possible

8 Complete the sentences. Use the word in brackets to make a new word. All the new words are in the text.

1 _____ for the expedition began during the polar summer. (prepare)
2 They couldn't travel in the _____ of the polar winter. (dark)
3 Scott knew that _____ was near (die).
4 The expedition was _____ (disaster) but Scott is a legend in the world of _____ (explore).
5 His men are remembered for their _____ (brave) in the face of great _____ (difficult).

Speaking

9 Work in pairs. Take turns to say sentences about the two expeditions. Use words from Exercises 7 and 8.

Example
A *Amundsen was a great explorer.*
B *Yes, he prepared for his journey well.*

10 Work in pairs. Student A reads about Marek Kamiński on page 129. Student B reads about Helen Thayer on page 130.

Now find out about your partner's explorer. Ask questions about:

- nationality • age • main expeditions
- greatest journey • method of travel
- aims of the journey • other interests and activities

Example
Where is Helen Thayer from? How old is she?

QUOTE ... UNQUOTE
'The main thing is just to go!'
Marek Kamiński, Polish explorer. (1964–)

2 Travellers' Tales

Before you start

1 Read about the travellers and choose the best answers for these questions (a, b or c).

1 How do Christina and Benedict both make a living?
 a from charities
 b from their books and TV
 c by meeting exotic people
2 Where have they both been?
 a New Guinea b the Amazon
 c Antarctica
3 What are they both *not* doing at the moment?
 a promoting books b working for radio c travelling

2 Read these questions and answers. Match the answers with Christina (C) or Benedict (B).

1 Do you get lonely?
 ☐ No, because I make friends on my journeys.
2 Where do you live?
 ☐ On a farm.
3 Are you doing any radio programmes at the moment?
 ☐ Yes, I'm doing a programme about Ethiopia.
4 Have you ever been to the Arctic?
 ☐ No, I haven't been there.
5 How long have you been a travel writer?
 ☐ Since my mid-twenties, I suppose.

Christina Dodwell was born in Nigeria and has always loved travelling. She has been a traveller and travel writer since her mid-twenties. She has made journeys by horse around Africa, New Guinea and Turkey. She has also travelled by canoe, dog sledge and microlight in China, Kamchatka and West Africa, though she hasn't been to the Poles.

Christina once spent time with cannibals but doesn't worry about danger. She never shows fear and when she thinks there could be trouble, she says, 'My husband is a policeman. He's waiting for me in the next village.'

Christina lives with her husband on a farm surrounded by horses and cattle. She works for a charity that she set up to help the Third World and she often makes TV and radio programmes. She is now working on a programme for BBC radio about indigenous culture in Ethiopia. Her books have been translated into several languages.

Benedict Allen is an experienced explorer who has visited remote natural environments all over the world. He has lived with the Amazon Indians, with a tribe in New Guinea and with Aborigines in Australia. He has crossed the Amazon forest with no map or compass, walked across the mountains of New Guinea and canoed from New Guinea to Australia. He has also made journeys across the Gobi and Namib deserts on foot and by camel and trekked across the Arctic. He has been lost in the jungle more than once and survived by copying the local tribes and eating plants.

Benedict doesn't like travelling with people and he usually makes films of his journeys without a film crew. He doesn't get lonely because he makes friends wherever he goes, even of his camels! He also talks to his video camera.

'It's getting hot out here. Hotter than I've ever been,' he said on his trip in Namibia when temperatures reached 50°C.

Benedict has worked for the BBC for years and has made several television series. He has also written nine books. His TV programmes and books have made him very popular in the UK. He isn't travelling at the moment but is promoting his latest book, *Icedogs*, about a 1,000-mile trek through Siberia.

Presentation

3 Name the tenses in the sentences <u>underlined</u> in the texts. Then match them with the uses (a–g).

a activities that happen regularly
b permanent situations/states
c things that started in the past and continue up till now
d past events that have clear results in the present
e events that happened in the past but it doesn't matter when
f activities happening now, at the time of speaking
g activities happening during a limited period of time around the present.

Find more examples of these tenses in the texts. Identify their uses (a–g).

Practice

4 Look at the sentences and decide which of the people <u>couldn't</u> say them. Explain why.

1 I'm living in Dublin.
a a Dubliner   b an exchange student studying in Dublin   c someone on a one year contract in Dublin
2 I work in an office.
a a student on a holiday job   b a secretary   c an accountant
3 I've been a traveller since I was 18.
a a traveller   b a travel writer   c a retired traveller

5 Put the verbs in brackets into the Present Simple, the Present Continuous or the Present Perfect.

I **1**_____ (work) as a botanist since graduation. I **2**_____ (teach) students at the university but I also **3**_____ (spend) a lot of time travelling. I **4**_____ (have) some professional success – I **5**_____ (just discover) an unknown orchid in Indonesia. At present, I **6**_____ (study) a rare Asian plant which Chinese medicine **7**_____ (use) to cure rheumatism. I **8**_____ (collect) leaves and flowers to examine their properties. I **9**_____ (examine) over ten plants so far. I **10**_____ (believe) my job is interesting and useful.

6 Use the notes about a scientist's life to write sentences in the Present Simple, the Present Continuous or the Present Perfect.

Example
1 *I've already done a lot of research on Australian culture.*
I regularly work for animal organisations.
I'm doing very little academic work at the moment.

1 do
a lot of research on Australian culture already
work for animal organisations regularly
very little academic work at the moment

2 be
a traveller and a scientist
interested in Australia all my life

3 work
as a scientist since 1991
at Lancaster University as an ethnographer
on a book about Australian food and drink

4 write
more than twenty articles about Australia
books on Australian customs
a book on the life of Australian Aborigines

5 live
in Lancaster
in the UK for twenty years
among Australian Aborigines in order to do research for the book

7 Use the cues below to write a travel questionnaire. Add more questions if you like.

1 ever travel abroad?
2 ever live abroad?
3 how many countries/be to?
4 like travelling?
5 plan a trip/holiday anywhere at the moment?
6 how many languages/speak?
7 what languages/learn at the moment?
8 interested in any country/culture?

Now work in pairs. Ask and answer questions. Tell the class something about your partner.

8 Personalisation Work in pairs. Think of a person that you know. Write sentences about what he/she *does, is doing* and *has done* in his/her life. Tell your partner.

Example
My aunt Monica teaches archaeology at the university. She is learning to hang-glide. She has climbed some of the highest mountains in Europe.

Pronunciation: Contractions

9 Read the sentences and decide what 's stands for, *has* or *is*.

1 He's gone abroad.
2 She's got a new car.
3 John's having a shower.
4 Pat's done a lot for her school.
5 Mike's a nice man.
6 The cat's drinking milk.

Listen to how 's is pronounced in the sentences and mark them with /s/ or /z/. Listen again and repeat the sentences.

SKILLS FOCUS

3 Extreme Sports

Before you start

1 Look at the photos and the Key Words. Answer the questions.

1 What is happening in each photo?
2 How do you think the people feel?
3 Which sport do you think is the most dangerous? Why?
4 Have you ever tried any of these extreme sports? Which ones? What was it like?
5 Which sports would you like to try? Why?

KEY WORDS: Extreme Sports

bungee jumping, extreme mountain biking, extreme skiing, ice-canyoning, ice diving, skysurfing, snowboarding, snowrafting, white water rafting

Are any of the Key Words similar in your language?

Listening

2 Read the Strategies.

LISTENING STRATEGIES: Preparation

- Before you listen, always look for clues that will help you understand what you are going to listen to (e.g. the title, captions, pictures, etc.).
- Read the questions carefully to help you listen for specific/relevant information.
- Use your knowledge of the world to try to predict answers to the questions.
- Guess the answers which you can, then check when you are listening.

3 Use the Strategies to answer the questions below.

1 People do extreme sports in order to feel …
   a excited.   b nervous.   c happy.
2 Extreme sports have become popular in the last …
   a 5 years.   b 10 years.   c 20 years.
3 People usually bungee jump from …
   a aeroplanes. b high buildings. c bridges.
4 In skysurfing people do mid-air …
   a gymnastics.   b dancing.   c swimming.
5 Skysurfing has similarities with …
   a skiing.   b surfing.   c canoeing.
6 Snowrafting is …
   a quite dangerous.   b very dangerous.
   c not very dangerous.
7 For white water rafting you need …
   a a big river.   b a warm river.   c a mountain river.
8 Ice divers …
   a swim under the ice.   b walk on the bottom of lakes.   c walk upside down under the ice.

🎧 **Listen to a TV programme and check your answers.**

🎧 **4 Listen to two people talking about extreme sports. Complete the table.**

Sports	Carol	Jonathan
likes		
doesn't like	*tennis*	
would like to try		
wouldn't like to try		*bungee jumping*

🎧 5 Listen again. Complete the Function File with the following words.

quite like, 'd love, can't stand, love, like, wouldn't like, 'd quite like, prefer, hate, 'd prefer

FUNCTION FILE

Preferences

+ 'ing' or noun	+ to + infinitive
I ¹_____ bungee jumping.	I ²_____ to try skysurfing.
	I ³_____ to do snowrafting.
I ⁴_____ doing boring sports.	I ⁵_____ to stay at home.
I ⁶_____ winter sports.	
I ⁷_____ going skiing.	
I ⁸_____ snowboarding.	
I ⁹_____ slow sports.	I ¹⁰_____ to go ice diving.

6 Use these words to write sentences about your preferences.

skiing, rock climbing, playing basketball, bungee jumping, swimming, sailing, snowboarding, playing tennis, ice-skating, ski-jumping

Examples
I love skiing. (You often ski.)
I'd love to try skiing. (You have never skied.)

Vocabulary: Multi-part Verbs (1)

7 Replace the verbs in *italics* with the words below in the correct form. Use the Mini-dictionary to help you.

not to do it, organise, love, arrive, wear, do (it) as planned, explain, start doing

I decided to ¹*take up* bungee jumping and now I ²*am* (really) *into* it. When I ³*turned up* for my first jump, I was so nervous that I tried ⁴*to back out* but my friends persuaded me to ⁵*go through with* it. You don't have to ⁶*put on* any special clothes, just a sweater and jeans but obviously you need a lot of time to ⁷*set up* the equipment. But it's worth waiting for. It's difficult to ⁸*get across* the excitement of bungee jumping.

8 Complete the sentences with a multi-part verb from Exercise 7 in the correct form.

1 Ann waited for Tom for ages but he didn't _____.
2 What kind of music _____ you _____?
3 A friend of mine has just _____ jogging to get fit.
4 Why don't we _____ our computer in the study?
5 He said he would help but _____ at the last minute.
6 She had to make a speech but got so nervous she couldn't _____ it.

🎧 9 Pronunciation Listen to the questions below. In which of them does the intonation go up at the end?

SPORTS QUESTIONNAIRE

1 What sports do you like doing?
2 Do you like watching sport on TV?
3 Have you ever turned up late for a match?
4 If you are in a school team, would you ever try to back out? Why?
5 Do you think you'll ever take up a dangerous sport?
6 What extreme sports would you like to try?
7 What extreme sports couldn't you go through with?
8 Have you ever watched extreme sports on TV?

🎧 Listen again and repeat the questions.

Speaking

10 Work in pairs. Use the questionnaire to interview your partner.

Example
A *What sports do you like doing?*
B *I'm really into ice hockey.*

Is your partner:
a very/quite/not very keen on sport?
b very/quite/not very interested in extreme sports?

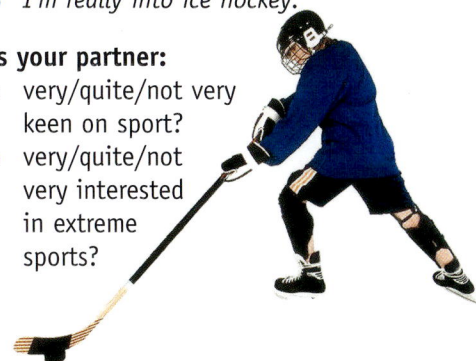

QUOTE ... UNQUOTE
'Adventure is the champagne of life.'
G.K. Chesterton, English writer
(1874–1936)

4 Communication Workshops

Speaking

Before you start

1 Read the holiday adverts (A–D). Which holiday …

1 is the cheapest?
2 offers the longest holiday?
3 doesn't mention flights?
4 offers some hotel accommodation?

2 Now listen to the dialogue and answer these questions.

1 Which holiday do Ricky and Shulah choose?
2 What reasons do they give?

3 Pronunciation: showing interest Listen to how Ricky and Shulah show that they are listening to each other.

Really?, Mm, Yes?, True, Yeah, That's true, No, I know

Listen again and repeat the words and sounds.

Choosing a Holiday

You have won a holiday. Work in pairs and negotiate the best holiday to go on together. Follow the stages.

Stage 1

Choose one of the trips you want to go on and one you don't. Look at the Key Words and make notes about your reasons:

• the trip   • the activities   • the accommodation
• the price • the weather

KEY WORDS: Opinions
boring, changeable, cold, comfortable, dangerous, difficult, educational, exciting, expensive, good value for money, interesting, lots of variety, luxurious, no privacy, rainy, reasonably priced, safe, sunny, tiring, uncomfortable

Example
A trip I'd like to go on : the Turkish trip
exciting – white water rafting
lots of variety – rafting, exploration, archaeology
comfortable – guest houses

Stage 2

Use your notes and the Function File on page 15 to prepare what you are going to say. Practise saying some sentences. Don't write down everything!

Eco-tourism in Sri Lanka Explore the beautiful island of Sri Lanka. See rare and exotic plants and animals. Relax at night around the camp fire. Visit ancient temples and palaces. Two weeks shared accommodation in tents. Experienced guides. €2,100.

A

WILDLIFE SAFARI

€2,250

Food and flights included.

Extra option of river canoeing.

Two weeks on safari in the reserves of South Africa. Open-topped vehicles for observing animals. Accommodation in four-star hotels and tents.

B

WHITE WATER EXPERIENCE

Two weeks rafting on the Çoruh River in Turkey. Explore this remote area. Meet friendly villagers and visit the ruins of Byzantine castles.

Experienced instructors. Accommodation in comfortable guest houses. €1,750. Flights and food included.

Extra options: four days in Istanbul or walking in the Kaçkar Mountains.

C

Patagonian Adventure Explore southern Argentina and Chile.

Three-week trips. Accommodation in tents. Transport by four-wheel-drive vehicles. Experienced guides. €2,800. Food and flights included. Mountaineering and skiing are extra options.

D

Stage 3

Read the Strategies.

Now, in pairs, try to agree on a choice of holidays.
- **A** – suggest a holiday and give your reasons.
- **B** – reject A's suggestion and give reasons. Suggest an alternative holiday.
- **A and B** – try to agree on one of the holidays or an alternative one.

Talkback

Tell the class which holiday you chose. Which are the most popular and least popular holidays?

Listening

Before you start

1 How do you think polar expeditions now are different from those in Captain Scott's time?

A Radio Programme

Listen to the programme about Marek Kamiński.

🎧 **2 Listen to the interview and answer these questions.**

1 Marek's two most famous polar expeditions were in …
   a 1991.   **b** 1995.   **c** 1999.
2 He went to the two Poles in …
   a May and November.
   b March and December.
   c May and December.
3 His biggest problem on the journey to the Antarctic was …
   a the strong wind.   **b** the low temperature.
   c the rough ground.
4 At university, Marek Kamiñski studied …
   a languages.   **b** literature.
   c philosophy.
5 He believes the key to a successful expedition is your …
   a legs.   **b** brain.   **c** heart.

3 Work in groups. Discuss Marek's statements.

- 'The limits are in us, not outside us.'
- 'The most important thing is your dreams.'

Writing

Before you start

1 Read Janet's letter and match the parts (1–6) with these topics (a–f).

a an excuse to stop writing	**d** extra information
b introductory questions	**e** what they are doing
c the people in the group	**f** where they are

> Hi Tania!
>
> ① *How are you? I hope the summer job is going well. Have you decided where to go on holiday? That skiing break sounds the best, doesn't it?*
>
> ② *Anyway, as you know, we're camping here on the Isle of Skye. We're staying on a campsite in the middle of nowhere. We've been here for five days but it feels longer. It's rained every single day! Everything is wet – our shoes, sleeping bags, all our clothes!*
>
> ③ *Luckily, we didn't come here for the nightlife! Actually, there isn't any! But then we're all too tired at the end of the day anyway. We go walking every day and yesterday we saw some seals. We've all tried windsurfing, but we're not very good. This afternoon I fell into the sea five times!*
>
> ④ *Our news: Predictably, Tim has fallen in love with half the girls on the campsite. Tom is complaining about everything and Colin is still trying to be funny all the time. So you can imagine what it's like!*
>
> ⑤ *Well, I must finish – it's my turn to cook tonight. Write back soon – I'll be home on Monday (15th).*
>
> Cheers, Janet.
>
> ⑥ *P.S. Brian phoned before we left – he wants you to get in touch.*

2 Find examples of informal style in the letter.
- greetings and goodbyes
- linking words at the beginning of sentences (e.g. *Anyway* …)
- contractions (e.g. *we're*)

A Personal Letter (1)

Write a letter to a friend. Follow the stages and use Writing Help 1 on page 140.

Stage 1

Imagine you are on an adventure holiday. Make notes on:

- the time of year, the place and what it is like
- the weather and how you are spending your time
- the people you are with and what they are like
- the people you have met and something interesting about them

Stage 2

Use your notes to plan paragraphs like Janet's and write your letter. Use linking words.

Stage 3

Check your letter.

Talkback

Work in groups. Read each other's letters. Which holiday sounds the most interesting?

Language Problem Solving 1   State and activity verbs

Himalayan Adventure

Are you bored and fed up? Are you dreaming about exciting holidays? Are you thinking of getting away from it all?

Come to the Himalayas with us! At *Adventure Holidays*, we **understand** the needs of trekkers. We **realise** that trekking can be hard work and think that trekkers need our help. Our guides have several years' experience and **know** the best routes; our cooks **prepare** local meals – they are spicy and **taste** delicious; our porters **carry** your luggage which **means** that you can simply enjoy the experience. There are also special offers for people who **don't want** to go straight home afterwards. If you **like** history, there is a trip to northern India. For people who **prefer** to spend some time on the coast, we can organise your travel and accommodation.

The trek **costs** €4,000 and that includes all flights and accommodation.

Phone 0800 479324 for a free brochure.

1 Read the advert. Would you like to go on this holiday?

2 Which of the verbs in bold describe activities and which describe states/feelings? Copy and complete the table.

STATES/FEELINGS	ACTIVITIES
realise	carry

Add more verbs from the text to each column.

3 Read what a trekker has written in a postcard from Nepal. Which verbs in bold, state or activity, are used in the continuous tenses?

Hi Ellen,
It's amazing! Just imagine! I'm **sitting** in front of my tent and **looking** at Mount Everest. I just **don't believe** it. I'm **drinking** local tea, which **tastes** slightly smoky. Me, who never **drinks** tea at home. I **don't understand** what's happened to me. Pat and Jim **are taking** photos of the mountains, as Mount Everest **looks** absolutely stunning today. They **realise** they probably won't get another chance as it's our last day. You **know** I **miss** you.
                              Love Chris

Complete the rule with *state* and *activity*:

We can use _____ verbs in continuous and simple tenses and we use _____ verbs only in simple tenses.

4 Read these pairs of sentences. Translate the verbs in blue into your language. Does the verb mean the same in both sentences?

1 a Our guides have several years' experience.
   b Are you having dreams about holidays?
2 a We also think that trekkers need our help.
   b Are you thinking of getting away from it all?
3 a Mount Everest looks absolutely stunning today.
   b I'm looking at Mount Everest.

5 Which sentences cannot be changed into the Present Continuous?

a The coffee tastes awful.
b We have lunch very early.
c She thinks she is the best.
d I have a splitting headache.
e She thinks about her boyfriend all the time.

6 Read this interview with a Nepalese guide and put the verbs in brackets in the Present Continuous or the Present Simple.

Interviewer **1**_____ (you like) your job?

Guide Oh, yes. I **2**_____ (love) it. I **3**_____ (enjoy) meeting new people.

Interviewer What **4**_____ (you think) of the tourists who **5**_____ (come) to Nepal?

Guide Some of them **6**_____ (not know) much about mountains and **7**_____ (want) to see as much as possible. Right now, I **8**_____ (work) for a group of Austrian trekkers. They **9**_____ (understand) all about trekking and I'm sure they **10**_____ (enjoy) themselves. That's great because it **11**_____ (mean) that the trek is good fun for me, too.

Interviewer How **12**_____ (the tourists differ) from local people?

Guide Well, most of them **13**_____ (smell) funny, not like us. Really! They **14**_____ (eat) different food and **15**_____ (not dress) like us. My Austrians, for example, **16**_____ (drink) coffee for breakfast – it **17**_____ (not taste) too good to me but they **18**_____ (love) it.

7 Which of these verbs and expressions can be used in both the Present Continuous and the Present Simple, and which only with the Present Simple?

play football, think about, look awful, want, have a pet, look at, like, have a shower

Now use the verbs and expressions to write sentences about you.

Example
have a shower
I always have a shower in the morning.
I'm not having a shower now.

Canada – A Land of Adventure

Capital city: [1]_____.

Area: 9,976,169 sq km.

Population: [2]_____ million.

Official languages: English and [3]_____.

National symbol: The maple leaf.

Political structure: A constitutional monarchy. The Head of State is the king or queen of [4]_____.

Society: Number [5]_____ on the UN 'Human Development Index' and particularly advanced in health and education.

Environment: 4 million sq km of forests; nearly a million sq km of rivers and lakes. Longest river: the Mackenzie River, [6]_____ km long.

Highest mountain: Mount Logan, nearly [7]_____ metres high.

1 Listen to a quiz and complete the information about Canada.

2 Work in pairs. Look at the photos and discuss these questions.

1 Would you like to go to Canada? Why or why not?
2 Where would you like to go in Canada?
3 Why do you think Canada might be a good place to live?

3 Listen to a short biography of the explorer, Alexander Mackenzie. Order these events in his life.

Example d = 1

a He went back to Britain to study astronomy and geography.
b In his first expedition, he travelled down a river by canoe.
c There his men wanted to turn back but he persuaded them to go on.
d Alexander Mackenzie went to America when he was ten.
e They got to the ocean but it was the Arctic – the wrong one!
f In his second expedition, he went west to the Rockies.
g The expedition finally reached the Pacific Ocean.
h He worked for a company that traded in furs.

4 Listen again. Write notes about these things. Then compare your notes with a partner.

• Mackenzie's family
• the importance of his second expedition
• his personality
• his attitude to Native Americans

Comparing Cultures

Compare travellers or explorers from your country's history with the explorers in this module.

• Work in pairs. Choose your person. Look for information in magazines, books, encyclopaedias and on the Internet. Write notes about these things.
   where he/she was born; family/early life; what places he/she went to; what he/she did; his/her personality; where/when he/she died; his/her importance
• Decide which parts you will each talk about.

Work in groups with two other pairs.
• Tell the others what you have found out.
• What are the differences and similarities between your traveller/explorer and the other travellers and explorers in this module?

Review 1

Grammar

1 Complete the text with the verbs in brackets in the Present Simple, the Present Continuous or the Present Perfect.

Antarctica is an inhospitable place. There are no towns or cities. In fact, nobody **1**_____ (live) there permanently, except for a few scientists. They **2**_____ (work) on special bases, studying the climate and the ecosystem. However, things **3**_____ (begin) to change now. Since the 1980s, polar tourism **4**_____ (grow) rapidly. Recently, polar cruises **5**_____ (become) popular because of the beauty of the landscape and the wildlife, such as penguins, whales and dolphins. Cruises **6**_____ (cost) a lot because the ships **7**_____ (need) to be very strong to break the ice. However, tourists **8**_____ (go) on them more and more. Unfortunately, this tourism **9**_____ (not do) any good so far. Scientific studies show that the tourists **10**_____ (now destroy) the ecosystem of the Antarctic. For example, the numbers of some species of wildlife **11**_____ (go down) rapidly. Many ecologists now **12**_____ (believe) that we should leave this beautiful continent alone.

2 Game Work in a group of two pairs, Team A and Team B.

- A player from Team A thinks of a verb and 'serves', by saying a sentence in the Present Simple.
- A player from Team B 'returns' by saying a sentence in the Present Continuous.
- A player from Team A 'hits' back, by saying a sentence in the Present Perfect.
- A player from Team B now thinks of a new verb to continue the game.
- If you make a mistake, the other team gets a point.

Example

A *We do gymnastics every Friday.*
B *I am doing a history project at the moment.*
A *She has done her homework.*
B *I play the electric guitar.*
A *We're playing a match on Saturday.*
B *I've never played* …

Vocabulary

3 Use the words in brackets to make adjectives to complete the sentences.

1 He was very _____ – he wanted to be the first to the South Pole. (ambition)
2 The exploration was a difficult and _____ experience. (challenge)
3 The weather was awful but we were _____ in our tents. (comfort)
4 Snowboarding is quite a _____ sport. (danger)
5 It was a _____ trip – everything went wrong. (disaster)
6 It was a very _____ video about Everest. (enjoy)
7 He was absolutely _____ at the end of the marathon. (exhaust)
8 She lives in a _____ apartment. (luxury)

4 Multi-part verbs Choose the correct alternative from the brackets.

1 I was frightened and wanted to back (in/out/up) of jumping off the bridge.
2 That speaker gets (across/away/through) her message very well.
3 He was very nervous and couldn't go through (by/to/with) the bungee jump.
4 I love music. I'm really (into/out of/onto) Iron Maiden.
5 The doctor advised him to take (in/on/up) cycling.
6 He always turns (in/out/up) late for our matches.

Pronunciation: Consonant Sounds

5 Look at the pairs of words. Try to pronounce them. Then listen and underline the one you hear.

three/free, ten/then, sink/think, clothes/close, dirty/thirty, worth/worse, van/than, thank/sank, mouth/mouse, bread/breath, debt/death, thick/sick, those/toes, dare/there, fought/thought

Listen again and repeat the pairs of words.

6 Can you say this proverb? Use the Phonetic Chart in the Mini-dictionary to help you. What does the proverb mean?

/nʌθɪŋ ventʃəd nʌθɪŋ geɪnd/

Check Your Progress

Look back at the Module Objectives on page 9.
- Which activities did you enjoy most?
- Which activities did you have problems with?
- Which grammar area do you need to practise more?

2 Stories

In this module you will...

- **tell** stories; **practise** giving opinions about films and books
- **listen to** stories, cinema information, a film plot and a song
- **read** stories
- **write** an adventure story
- **learn about** the Past Perfect tense and *would* and *used to*

Warm-up

1 Look at the photos (A–C) and answer the questions.

1. What are the people doing?
2. Have you heard of the stories, read them or seen the films?
3. Where do you think the stories take place?
4. What do you know about the characters or the stories?

2 Match the information in the table with the three novels.

a Don Quixote **b** Anna Karenina
c Wuthering Heights

WRITERS	SETTINGS	CHARACTERS
Emily Brontë	Russia	Sancho Panza
Miguel de Cervantes	England	Cathy
Tolstoy	Spain	Anna Karenina
		Vronsky
		Don Quixote
		Heathcliff

🎧 **Listen to the people talking about the stories and check your answers.**

3 Read the questions and think about the answers. Use the Key Words to help you.

1. What kinds of stories do you enjoy most?
2. Who is your favourite writer?
3. Have you read any books in English? Which ones?
4. What was the last book you read? What was it about?
5. What is the best book you've ever read? Why did you like it?
6. What is the best film or play you've ever seen? Why did you like it?

Now work in pairs. Talk about your answers with your partner.

B

C

KEY WORDS: Stories
Kinds of story: adventure, crime, detective, ghost, historical, horror, love, science fiction, spy, travel
Adjectives: boring, complicated, educational, exciting, fantastic, fascinating, funny, hilarious, imaginative, interesting, outstanding, romantic, scary

21

SKILLS FOCUS

5 The Chase

Before you start

1 Describe what is happening in the pictures.

KEY WORDS
Nouns: cab, laboratory, microscope, slide, slippers, test tube, top hat
Verbs: get out of, hold, look at, wave goodbye

Reading

2 Read the Strategies.

READING STRATEGIES: Paragraph gaps
- First, read the text to get the general idea of the story and characters.
- Then read the gapped paragraphs.
- Read the paragraphs before and after the gaps.
- Look at linkers (e.g. *when*) and reference words (e.g. *he/him*). Use them to help you match paragraphs with the gaps.
- Make sure that one paragraph does not fit.
- Finally, read the story again and check it makes sense.

Use the Strategies to match the paragraphs (1–5) below with the gaps (A–D) in the story. There is one extra paragraph.

1 Minnie heard the door close very violently. She went to the window and looked out. The young man was getting into a cab and her husband, in his slippers, was running after him, shouting.

2 Just then the first cab went around a corner and stopped. The young man got out and immediately ran into a shop holding the test tube in his hand. 'You're all in my control!' he shouted to the astonished shoppers.

3 Then, he realised that there was no need to get away. He told the driver to stop and got out. He waited for the scientist's cab and said to him, 'It is too late. I have drunk it. I'll be the first person with cholera!'

4 Just then there was a knock on the lab door. The scientist immediately got up and opened it. 'Just a minute, dear,' he whispered to his wife, Minnie.

5 Suddenly, the scientist saw Minnie holding his top hat, shoes and coat. 'Very good of you to bring my things,' he said. They got into his cab and asked the driver to take them back home. Minnie was now absolutely convinced that her husband was totally mad.

'This,' said the scientist taking a glass slide and putting it under the microscope, 'is the famous cholera bacillus.'

The young man looked into the microscope. 'Little pieces of pink,' he muttered, 'and yet they could destroy a city. Are these dangerous now?'

'No, not very dangerous. But here is the living thing.' The scientist picked up a test tube. 'This is bottled cholera.'

The rather nervous young man looked at the test tube with satisfaction. He was at the scientist's house that afternoon with a letter of introduction from an old friend. The scientist explained the terrible effects of cholera and added, 'But it is very safe here, you know, very safe.'

A _____ ...
When he came back, his visitor was looking at his watch. 'I must be going,' he said.

The scientist showed him out of the house but when he got back to the laboratory, he suddenly had a really horrible thought. 'Oh no!' he cried and rushed after the young man.

B _____ ...
'He has gone *completely mad*!' said Minnie. 'It's that horrid science of his.' The horse and cab left and then her husband stopped another cab and followed it. 'I know he is a bit eccentric,' Minnie said to herself, 'but this!' She put on her coat and hat, picked up her husband's shoes and went out. She stopped a passing cab. 'Drive me up the road,' she said. 'I am looking for a gentleman with no shoes and hat.'

By this time, three cabs were driving extremely fast through the streets of London. The man in
35 the first cab sat holding the test tube. He was quite afraid, but also incredibly excited. He was the first anarchist to do such a thing. He had planned everything brilliantly, forging a letter of introduction for the scientist. Now, he would be
40 famous if he could put the contents of the tube into the water supply.

The anarchist looked back. The scientist's cab was catching up. He stood up and gave the driver more money saying, 'Hurry up! Faster!' The cab
45 moved suddenly and when the anarchist put his hand down to keep his balance, he broke the test tube. He looked at the two or three drops of liquid on his hand. 'Well, I'll be the first to die,' he said and drank the remaining drops.
50 C _____ ...

The scientist looked at him. 'I see now.' Then a big smile came over the scientist's face. The anarchist waved goodbye and walked away.
D _____ ...
55 'You see, that man who came round to the house is an anarchist, though I didn't know that at the time. I was showing him a new bacteria we have that makes monkeys turn blue. Like a fool I said it was cholera. And he stole it and ran away, probably
60 to poison the water of London. And now he has drunk it. And he'll turn blue! But my problem is I'll have to prepare more bacteria. What? Put on my shoes and coat? Oh! Very well, dear.'

(From *The Stolen Bacillus*, by H.G. Wells)

3 Answer these questions in your own words.

1 Why did the young man go to visit the scientist? What did he plan to do?
2 What did the scientist explain to him?
3 Why did the scientist suddenly run out of the house after the young man?
4 What did the scientist's wife, Minnie, think about what happened?
5 How did the young man break the test tube? Why did he drink the liquid?
6 Why did the scientist think it was funny in the end? What do you think happened to the young man?

Vocabulary: Modifiers

4 Look at the <u>underlined</u> modifying adverbs from the text. Do they modify adjectives or adverbs?

1	<u>a bit</u> eccentric	7	<u>not very</u> dangerous
2	<u>completely</u> mad	8	<u>totally</u> mad
3	<u>rather</u> nervous	9	<u>extremely</u> fast
4	<u>very</u> violently	10	<u>really</u> horrible
5	<u>absolutely</u> convinced	11	<u>very</u> safe
6	<u>quite</u> afraid	12	<u>incredibly</u> excited

Which of the modifiers make words stronger and which make them weaker?

Example
a bit eccentric → *weaker*

5 Some modifying adverbs do not go with some strong adjectives. Look at these examples.

~~very horrible/extremely fantastic~~

6 Write about five things that you did last week. Use modifiers.

Example
I went to a football game on Saturday. It was <u>really</u> cold and the game was <u>rather</u> boring.

Speaking

7 **Game** Work in groups. Close your books and try to retell the story of *The Stolen Bacillus*. Take turns to say sentences. You get a point for every correct sentence.

Example
A *A rather nervous young man went to a scientist's house.*
B *He had a letter of introduction.*
C *The scientist showed him a test tube.*

GRAMMAR FOCUS:

6 A Memory

Before you start

1 Work in pairs. Tell your partner about one of your first memories.

- When and where did it happen?
- What happened?
- How did you feel?

2 Read the extract from Groucho Marx's autobiography. Which of these titles do you think is the best? Why?

- A Night at the Theatre
- My First Date
- Young Love

Times Square, 1890s

'Love hit me when I was twelve. I was still in shorts but little hairs were starting to grow on my upper lip. A young girl, Lucy, lived in the flat above ours. She was pretty with lovely, brown hair and perfect teeth. One day, after I had saved my pocket money for some time, I invited Lucy to go to a variety show with me. I only had seventy cents but I had worked it all out: two tickets for the theatre, fifty cents, and four tram tickets, twenty cents.

It was January and it had snowed earlier that day so we took the tram. Lucy looked charming and I looked handsome as we got off in Times Square. Unfortunately, a candy vendor was standing outside the theatre. I hadn't thought about that. Lucy saw her favourite coconut candy and asked for it. Like a fool, I bought it for ten cents.

We were miles away from the stage and the noise of Lucy eating her candy was louder than the actors' voices. During the performance, Lucy ate every single bit of the candy. On the way out, I was a bit upset about the candy. But then I realised I only had enough money for one ticket back home. Today I feel terrible about this, but remember, I was only twelve, it was very cold and Lucy had eaten all the candy.

I turned to her and said, "Lucy, when we left home I had seventy cents, enough for the tickets and the tram fare. I hadn't planned on candy. I didn't want candy. You wanted candy and you had all the candy. I have every right to go home by tram and leave you to walk. But, you know I'm mad about you. So I'm going to give you a fair chance. I'm going to toss this coin. If it's heads, you get to ride home. If it's tails, I ride home." It was tails. For some curious reason, Lucy never spoke to me again. What had I done wrong?'

(From *Grouncho and Me*, by Groucho Marx)

3 Are these sentences true (T) or false (F)? Correct the false ones.

1. ☐ Groucho waited for some time before he invited Lucy out because he was nervous.
2. ☐ He offered to buy Lucy some candy.
3. ☐ He was upset because Lucy ate all the candy.
4. ☐ Lucy went home by tram.
5. ☐ She was angry with him.

Presentation

4 Complete the table with: *hadn't, had, snowed, planned, eaten, saved.*

Past Perfect
Affirmative
It had **1**_____ earlier that day.
Lucy had **2**_____ all the candy.
Negative
I **3**_____ thought about that.
I **4**_____ **5**_____ on candy.
Question
Had he **6**_____ any money?
What **7**_____ I done wrong?

5 Put the activities below in the order in which they really happened. What tenses are used in the story to refer to each activity?

a I was upset about the candy.
b I bought the candy.
c Lucy ate all the candy.
d I didn't plan on the candy.
e It snowed.
f I realised I had money for one ticket.
g We took the tram.
h I invited Lucy to the theatre.

6 **Read the sentences (1–3).**

1 I **had worked** it all out: two tickets for the theatre, fifty cents, and four tram tickets, twenty cents.
2 I **bought** the candy for ten cents.
3 A candy vendor **was standing** outside the theatre.

Which tense talks about:

a a single event in the past?
b an activity which continued for some time in the past?
c an event that happened earlier, before other events in the past?

Practice

7 **Which of the two sentences (a or b) best describes each picture (1–2)?**

1

a The film began when they arrived at the cinema.
b The film had begun when they arrived at the cinema.

2

a The students were leaving the class when the teacher arrived.
b The students had left the class when the teacher arrived.

8 **Finish the sentences using the Past Perfect. Use the text to help you, if necessary.**

1 Groucho invited Lucy as soon as _____.
2 They took a tram because _____.
3 Groucho was upset because _____.
4 He didn't have money for two tram tickets back home because _____.
5 Lucy never spoke to him again because _____.

9 **Put the verbs in brackets in the Past Perfect. Pay attention to the position of the adverbs.**

1 Nobody believed him because he *had often lied* (often lie) before.
2 They weren't surprised at all. _____ (they hear) the news earlier?
3 John wasn't there when I came. He _____ (already leave).
4 I first met her at a party. I _____ (never see) her before.
5 She was very hungry; she _____ (not eat) anything yet.
6 I decided to see the film after I _____ (read) the review.

10 **Use the cues in brackets and the Past Perfect to explain the situations (1–4). Add another possible explanation.**

Example

1 The police stopped the car *because the driver hadn't stopped at the red light.*
The police stopped the car *because someone had stolen a white Mercedes earlier.*

1 The police stopped the white Mercedes. (driver/not stop at the red light)
2 A famous pop group split up. (their last album/not be successful)
3 A young man started stealing. (he/lose his job)
4 The Smiths went on a round-the-world trip. (Mr Smith/get a pay rise)

11 **Complete the story with the verbs in brackets in the Past Simple, the Past Continuous or the Past Perfect.**

One day, when Albert Einstein **1**_____ (go) round the USA on a speaking tour, his driver, who often **2**_____ (sit) at the back of the hall during his lectures, **3**_____ (remark) that he could probably give the lecture himself because he **4**_____ (hear) it so many times. Sure enough, at the next stop on the tour, Einstein and the driver **5**_____ (switch) places and Einstein **6**_____ (sit) at the back of the lecture hall in the driver's uniform. After the driver **7**_____ (deliver) a brilliant lecture, a member of the audience **8**_____ (ask) him a difficult question. 'Well, the answer to that question is quite simple,' he **9**_____ (reply) casually. 'I bet my driver, sitting up at the back there, could answer it ...'

12 **Personalisation Work in pairs. Tell your partner a funny story from your life. Use the cues and each past tense at least once.**

• scene • people involved • what happened
• what had happened before • ending

7 Films

Before you start

1 What kinds of films do you like?
Use the Key Words and tell the class.

KEY WORDS: Films

action, cartoon, comedy, disaster, fantasy, historical, musical, romantic, science fiction, thriller, war, western

2 Look at the photo and answer the questions.

1 Do you know the actor in the photo? Have you seen any of his films?

2 What kind of film do you think the photo is from?

3 What is happening in the scene? How do they feel about each other?

Listening

3 Listen to the recorded message and complete the cinema information for the Picture House.

4 Which of the Key Words below are similar in your language? Use the Mini-dictionary to help you.

KEY WORDS

actor, actress, character, costumes, dialogues, music, part, photography, plot, scene, situation, special effects

---

PICTURE HOUSE

15 Broad Street, Telford

FILMS

1 _____ to 30 November.

Screen 1: *Love Actually*: 12.30, 15.00, **2** _____, 20.00
Screen 2: *The Incredibles*: 14.00, **3** _____, 18.00
Screen 3: *The Aviator*: 12.30, **4** _____, 17.00, 19.15

PRICES

5 £_____.   Late show: **6** £_____.
Students/Old Age Pensioners: **7** £_____.

SYNOPSIS

Love Actually: Romantic comedy. Written and **8** _____ by Richard Curtis and **9** _____, amongst others, Hugh Grant, Emma Thompson and Liam Neeson. The film is set mainly in London six weeks before Christmas and there are **10** _____ different storylines – all about love and romance.

5 **Listen to Christine and Malcolm talking about the film *Love Actually*. Which of them:**

1 ☐ loved the film?
2 ☐ thought the story was *not* very good?
3 ☐ thought the dialogues were very clever?
4 ☐ did not like the ending very much?
5 ☐ really liked Emma Thompson?
6 ☐ thought the scenes with Liam Neeson and his son were touching?

6 **Listen to the dialogue again and complete the Function File.**

> **FUNCTION FILE**
>
> **Giving opinions about films**
> What did you think of the film?
> I thought it was absolutely brilliant.
> 1 _____?
> Some of it was quite funny, 2 _____.
> But the plot was nothing special, 3 _____?
> And the whole film was really great, 4 _____.
> The dialogues were very clever. 5 _____ the ones with the rock singer.
> 6 _____, there were some good dialogues.
> But the plot was silly. 7 _____ the bit about the writer and the Portuguese maid.
> I thought that was awful!
> Oh 8 _____?
> That's not very original, 9 _____?
> That's not 10 _____, Malcolm. Some of the stories were really funny. 11 _____, the one with the prime minister.
> She's just an amazing actress, don't 12 _____?
> Yeah, I 13 _____.
> 14 _____! He was really good in this one!
> Well, 15 _____ he was quite good in one scene.

What tense do we use to express opinions about films? Which words do we use to give examples?

7 **Complete the dialogues with expressions from the Function File.**

1 A I thought she was great, *didn't* you?
   B Yes, I _____.
2 A I thought the ending was terrible.
   B Oh _____ you?
   A Yes, I did.
3 A The film was great, I _____.
   B It wasn't bad, I _____.
4 A He was really good, _____ you think?
   B I _____ so.

8 **Use expressions from the Function File, Key Words from Exercise 4 and modifiers on page 23 to write five opinions about films and film stars. Then read your sentences to the class.**

Example
I thought The Aviator was really fantastic. For me, Leonado DiCaprio is an absolutely brilliant actor.

Speaking

9 **Work in pairs. Choose two films that you have both seen recently. Use the Key Words and expressions from this lesson to discuss them.**

Example
A *I thought the plot was really exciting. What about you?*
B *Well, it was quite a good story. But I thought the special effects were brilliant.*
A *That's true. And the music was really good, too. ...*

Vocabulary: Multi-part Verbs (2)

10 **Read the sentences (1–5) from the film dialogue in Exercise 5. Which alternative (a or b) means the same as the underlined verbs?**

1 I met him at a concert and I <u>fell for</u> him immediately.
   a I quite liked him.   **b** I thought he was very attractive.
2 I started to <u>go out with</u> him two months ago.
   a We began a relationship.   **b** We started living together.
3 Then we both <u>fell in love</u>.
   a We started liking each other.   **b** We started loving each other.
4 We had an argument and I decided to <u>break up with</u> him.
   a stop the relationship   **b** go home on my own
5 Now I don't know what I <u>saw in</u> him.
   a why I thought he was attractive   **b** what he was really like

11 **Write real or imaginary sentences about your life. Use the multi-part verbs in Exercise 10. Then work in pairs and guess if your partner's sentences are true or false.**

Example
Last year, Nicole Kidman fell in love with me. (false)

> QUOTE ... UNQUOTE
> 'Drama is life with the dull bits left out.'
>   Alfred Hitchcock, British film director, (1899–1980)

8 Communication Workshops

Listening

Before you start

1 Which of the groups (1–4) can you see in the photos (A–C) from the film *Mississippi Burning*?

1 FBI agents
2 the Ku Klux Klan
3 the civil rights movement
4 a town sheriff and deputies

2 Read the Strategies.

> **LISTENING STRATEGIES: Listening for important words**
>
> - When you listen in English, don't worry if you do not understand all the words.
> - Pay attention to stressed words. These give the most important information (e.g. *I saw a great film last night on telly.*).
> - Before you answer multiple-choice questions, read them and <u>underline</u> important words (e.g. *activists*).
> - Listen out for these words or synonyms of them when you are listening.

A Film Plot

Listen to somebody talking about the film.

3 Listen to the dialogue. Use the Strategies to answer the questions.

1 When does the story take place?
   a the 1950s   **b** the 1960s   **c** the 1970s
2 How many young activitists are killed?
   a two   **b** three   **c** four
3 Who are the activists killed by?
   a the FBI   **b** the local people   **c** the local police
4 Where is the FBI man played by Gene Hackman from?
   a the South   **b** the North   **c** the West
5 How helpful is the town sheriff to the FBI men?
   a very helpful   **b** not very helpful
   c not at all helpful
6 What do the Ku Klux Klan attack?
   a a church   **b** a hotel   **c** a shop
7 Who decides to give information to the FBI?
   a one of the deputies   **b** one of the deputies' wives
   c one of the victims' friends
8 What happens to the character played by Frances McDormand?
   a She leaves the town with Gene Hackman.
   b She goes to prison.   **c** She stays in the town.

Would you like to see the film? Why or why not?

Speaking

Before you start

1 What do you do when you think you have made a mistake while speaking English?

2 Read the Strategies.

SPEAKING STRATEGIES: Dealing with mistakes

- If you think you have made a mistake but are not sure, don't worry. Continue speaking.
- If you know that you have made a very simple mistake, correct yourself.
- If someone does not understand you, try to say it again using different words.
- Use these expressions: *I mean …/What I mean is …*

Telling a Film Plot

Tell your partner the plot of a film. Follow the stages.

Stage 1

Choose a film you have seen recently. Write notes on these:
- what kind of film it is
- when and where it takes place
- the main characters
- what happens to start with
- what happens next
- what happens in the end
- your opinions about the film (story/acting/music, etc.).

Stage 2

Work in pairs. Take turns to tell each other about the plot of your film. Use the Present Simple and the Present Continuous.

Example

Well, it takes place in the South of the USA. It starts with a scene at night. These three civil rights activists who are driving along …

Talkback

Tell the class which film your partner chose. Vote for the best film in the class.

Writing

Before you start

1 Read the story below. Match the paragraphs (A–D) with these headings.
- ending to the story • setting the scene
- developing the story • what happened to start with

A   It was a beautiful day in spring and the sun was shining. The night **1**_____, my cousin Sam, my boyfriend Tom and I had decided to go canoeing. We had arranged to meet up at eight o'clock. I was a bit late and **2**_____ I arrived at the river, Sam and Tom were already waiting.

B   We got everything ready and set off. We had canoed a few miles **3**_____ we noticed that the sky was very cloudy. **4**_____, it started to rain heavily. We carried on and twenty minutes **5**_____ we came to some rapids. I was absolutely terrified. **6**_____, Sam shouted: 'Look over there! It's Tom's helmet!' **7**_____ that, we saw his canoe floating down the river.

C   We got out of the river and walked back to look for Tom. There was no sign of him anywhere so we decided to get help. **8**_____, I had my mobile phone and I rang the emergency services. Then we heard cries from some bushes. **9**_____, we ran towards them and saw Tom lying on the ground. His canoe had turned over and he had hit a rock. **10**_____, he had managed to swim to the bank.

D   Tom was weak and had hurt his leg so we kept him warm and waited for help to arrive. **11**_____, we saw some people coming towards us. They took us to the local hospital and checked Tom's injuries. He was OK and that evening they let him out. **12**_____, our parents came to collect us. **13**_____ we were going home, we talked about how lucky Tom had been. We all felt very happy to be back home.

2 Complete the story with the linking words below.
⇨ **Writing Help 2 (linking) on page 140.**

after, at last, before, by the time, immediately, in the end, just then, later, luckily, somehow, suddenly, when, while

An Adventure Story

Write a story beginning, 'It was a beautiful spring day … .' Follow the stages below and see Writing Help 2 on page 140.

Stage 1

Make some notes about your story:

- when and where it took place • who else was in it
- what was happening at the start • what happened next
- what happened in the end • how you felt in the end

Stage 2

Write your story in four paragraphs. Use linking words. Then check your story for mistakes.

Talkback

Work in groups. Read each other's stories. Decide which story is the best.

Language Problem Solving 2 *used to and would*

1 Read what Groucho Marx said about his parents. Who was a more popular person, his mother or his father?

'We **used to** live in a crowded flat in New York. People **used to** visit our house day and night. All our visitors **would** always come to see my mother. She was amazing. She **used to** have more friends than anyone else I've known and she **used to** give them all advice. They loved her and **would** come back again and again for more!

My father was different. He **didn't use to** like talking to people very much and he **wouldn't** help anyone unless he had no choice. He was probably the worst tailor in our part of New York. He thought he could measure a man by just looking at him so he **didn't** even **use to** have a tape measure. You could easily recognise his customers. They **would** all walk around with one trouser leg or sleeve shorter than the other!'

2 Read the text again and complete the table with *used to, use to, would* or *wouldn't*.

Affirmative
We **1**_____ live in a crowded flat.
They **2**_____ walk around with one sleeve shorter.
Negative
He didn't **3**_____ like talking to people very much.
He **4**_____ help anyone.
Question
Did we **5**_____ live in a crowded flat?
6_____ they come to see your father?

Find more examples of *used to* and *would* in the text. Did the people do these things just once or regularly?

3 Read the sentences (a–d). What verbs cannot follow *would* – verbs expressing states or actions?

a We **used to/~~would~~** live in a crowded flat in New York.
b They **used to/would** walk around with one trouser leg or sleeve shorter than the other.
c She **used to/~~would~~** have more friends than anyone else.
d People **used to/would** visit our house day and night.

4 Complete the sentences with *used to/didn't use to* or *would*. In some cases both *used to* and *would* are possible.

1 We _____ live in a small flat but last year we bought a house.
2 Whenever I walked past his desk, he _____ look up and smile.
3 Peter and John _____ be best friends but then they fell in love with the same girl.
4 In the morning, we _____ always sit together and eat breakfast.
5 Mr Smith _____ watch TV all day before he lost his sight.
6 I _____ eat seafood but now I just love it.
7 This town is very quiet now but before the war it _____ be a popular seaside resort.
8 Harrison Ford _____ accept all sorts of jobs before he became an actor.

5 What would these people say about their past habits?

Example
1 *I would play golf every Saturday.*
   I didn't use to drive a small car.
   I used to have five secretaries.

1 a millionaire who has lost all her money
2 a retired soldier
3 a student who has just begun work
4 a retired pop star
5 a mother of triplets

6 Look at the two pictures of the same street taken in 1900 and 2000. Compare the pictures using *used to* and *would*.

Example
The street used to be nice and quiet. There didn't use to be any cars. People would chat in the middle of the road.

2000

1900

Culture Corner 2

$500 REWARD

For the Arrest and Conviction of

JESSE JAMES

St. Louis Midland Railroad

1 Read about Jesse James. Find the Key Words in the text and guess the meaning. Use the Mini-dictionary to check your answers.

KEY WORDS: Crime
Verbs: arrest, get away, rob, shoot, steal
Nouns: gang, outlaw, victims
Adjectives: wanted

2 Read the text again. Choose from reasons (a–f) why you think Jesse James became a 'hero' in Missouri.

a Jesse and Frank were educated.
b They robbed unpopular companies.
c They did not steal from the poor.
d They represented the Confederate South.
e They were violent criminals.
f Jesse died young.

3 Read the song and check new words in the Mini-dictionary. Then listen and put the verses (A–E) in the correct order.

4 What new information can you find in the song about Jesse James?

Example
Robert Ford was staying at his house when he killed him.

Cole Younger | Jesse James | Frank James | Rob Younger (rear)

The Ballad of Jesse James

Chorus
Poor Jesse had a wife to mourn for his life,
Three children, they were brave;
But the dirty little coward that shot Mr Howard
Has laid Jesse James in his grave.

A Jesse was a man, a friend to the poor,
He'd never see a man suffer pain;
And with his brother Frank, he robbed the Chicago bank,
And stopped the Glendale train.

B Yes, it was on Saturday night and Jesse was at home
Talking with his family brave,
Robert Ford came along like a thief in the night
And laid poor Jesse in his grave.

C Jesse James was a lad that killed many man,
He robbed the Danville train,
He stole from the rich and he gave to the poor,
He'd a hand and a heart and a brain.

D It was Robert Ford, that dirty little coward,
I wonder how does he feel,
For he ate of Jesse's bread and he slept in Jesse's bed,
Then he laid poor Jesse in his grave.

E It was on a Wednesday night and the moon was shining bright,
They robbed the Glendale train,
And the people they did say for many miles away,
It was robbed by Frank and Jesse James.

This song was written just after the death of Jesse James in 1882. Jesse, his brother Frank and their gang had been the most wanted and violent outlaws of the American West for fifteen years. The James family were small farmers in Missouri and the brothers grew up to be educated men who did not smoke or drink. During the American Civil War, they fought for the Confederate South against the Union armies of the North. After the defeat of the South, the James brothers set up their own gang. Their favourite victims were the 'Yankee' or northern banks and railroad companies which were hated by the local people. It is true that the James brothers 'stole from the rich and gave to the poor', as there was no point in stealing from the poor farmers who often helped them. Most of the gang were arrested after robbing a bank in Ohio. Jesse got away but was later shot in the back by a member of his own gang, Robert Ford, while at home. After his death, at the age of 35, Jesse James soon became a hero for the poor farmers of Missouri. Recent versions of the *Ballad of Jesse James* have been performed by singers like Bruce Springsteen. The legend of Jesse James lives on.

5 Explain this sentence about Jesse James from the song. 'He had a hand and a heart and a brain.'

6 Your Culture Are there any famous outlaws in your country? When did they live and what did they do?

31

Review 2

Grammar

1 Complete the story with the verbs in brackets in the Past Simple, the Past Continuous or the Past Perfect.

Amazing But True!

One day, a fisherman on the Aral Sea **1**_____ (sail) home after a day's work. It **2**_____ (rain) and he **3**_____ (not feel) very happy. He **4**_____ (not have) a very good day and **5**_____ (not catch) very many fish. Suddenly, he **6**_____ (hear) a strange noise. A cow **7**_____ (fly) towards his boat! The cow **8**_____ (hit) the boat and nearly **9**_____ (destroy) it. When the fisherman **10**_____ (get back) home, people **11**_____ (not believe) his story. Then, some time later, the US Air Force **12**_____ (show) that the fisherman **13**_____ (tell) the truth. While one of their transport planes **14**_____ (fly) over the Aral Sea, a cow on the plane **15**_____ (go) mad and the pilot **16**_____ (throw) it out into the sea!

Pronunciation: Contractions

2 Listen to the story from Exercise 1 and check your answers. Write down the contractions you hear.

3 Listen to six sentences with the contraction *'d*. Which auxiliary (*would* or *had*) does it replace in each sentence?

4 Read the notes on the right about two famous people in Hollywood years ago. Write the notes as sentences, using *would*, *used to* or the Past Simple.

Example

The actress Jayne Mansfield used to love the colour pink.

Vocabulary

5 **Multi-part verbs** Complete the story below.

'I fell **1**_____ this beautiful girl when I was doing a French course in the evenings. We arranged to meet one weekend and went ice-skating. It was a complete disaster and I broke my leg! But she came to visit me in hospital and I fell **2**_____ love _____ her immediately. Then I started going **3**_____ _____ her and we got married six months later. I know some of her friends don't understand what she sees **4**_____ me, but I can tell you, we are the happiest couple on earth!'

6 Evaluate the stories you have heard or read about in this module. Use modifiers (*very, quite, really, etc.*) and adjectives (*amusing, dull, great, etc.*).

- The Stolen Bacillus
- Groucho Marx's Date
- Mississippi Burning
- Amazing But True!

Example

The Groucho story was quite funny.

Pronunciation: Vowel Sounds (1)

7 Classify the sounds in the irregular verbs below.

Group 1/ əʊ /, e.g. go   Group 2/ ɔː /, e.g. four

Example *broke – group 1*

broke, bought, caught, chose, drove, rode, saw, spoke, taught, told, thought, woke, wore, wrote

Listen and check your answers. Repeat the words.

8 Can you say this proverb? Use the Phonetic Chart in the Mini-dictionary to help you. What does the proverb mean?

/ðeɪ ɪz nəʊ sməʊk wɪðaʊt faɪə/

Check Your Progress

Look back at the Module Objectives on page 21.
- Which activities did you enjoy most?
- Which activities did you have problems with?
- Which grammar area do you need to practise more?

Actress Jayne Mansfield: love the colour pink; live in a pink house; her rooms painted pink; have pink furniture; always wear pink clothes; drive everywhere in a pink car; take dog for walks – dog pink, too!

Director Alfred Hitchcock: always had small parts in his own films; not speak, but appear in some part of the film; sometimes be a man standing on a street corner; other times sit on a train or bus; in one film appear in a newspaper advertisement for losing weight

3 Travel

In this module you will...

- **read** an extract from a travel book, a magazine article, a report and tourist information
- **talk about** travel and **do** travel roleplays; **practise** travel situations
- **listen to** monologues, airport announcements, travel situations and tourist problems
- **write** a report about tourism in your area
- **learn about** the Present Perfect Simple and Continuous and pronouns

Warm-up

1 Look at the photos and the Key Words. Use your Mini-dictionary to check the words you don't know.

KEY WORDS: Transport

Verbs: go on foot; go by bus/train/plane; go on a bus/train/ship/car/tram; go in a lorry/taxi/car
Types: balloon, ferry, helicopter, hovercraft, lorry, ship, the underground, van, yacht
People: commuter, cyclist, lorry driver, motorist, motorcyclist, passenger, pedestrian

2 Work in pairs. Say which types of transport:

- you have travelled in or on once or twice
- you use regularly
- you would like to travel in or on

3 Listen and identify the five people in the Key Words in Exercise 1.

4 Complete the sentences with the words below. Check differences in meaning in the Mini-dictionary.

drive, flight, journey, travel, trip

1 Air _____ is safer than many people think.
2 When we arrived at the airport, we discovered our _____ had been cancelled!
3 We went on a school _____ to the planetarium.
4 They went for a _____ in the country in their new car.
5 It's a boring 18-hour _____ by train.

9 Problems

Before you start

1 Your Culture Work in pairs. Use the Key Words to discuss the answers to these questions.

1 What is the best way of travelling round your country? (rail/road/air) Why is it better than the others?
2 What are the biggest transport problems in your country?

KEY WORDS: Transport Problems
accidents, air pollution, dangerous driving, delays, lack of motorways, narrow roads, overcrowding, queues, roadworks, ticket prices, traffic jams

Reading

2 Read the text quickly. Do not worry about the gaps. List two problems Bill Bryson had.

Bill Bryson, a travel writer, starts his trip around Europe in Norway.

In winter, Hammerfest is a thirty-hour ride by bus from Oslo, though why anyone would want to go there in winter is a question worth considering. **1**_____, the northernmost town in Europe, as far from London as London is from Tunis, a place of dark and brutal winters, where the sun sinks into the Arctic Ocean in November and does not rise again for
5 ten weeks.
      I wanted to see the Northern Lights … but now as I picked my way through the grey, late-December slush of Oslo, I was beginning to have my doubts.
      Things had not started well. **2**_____, missing breakfast, and had to leap into my clothes. I couldn't find a cab and had to drag my overweighted bag eight blocks through the
10 slush to the central bus station. I had had huge difficulty persuading the staff at the Kreditkassen Bank on Karl Johans Gate to cash sufficient traveller's cheques to pay the extortionate 1,200-kroner bus fare – they simply could not be made to grasp that the William McGuire Bryson on my passport and the Bill Bryson on my traveller's cheques were both me – and now here I was arriving at the station two minutes before departure … and the girl at
15 the ticket counter was telling me that she had no record of my reservation.
      'This isn't happening,' I said. 'I'm still at home in England enjoying Christmas …' Actually, I said, 'There must be some mistake. Please look again.'
      3_____. 'No, Mr Bryson, your name is not here.'
      But *I* could see it, even upside-down. 'There it is, second from the bottom.'
20   'No,' the girl decided, 'that says Bernt Bjornson. **4**_____.'
      'It doesn't say Bernt Bjornson. It says Bill Bryson. Look at the loop of the *y*, the two *l*s. Miss, please.' But she wouldn't have it. 'If I miss this bus, when does the next one go?'
      'Next week at the same time.'
      Oh, splendid.
25   'Miss, believe me, it says Bill Bryson.'
      'No, it doesn't.'
      'Miss, look, I've come from England. I'm carrying some medicine that could save a child's life.' She didn't buy this. 'I want to see the manager.'
      'He's in Stavanger.'
30   'Listen, **5**_____. If I don't get on this bus, I'm going to write a letter to your manager that will cast a shadow over your career prospects for the rest of this century.' **6**_____. Then it occurred to me. 'If this Bernt Bjornson doesn't show up, can I have his seat?'
      'Sure.'
      Why don't I think of these things in the first place …?
35 'Thank you,' I said …

(Adapted from *Neither Here Nor There* by Bill Bryson.)

3 Read the Strategies.

READING STRATEGIES: Sentence gaps
- Read the text to get the general idea.
- Read a section of the text with a gap and identify the topic (e.g. the location of a place).
- Read the sentences before and after the gap and look for clues about the missing sentence (e.g. Is it an example of what was mentioned before?).
- Certain words may help you (e.g. time references: *then* and pronoun references: *it, that*).
- Decide which sentence goes in the gap. Check that it fits with the sentences before or after it.
- Check that the extra sentence does not fit in one of the gaps.

Use the Strategies to match the sentences (a–g) with the gaps (1–6) in the text. There is one extra sentence.

a   The girl studied the passenger list
b   It is on the edge of the world
c   This clearly did not alarm her
d   That's a Norwegian name
e   I had arrived late the night before
f   I had overslept at the hotel
g   I made a reservation by telephone

4 Read the text again and answer the questions.

1   Why did the writer want to go to Hammerfest?
2   Why did he walk to the station from the hotel?
3   Why did the bank staff not want to cash his traveller's cheques at first?
4   Why was he so worried about missing the bus?
5   Why did he say he was carrying medicine and that he would write a letter to the manager?
6   How did he finally persuade the girl to get him a seat?
7   How did the writer feel:
   • while he was talking to the girl?
   • after he left the ticket counter?
   Which words/expressions from the text tell you this?

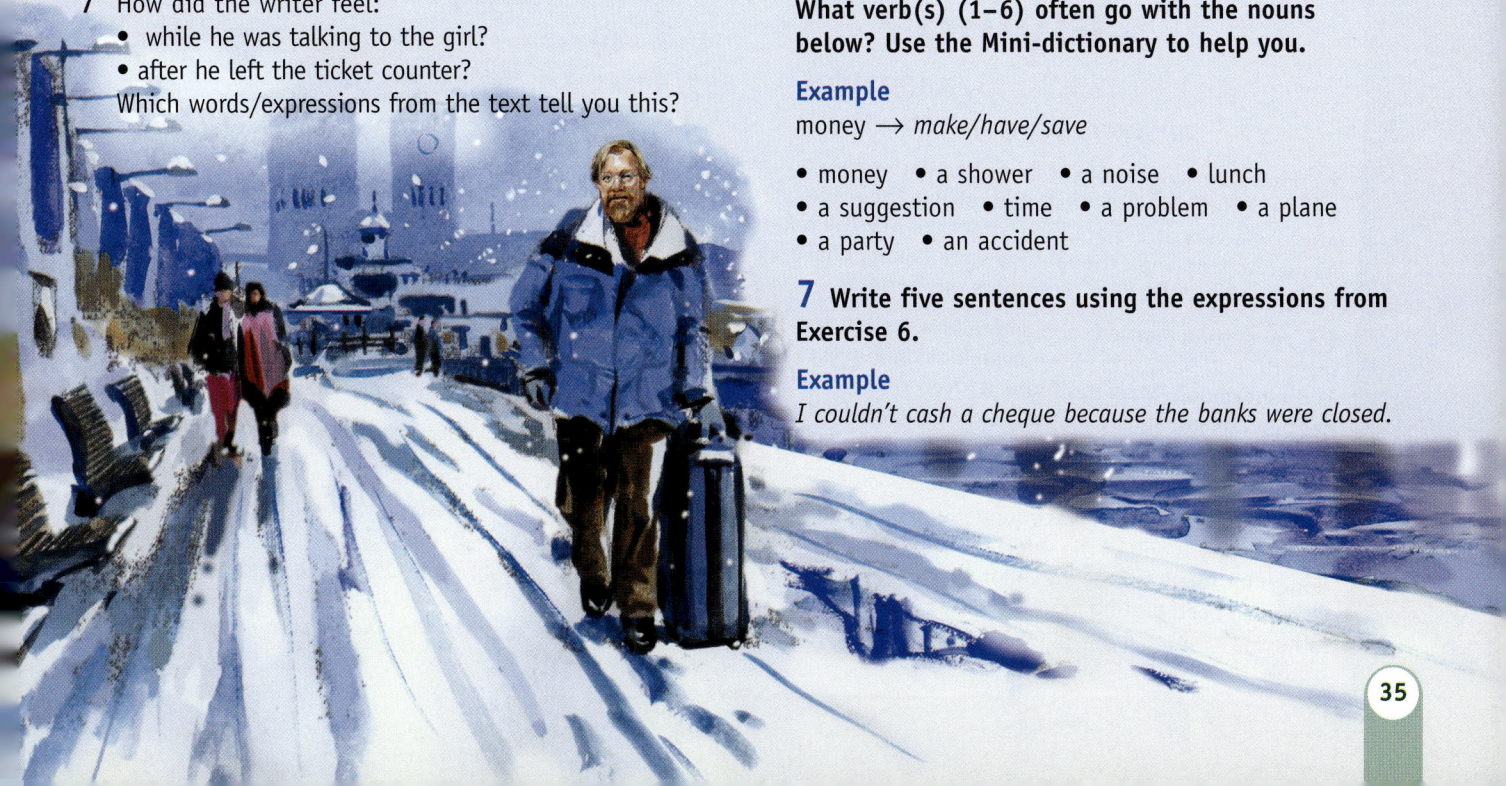

Speaking

5 Work in pairs. Act out conversations similar to the one in the text.

1

Student A
You have come to the station to collect your ticket. Decide on your destination.

Student B
You work in the ticket office. The customer's name is not on your passenger list.

2

Student A
You work in a bank. The name on a customer's passport is slightly different from the name on the traveller's cheques.

Student B
You want to cash €100 of traveller's cheques in a bank. Your full name is 'Christina Ruth Smith/ Christopher Anthony Smith'. The name on the traveller's cheques is 'Chris Smith'.

Vocabulary: Collocation

6 In English some words often go together.

Example
do some exercise

Match the words below from the text.

1   make   a   doubts/difficulty/no record
2   have   b   a bus/breakfast
3   cash   c   a life
4   miss   d   a reservation
5   save   e   a bus
6   get on   f   a cheque

What verb(s) (1–6) often go with the nouns below? Use the Mini-dictionary to help you.

Example
money → *make/have/save*

• money • a shower • a noise • lunch
• a suggestion • time • a problem • a plane
• a party • an accident

7 Write five sentences using the expressions from Exercise 6.

Example
I couldn't cash a cheque because the banks were closed.

GRAMMAR FOCUS:

10 Fear of Flying

Before you start

1 Look at the photo. Have you ever been on an aeroplane? How many times? Were you nervous? Tell the class.

Something has been interfering with our flight controls. Have you been using your mobile phone, sir?

No, I haven't been using it! My son's got it.

Yes, I've been playing space invaders on it!

2 Which of the Key Words are related to safety? Use the Mini-dictionary to help you.

KEY WORDS: Air travel

aisle, emergency exit, flight attendant, food tray, life jacket, overhead locker, oxygen mask, pilot, seat belt

3 Match the questions from the readers (1–3) with the pilot's answers (A–D). There is one extra answer.

Are You Afraid of Flying?

Captain Tom Yates, a top pilot, answers your questions.

1 I have flown a couple of times and each time I got nervous when the flight attendant started talking about life jackets! Also, I was very afraid not long after take-off. The engines seemed to stop and I thought we were falling. I have been thinking about this a lot recently. Is this normal?

2 I'm getting married soon and during the last few months, my girlfriend Mary and I have been looking at places to go for our honeymoon. Mary has found a lovely place in Cuba and she has been telling all our friends about it for weeks. There's just one problem – I've never been on an aeroplane before. I get claustrophobic and I'm terrified!

3 I used to fly when I was younger and didn't use to be afraid. I know flying is one of the safest forms of transport and I have done a lot to encourage my children to fly. But in the last few years, I've been getting more and more frightened about flying. In fact, I've missed many opportunities to see the world because of this. My children think I'm crazy! Am I?

A No, you're not, you're just very imaginative! Many older people have written to me with this problem. Because you're older, you're more aware of things that can go wrong and this leads to physical tension. So, to stop this process, keep your mind busy – buy lots of magazines for the flight and take a walkman with several tapes – this will help you to stop imagining 'disasters'!

B We have been running a strict no-smoking policy for years and this has improved air quality on our flights for all our customers. So, when you start to get nervous, the best thing to do is to have some nicotine chewing gum. Whatever you do, don't smoke in the toilets!

C It's natural to be nervous when you do something for the first time. But let me tell you something – I wouldn't do this job if it wasn't safe, and I've been flying planes for over fifteen years! As for the claustrophobia, get a seat near the aisle or near an emergency exit – there's more room there. So don't worry – enjoy your honeymoon!

D Yes, it is. After we have reached about 1,000 feet, we always reduce power to reduce engine noise – we have been doing this ever since the mid-90s to comply with noise pollution laws.

Presentation

4 Complete the sentences from the cartoon in the Present Perfect Continuous.

Affirmative: I've been **1**_____ space invaders.
Question: Have you **2**_____ using your mobile phone?
Negative: No, I **3**_____ been using it.

5 Complete the sentences with the correct forms of the tenses.

PRESENT PERFECT CONTINUOUS
She **1**_____ (tell) all our friends about it for weeks.
We **2**_____ (do) this for years.
I **3**_____ (fly) planes for over fifteen years!

PRESENT PERFECT
My girlfriend **4**_____ (find) a lovely place in Cuba.
I **5**_____ (do) a lot to encourage my children to fly.
I **6**_____ (fly) a couple of times.

6 Look at the completed examples in Exercises 4 and 5. Which of the two tenses refers to:

a a finished event or events?
b an activity that may not be finished?
c an activity continuing or repeated over a period of time?

Practice

7 Complete the sentences using the verbs in brackets in the Present Perfect Continuous.

1 You look very tired. _____ (you drive) for a long time?
2 Mike has a nice tan. He _____ (cycle) everywhere for the last two months.
3 She's just got her driving licence. She _____ (not drive) for very long.
4 Why are the police looking for him? _____ (he sell) stolen cars?
5 The traffic in this town is impossible. We _____ (sit) in a traffic jam all morning.

8 Use the cues to explain what has been happening. Then add your own explanations.

Example
1 *She's been waiting for her children all day.*
She's been looking for her passport.
She's been reading about AIDS.

1 A woman is worried. (wait for her children all day)
2 A man, all wet, is coming out of the pond in the park. (look for a ring)
3 A woman in a track suit is going on the bus with a huge bag. (play tennis)

9 Work in pairs. Student A turns to page 129, Student B turns to page 130. Read their cues and then act out the dialogues.

Example
A *Peter, your hands are very dirty! Have you been working in the garden?*
B *No, I haven't. I've been repairing my bike.*

10 Which sentence (a or b) would sound better in each situation?

1 You want to find out why someone is late.
   a What have you been doing?
   b What have you done?
2 You want to talk about your success in your training programme.
   a I've been running today.
   b I've run three miles today.
3 You want to complain about your garage.
   a They've been fixing my car for a week.
   b They've fixed my car.

11 Read this interview with a traveller and put the verbs in brackets in the Present Perfect Simple or Continuous.

Interviewer: Your new book **1**_____ (just be) published. We **2**_____ (wait) for it for almost a year! **3**_____ (you write) all this time?
Traveller: Well, not really. I **4**_____ (travel) most of the time.
Interviewer: Where **5**_____ (you be)? Is there any place at all where you **6**_____ (not be) yet?
Traveller: Oh yes, there are lots of places I **7**_____ (not visit). But over the last ten months, I **8**_____ (collect) photos of places I **9**_____ (never be) to before.
Interviewer: Your new book is about Australian Aborigines and their lifestyle. **10**_____ (you meet) many Aborigines in your life?
Traveller: Yes, actually, I **11**_____ (live) in the Australian outback for the last few months and I **12**_____ (make) a lot of friends among the Aborigines. They are very friendly people and **13**_____ (help) me a lot.
Interviewer: What's your next book about?
Traveller: Well, for years, I **14**_____ (plan) to write about Siberia. I **15**_____ (not start) yet but I **16**_____ (think) about it a lot.
Interviewer: Well, thank you and good luck with your next project.

12 **Personalisation** Write about things that you started doing in the past and haven't finished yet. Use the Present Perfect and the Present Perfect Continuous.

Example
I've been reading Don Quixote for some time.
I've read fifteen chapters so far.

Module 3

11 On the Move

Before you start

1 Look at the photo and answer the questions.

1 Where are the people? What are they doing?
2 Have you ever been abroad? Where did you go?
3 Have you ever travelled a long distance on your own? How did you travel? Did you enjoy it? Why? Why not?

2 Put the Key Words into the correct column in the table. Use the Mini-dictionary to help you.

KEY WORDS: Travel
baggage (luggage), boarding card, carriage, check-in, customs, flight, gate, information desk, passenger, passport control, platform, seat, ticket, ticket collector, trolley

AEROPLANES/ AIRPORTS	TRAINS/ STATIONS	BOTH
boarding card	Carriage	baggage

3 Listen and complete the information.

DEPARTURES

Flight	Destination	Gate
AF 2146	Ottawa	_____
_____	Budapest	_____
LO 1473	_____	_____
_____	_____	13
_____	Istanbul	_____
_____	_____	9

4 Read the Strategies.

Listening Strategies: Matching Information and Dialogues

- When you listen to dialogues, think about where they take place (e.g. on a bus).
- Focus on the language the people use (formal or informal).
- Think about the mood of the speakers (e.g. polite, angry, happy, nervous).
- Use this information to match the information with the dialogues.

Now listen to three dialogues. Use the Strategies to match the information (a–f) with the dialogues 1, 2 or 3.

Place
a ☐ airport
b ☐ plane
c ☐ railway station

Topic
d ☐ seat numbers
e ☐ ticket
f ☐ checking in

Listen again and match the speakers with their moods (a–f).

Speaker		Mood
Woman (1)	a	happy
Man (1)	b	unhappy
Woman (2)	c	rude
Man (2)	d	polite
Woman (3)	e	sleepy/bored
Man (3)	f	nervous

5 Listen to the first two dialogues again and complete the Function File.

FUNCTION FILE

Travel Situations
Dialogue 1

Woman	Hello. I'd like **1**_____ to Newcastle, please.
Man	Single or **2**_____, madam?
Woman	Single, please.
Man	**3**_____ or non-smoking?
Woman	Non-smoking, please.
Man	That'll be **4**_____ pounds, please.
Woman	What time does it <u>get to</u> Newcastle?
Man	At **5**_____. But you have to change at York.
Woman	Oh do I?
Man	That's right, madam. <u>Get off</u> at York and <u>get on</u> the **6**_____ from London to Newcastle. But you'd better be quick. It <u>goes off</u> in **7**_____ minutes.
Woman	Oh really? What **8**_____ does it <u>go from</u>?
Man	Number **9**_____, over there.
Woman	Thanks very much.

Dialogue 2

Woman	Good morning, sir.
Man	Can I <u>check in</u> here?
Woman	Yes, you can. How much luggage have you got, sir?
Man	I've just got **10**_____ to check in and a laptop for hand baggage. That's OK, isn't it?
Woman	Of course. Did you pack your case yourself, sir?
Man	Yes, I did.
Woman	And could I see your **11**_____, please? Great, that's fine.
Man	The plane's going to <u>take off</u> late, isn't it?
Woman	Yes, sir but it's only **12**_____ minutes late. Here is your boarding card. <u>Go through</u> **13**_____ now. It goes from gate number twenty-one.
Man	OK. Thank you.
Woman	Not at all, sir.

6 Pronunciation The meaning of a sentence can change if you put the stress on a different word.

1 I want <u>two</u> return tickets to Liverpool. = Not <u>one</u> ticket.
2 I want two <u>return</u> tickets to Liverpool. = Not <u>single</u> tickets.
3 I want two return tickets to <u>Liverpool</u>. = Not <u>Manchester</u>.

Listen to three situations and choose the correct meaning, a, b or c.

1 Eric wants to go to Rome by train.
   a Not Sarah **b** Not Milan **c** Not by bus
2 I'd like a single ticket for a morning train in a non-smoking compartment.
   a Not a return ticket **b** Not an afternoon train **c** Not in a smoking compartment
3 A man told me to go to gate number two at three o'clock.
   a Not a woman **b** Not to gate four **c** Not at half past two

Vocabulary: Multi-part Verbs (3)

7 Look at the <u>underlined</u> verbs in the Function File. Match them with the definitions (1–8).

1 leave a place
2 enter (a train/plane)
3 leave (a train/plane)
4 leave the ground
5 leave from a specific place
6 to pass through a place
7 to arrive in a town
8 to register your ticket and give in your luggage

Speaking

8 Work in pairs. Student A turns to page 129 and Student B turns to page 130. Read Roleplays 1 & 2 and act out the situations. Use expressions from the Function File to help you.

9 Imagine you have lost something on a flight. Make notes about the following things:

1 your flight number and where you have flown from (e.g. BA 528 from Manchester)
2 what you have lost (e.g. suitcase/rucksack/bag) and the colour and size
3 contents of your luggage (e.g. clothes/books)

Now, work in pairs. Take turns to act out the situation at the lost luggage counter at the airport.

Example
A *Can I help you?*
B *Good morning. Yes, I've lost my ...*

QUOTE ... UNQUOTE
'He travels the fastest who travels alone.'
Rudyard Kipling, British writer (1865–1936)

12 Communication Workshops

Listening

Before you start

1 Which of the Key Words might you use in the situations in the photos (A–C)? Use the Mini-dictionary to help you.

KEY WORDS

accident, after-sun cream, a cold, a headache, mugging, museum, path, pedestrian crossing, sore throat, sunburn, tablets, theft, traffic lights, tube station, upset stomach

Tourist Problems

Listen to three conversations with tourists in London.

2 Listen to the dialogues and match the words (a–c) with the three tourists.

Example

b → *Tourist 1*

a happy and relaxed
b upset and rude
c nervous and in a hurry

3 Listen to the dialogues again and complete the information.

Dialogue 1
1 The stolen bag contained a passport, traveller's cheques and _____.
2 The theft happened outside the _____.
3 The thief was wearing a black woolly hat, _____ and _____.

Dialogue 2
4 The woman has got _____.
5 The chemist gives her some _____.
6 She has to take one a day for _____.
7 Her little boy needs something for _____.

Dialogue 3
8 The man wants to go to the _____.
9 He should go right at the _____.
10 It costs _____.

Speaking

Before you start

1 Choose the correct option (a or b) to complete the Function File.

FUNCTION FILE

At the Police Station
- Good morning. I'd like to **1** a *report* b *tell* a theft from my car.
- What exactly was **2** a *lost* b *stolen*?
- It happened about two blocks **3** a *far* b *away*.
- Okay, sir, I'll get an officer to see you and **4** a *take* b *write* a statement.

At the Chemist
- Hello. Can you **5** a *give* b *sell* me something for a cold, please?
- And if you still **6** a *feel* b *look* bad, you should see a doctor.

Asking for and giving directions
- Go along this street **7** a *through* b *past* the hospital.
- You'll see a park **8** a *on* b *at* your right.
- Keep going **9** a *when* b *until* you get to some traffic lights.

2 **Pronunciation** Listen to six questions. Which of them are polite?

Listen and repeat the polite questions.

Tourist Problems

Imagine you are a tourist in London. Act out three roleplays. Follow the stages below.

Stage 1

Read the Strategies.

Speaking Strategies: Preparing for Roleplays

- Write notes with information about the situation and your role (e.g. the things you have lost, where you were, what you were doing).
- Decide if the situation is formal or informal (e.g. Who are you talking to?).
- Find useful expressions in Function Files from the lesson or module.
- Practise saying expressions politely to yourself.

Use the Strategies to prepare for these roleplays.

Roleplay 1
You have lost something or someone has stolen something.
- Where were you when it happened?
- What happened exactly?
- What clues can you give the police?

Roleplay 2
You need to buy some medicine.
- Ask for the medicine you want.
- Describe your symptoms.
- Choose something that the chemist suggests.

Roleplay 3
Decide which place you would like to visit in your town. You need to ask for directions.

Stage 2

Work in pairs. Act out each situation. Take turns to be:
1 the tourist and the police officer
2 the tourist and the chemist
3 the tourist and a local person in the street

Talkback

Which situation was the most difficult for you? Why?

Writing

Before you start

1 Read the parts of a report (A–E) and put them in the correct order.

2 Find the linking words in *italics* in the report.

Which do we use:

a to list ideas?
b to contrast ideas?

A Report

Write a report about tourism in your area. Follow the stages below. See Writing Help 3 on page 141.

Stage 1

Make a list of the pros and cons for tourists visiting your area. Think about the following things:

accommodation, buildings and monuments, information, local people, museums, night life, public transport, restaurants, shops, signposts, street crime, traffic, the weather

A

There are several positive things that tourists mention.
a The night life is excellent. There are world famous musicals, classical orchestras *plus* concerts for all musical tastes.
b There are many places to eat – *and* a great variety of international food, *too*.
c Travel in the capital can be expensive, *although* the cheap 'saver' tickets, especially for families, are a good idea.

B

To: the London Tourist Office
From: Malcolm Ryan
Date: 15.01.06
Subject: tourists' opinions of London

C

To sum up, *on the one hand* tourists find London an exciting capital city with lots of things to do and see. *On the other hand,* they think it is too expensive. *In addition,* they think London can be a dangerous place.

D

The aim of this report is to highlight what tourists like about London and to identify the main problems they have while visiting the city.

E

However, there are many things which tourists would like to improve.
a Accommodation is expensive *but* this is probably the same in all capitals.
b Tourists do not always feel safe, for example in some tube stations at night. *Also,* they think there should be more police officers on the streets.
c Public transport costs a lot. Tourists think the underground is old and crowded *as well as* expensive.

Example

Pros	Cons
historic church	*no night life*

Stage 2

Use your list to write a report. Use linking words.

Stage 3

Check your report.

Talkback

Work in pairs. Read each other's reports and compare the pros and cons you have mentioned.

Language Problem Solving 3

myself, yourself, themselves and each other/one another

myself, yourself, themselves, etc

1 Compare the meaning of the pronouns in these pairs of sentences. Which pronouns A or B show that the person is the object of their *own* action?

A	B
I sometimes talk to **myself**.	My parents often talk to **me**.
Peter cut **himself** with a knife.	Peter's sister cut **him** with a knife.
She looked at **herself** in the mirror.	He looked at **her** in the mirror.
You shouldn't blame **yourselves**!	No one should blame **you**.

Translate the pronouns in column A into your language.

2 Read the sentences (1–6). Match the words in bold with the correct use (a–c).

1 They succeeded because they believed in **themselves**.
2 Susan has a strange haircut – she probably cut her hair **herself**.
3 I **myself** have never been there so far.
4 Why don't you do it **yourself**! It'll be a waste of money to hire a decorator.
5 Before we started our presentation, we introduced **ourselves** to the audience.
6 The president **himself** visited the casualties in hospital.

a the person did something with no one's help or alone, on their own
b we want to put special emphasis on the fact that it was this person, not anyone else
c the person is the object of their own action/feeling

3 Complete these sentences with the correct pronouns, e.g. *myself, yourself*, etc.

1 They should feel responsible not only for _____ but for their employees, too.
2 Let's wait till we have a chance to talk to the winner _____.
3 Although she has a large family, she thinks only about _____.
4 Did you really cook it _____? It's delicious.
5 Andy drives too fast. He'll kill _____ one day.
6 Why do you think I didn't write this essay _____?
7 My sister and I really enjoyed _____ at your party.
8 We asked Nicole Kidman _____ why she had agreed to star in this film.

4 Complete the sentences with the correct pronouns, e.g. *me, myself, you, yourself*, etc.

1 I'm not going to help you; you have to do your homework _____.
2 He loves his children but he has very little time to play with _____.
3 We were hungry so we made _____ some sandwiches.
4 Sylvia watched the man who was sitting opposite _____.
5 You don't have to pay for me. I will pay for _____.
6 You failed because you convinced _____ that you couldn't succeed.
7 You should bring your friends with _____.
8 She cut _____ badly when she was preparing lunch.
9 They said the film was fantastic but we didn't like it very much _____.

each other/ one another

5 Match the pictures (1 and 2) with the captions (a and b).

a Peter and Mary are looking at themselves.
b Peter and Mary are looking at each other/one another.

6 Complete the sentences with o**urselves, yourselves, themselves** or **each other/ one another**.

1 You just don't know _____ if you think you can live on bread and water for ten days.
2 I think they love _____ very much.
3 We should take care of _____ rather than think about others all the time.
4 Mary and Tom had an argument last week and haven't spoken to _____ since then.
5 How long had they known _____ before they set up a business together?
6 Mountaineers have to wear special clothing to protect _____ against the cold and the wind.
7 In my office, people are very friendly with _____.
8 They laughed when they saw _____ in the photo.

Getting Around Britain

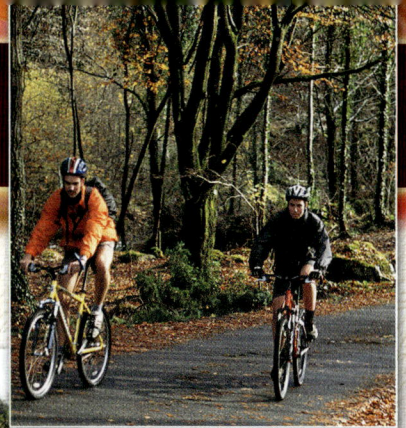

1 Read the text and answer these questions.

1 What is 'the knowledge'?
2 What are Britain's biggest transport problems?
3 Why is Britain good for cycling and walking?
4 What are the advantages of canal boats and steam railways?
5 Which places in the text would you like to visit? Why?

2 Your Culture Think of three differences and three similarities between transport in Britain and in your country.

3 Which of the sentences about Britain do you think are true?

1 Most phone boxes are red.
2 Phone calls are cheaper in the evening.
3 Restaurant tips are usually 10%.
4 'Bed and breakfasts' and youth hostels are not very expensive.
5 Plugs in Britain are the same as the rest of Europe.
6 In Britain it is usually between 25°C and 30°C in the summer.

4 Listen to a radio programme and check your guesses to Exercise 3.

Comparing Cultures

Find more information about visiting Britain. Think about these things.

• interesting places to visit
• adventure holidays
• shopping
• going out at night

Work in groups. Use your information to talk about these things.

1 What places would you like to visit in Britain?
2 What differences can you identify between Britain and your country?
3 What do you think you would find strange in Britain?

In Britain, we still calculate distances in miles and we still drive on the left. Though just to be difficult, there is one road in London, near the Savoy Hotel, where you have to drive on the right! Many of Britain's roads follow ancient Roman roads and you have to pay at some old toll bridges dating back hundreds of years. In London, we still have red double-decker buses and black London cabs. Before they can work, London cab drivers still have to spend about 18 months learning all about the streets of London to get 'the knowledge'.

However, not everything about British transport is as it used to be fifty years ago. There are now more than 25 *million* cars on our roads so traffic jams are common on Britain's motorways, like the infamous M25 around London. And even though we invented the railways, our train network is not in a terribly good state; you get delays caused by unpredictable events such as 'leaves on the lines' in autumn. To improve the situation in transport, the government is investing a lot of money in the railways and coming out with 'new' ideas like toll motorways and congestion charges in major cities like London.

Despite all of this, there are some fantastic ways of getting around the country and enjoying yourself at the same time. For example, you can go on a cycling holiday. Britain has thousands of miles of quiet country lanes and forest tracks which are ideal for keen cyclists. There are even more footpaths for walking holidays from one end of the country to the other, like Offa's Dyke Footpath on the lovely borders of England and Wales. For the more adventurous, there are plenty of places for horse riding and canoeing as well as hang-gliding, paragliding and ballooning.

If you want something a bit safer and less energetic, go on a narrow boat. Britain has a great network of canals, a lot of them going through spectacular countryside. Another relaxed option is to go on one of Britain's many steam railways like the Severn Valley Railway or the Snowdon Railway which goes up the highest mountain in Wales. Just sit back and enjoy it!

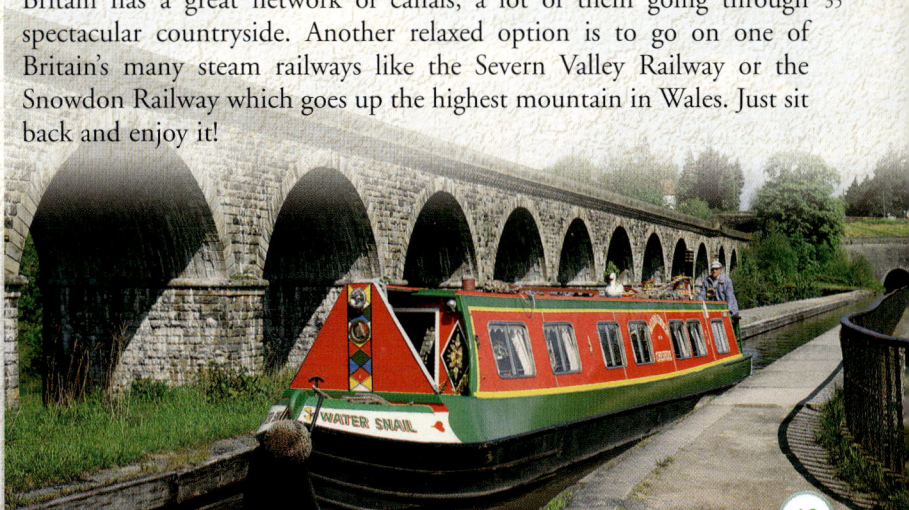

Review 3

Grammar

1 Complete the dialogue with the verbs in brackets in the Present Perfect Simple or Continuous.

A Hi, how are you?

B A bit nervous. I **1**_____ (wait) for days to hear about my exam results. I'm sure I **2**_____ (not do) very well. What about you? You look very pleased with yourself. What **3**_____ (you do)?

A Well, I **4**_____ (go out) with Susan for the last couple of weeks.

B You and Susan? But you've got nothing in common!

A Yes, we have. We **5**_____ (go) to the cinema a lot. We **6**_____ (see) about four films together already. And we **7**_____ (do) that history project together. We **8**_____ (work) hard but we **9**_____ (not finish) it yet.

B You mean Susan **10**_____ (work) very hard. I **11**_____ (never see) you work hard!

A I **12**_____ (change) completely. Since we got together, Susan and I **13**_____ (talk) a lot about the future. We **14**_____ (decide) we want to go to university together and study law.

B I don't want to think about university yet. I'm very busy. I **15**_____ (repair) my bike for the last couple of days. I **16**_____ (take) it to pieces and put it together again twice! Oh, here comes your new girlfriend. She doesn't look very pleased.

A Oh no, I forgot. She **17**_____ (wait) for me for twenty minutes. I **18**_____ (talk) too much, as usual!

2 Choose the correct words in *italics* to complete the sentences.

1 They haven't spoken to *each other/themselves* for two years.
2 She gave *me/myself* a birthday present.
3 He cut *him/himself* shaving.
4 They designed the garden *each other/themselves*.
5 I think you copied this. I don't think you wrote it *you/yourself*.
6 They were writing to *each other/themselves* for ages.
7 I bought a computer programme and taught *me/myself* to type.
8 He looked at *her/herself* in the mirror.
9 She broke her arm but drove *herself/her* to the hospital.
10 Susan and I work with *ourselves/each other*.

Vocabulary

3 Collocation Complete the sentences with the correct verb.

1 I _____ my train yesterday and had to wait three hours for another one.
2 She _____ the bus outside her house and went to work.
3 He _____ the reservation for the ticket six months early and _____ a lot of money.
4 If you drive like that, you are going to _____ an accident.
5 Do you know if there is a bank around here? I need to _____ a cheque.

4 Multi-part verbs Complete the advice for air travellers.

- Please **1**_____ two hours before your flight as there are sometimes queues at the desk.
- You should have your boarding card with you when you **2**_____ passport control.
- Make sure you **3**_____ the gate that your plane **4**_____ five or ten minutes before it is going to board.
- Fasten your seat belt before the plane **5**_____.
- Before you **6**_____ the plane, make sure you have all your possessions with you.

Pronunciation: Different words that sound the same

5 Listen to the sentences. <u>Underline</u> the words you hear.

1 our/hour
2 weather/whether
3 road/rode
4 know/no
5 buy/by
6 week/weak

6 Can you say this proverb? Use the Phonetic Chart in the Mini-dictionary to help you. What does the proverb mean?

/betə leɪt ðən nevə/

Check Your Progress

Look back at the Module Objectives on page 33.
- Which activities did you enjoy most?
- Which activities did you have problems with?
- Which grammar area do you need to practise more?

▶▶ Now read the story *Frankenstein*, Literature Spot 1, page 132.

4 The Media

- **read** newspaper stories, articles and a review
- **listen to** extracts from TV and radio programmes, a dialogue, a TV debate and a song
- **talk about** news and the media; **practise** giving opinions
- **write** a review of a film or a TV programme
- **learn about** passives and causatives

Warm-up

1 Which of the things from the Key Words can you see on this page?

KEY WORDS: The media

TV programmes: chat show, documentary, game show, reality show, soap opera, the news
Magazines about: cars, computers, current affairs, fashion, films, music, sport
Newspapers: local newspaper, popular newspaper, quality newspaper
The Internet: chatroom, newsletter, website
Mobile phones: text updates (e.g. news/traffic), text voting (interactive TV)

Which things in the Key Words have you seen, read or used?

2 Listen and identify the five types of TV programmes.

3 Read the questions. Then, in pairs, tell your partner about yourself.

Example

I listen to the radio every morning while I'm getting ready for school. And you?

1 Do you listen to the radio much? Which programmes?
2 How many hours of TV do you watch each week?
3 What are your favourite TV programmes?
4 What magazines do you read regularly?
5 Do you read a newspaper regularly? If yes, which one?
6 What do you use the Internet for? How much time do you spend on the Internet each week?
7 Do you use a mobile phone for information or entertainment? What kind of information would you like to get on your mobile phone?

13 What's in the Papers?

Before you start

1 Your Culture Make a list of the popular, quality and local newspapers and magazines in your country. Which do you like? Give reasons.

Example

There's a gossip magazine about celebrities called Heat *which I can't stand.*

Reading

2 Read the newspaper articles (A–C) and answer the questions.

1 Which headlines …
   a are in informal language?
   b are a full sentence?
   c play with words?
2 Which article is …
   a about celebrities?
   b of local interest?
   c of general interest?
3 Which newspapers …
   a use formal punctuation?
   b use capital letters for emphasis?
   c have short paragraphs?
4 Which type of newspaper are the articles from?
   a local b popular c quality

B

BRAD AND JEN PARTY TOGETHER

Brad and Jen in happier times

TWO LORRIES delivered ice to the house for the bottles of Krystal champagne.

One guest hinted Pitt made a special effort for the party. He told a friend as he was leaving: 'Brad looked absolutely amazing.'

Brad Pitt and Jennifer Aniston have thrown a huge party for her birthday – fuelling rumours they may get back together.

They spent **TWO DAYS** preparing the birthday bash at their Beverly Hills mansion on Saturday night, a day after *Friends* star Jennifer turned 36.

The couple, who separated after a four-year marriage, welcomed **FIFTY** guests. They included Morgan Freeman, Mel Gibson, Cindy Crawford and Arnold Schwarzenegger.

C

Cool idea for town centre ice rink

Cllr Ian Smart

Harford people will soon be able to enjoy skating on a synthetic ice rink in the town centre. The 100-square-metre rink will be in Peel Square.

A council spokesman said: 'It will be an all-weather ice rink – skaters will be able to use it in any weather. And trained monitors will be there to offer useful skating tips.' Skating will be free and the local council will provide skates.

But the idea has been criticised by opposition councillors. Cllr Ian Smart said: 'It's OK having a skating rink but my concern is they don't seem to be spending money on the serious issues, like housing.'

Another councillor opposed to the idea said: 'If they have money to spend, then they should spend it on other things like the Civic Theatre. It's barmy that we can afford to do this but we can't clean one of our oldest buildings. I can't believe it. We don't need an ice rink. Winters in Harford are always icy and old people have been skating all over the streets for weeks!'

A

Cadbury faces mobile menace

by Andrew Clark

Britain's teenagers are rejecting sweets in favour of mobile phone top-up cards, according to the multinational sweets company, Cadbury Schweppes, which has suffered a second consecutive year of flat UK sales. The company, which makes Dairy Milk chocolate and Creme Eggs, said the slowdown was 'unusual' in a market that has traditionally had modest but steady growth. It has been made worse by the closure of many smaller newsagents and corner shops.

Chief executive, John Sunderland said: 'Five years ago, I didn't imagine that today we'd be competing with mobile phone cards for teenagers' pocket money.' He was speaking as Cadbury announced annual pre-tax profits of £886m. Europe-wide sales rose 6% to

Cadbury is competing with mobile phones

£212m, despite the disappointing performance in Britain. Cadbury hopes to improve sales through new sales channels; it is introducing sweets machines in pubs and clubs and is advertising its snacks in mobile phone text messages.

The company admitted it also needed new thinking to put the sparkle back into its fizzy drinks operation in America, where Cadbury's 7 Up and Doctor Pepper are not doing well.

3 Read the Strategies.

4 Read the newspaper stories again. Use the Strategies to find examples of these things.

- an area of a city   • a building   • a company
- a famous person   • sweets or chocolate
- a drink   • the title of a TV Programme
- a town or city

5 Use the Strategies to answer these questions.

1 What are 'corner shops'? (text A)
   a large shops
   b local shops
   c newsagents
2 What are 'pubs'? (text A)
   a bars   **b** discotheques   **c** restaurants
3 What does 'fuelling rumours' mean? (text B)
   a making rumours weaker
   b making rumours stronger
   c ending rumours
4 What does 'bash' mean? (text B)
   a party   **b** separation   **c** wedding
5 What does 'barmy' mean? (text C)
   a boring   **b** crazy   **c** great
6 What is 'Cllr' short for? (text C)
   a chancellor   **b** councillor   **c** counsellor

6 Are these statements true (T) or false (F)?

1 ☐ Sales of sweets have been affected by teenagers using mobile phones.
2 ☐ Cadbury plans to use mobile phones to increase sales.
3 ☐ Cadbury hasn't done well in its UK market.
4 ☐ Jennifer Aniston had the party after her birthday.
5 ☐ Brad Pitt did his best for the party.
6 ☐ The ice rink in Harford will only open in winter.
7 ☐ Opposition councillors think that the ice rink is a waste of money.
8 ☐ Old people in Harford are experienced skaters.

Vocabulary: Compound Adjectives

7 Sometimes you can join words with a hyphen to make adjectives. Find phrases with compound adjectives in the texts, which mean:

1 cards that put money in your mobile phone account (A)
2 a company's profits before tax has been paid (A)
3 sales of a product throughout Europe (A)
4 a marriage that lasts four years (B)
5 an ice rink with an area of 100 square metres (C)
6 an ice rink you can use in all kinds of weather (C)

Notice how words after numbers are singular.

Example

a 100-square-metre rink (NOT *100-square-metres rink*)

8 Rewrite these sentences using compound adjectives.

Example

1 *We went on a two-week holiday.*

1 We went on a holiday for two weeks.
2 He broke the record for the 10,000 metres race.
3 She went for a walk early in the morning.
4 I saw a documentary about a man who is 120 years old.
5 He went on a journey of 3,000 miles.
6 She bought a house for a million pounds.

Speaking

9 Imagine you work for a *local* newspaper. Write notes about a real or imaginary news story. Choose one of these things:

- entertainment (e.g. a concert)   • a sports event (e.g. a local match)   • a story about a local person (e.g. local girl wins national chess competition)
- some good news (e.g. a new hospital is opened)
- some bad news (e.g. an accident)

Example

What?   24-hour rock concert
Who?   local groups, e.g. the Plastic Roses
When?   next Friday 8 pm – Saturday 8 pm
Where?   the local park
Why?   to raise money for charity
Comment brilliant idea

Now, work in pairs. Find out about your partner's news story.

QUOTE ... UNQUOTE
'It was long ago in my life, as a simple reporter, that I decided that facts must never get in the way of truth.'
James Cameron, British journalist. (1911–1985)

Module 4

14 Breaking News

Before you start

1 Do you ever find out news from the Internet? Which websites do you find useful?

2 Look at the photo and read the headline. Use the Key Words to answer these questions.

1 What do you think has happened?
2 What do you think is happening?
3 What do you think is going to happen next?

KEY WORDS: Disasters

aid, casualties, earthquake, homeless, rescue teams, ruins, tsunami, wave

3 Now read the article and answer these questions.

1 Why were there suddenly huge waves?
2 How big was the earthquake?
3 How are other countries going to help?

Presentation

4 Complete the sentences from the text with these words.

will be, are being, have been, were, is going to be, were being, can't be, is not, had been

STRUCTURE	THE PASSIVE
Present Simple	The area ¹ _is not_ often threatened by tsunamis.
Past Simple	Thousands of people ² _____ killed yesterday.
Present Continuous	Higher figures ³ _____ predicted.
Past Continuous	Problems ⁴ _____ made worse.
Present Perfect	Thousands more ⁵ _____ injured.
Past Perfect	Over 60,000 dead bodies ⁶ _____ found.
going to	Aid ⁷ _____ sent.
modal	Many others ⁸ _____ left homeless.
	The exact numbers ⁹ _____ confirmed.

Headlines

- Headlines
- News
- Business News
- Weather
- Sport
- Finance
- Community
- Interactive
- Bulletin
- Links

Search News

[Search]

120,000 killed by tsunami

Thousands of people were killed yesterday when an earthquake near Sumatra caused a massive 'tsunami'. The entire coastal area of the Bay of Bengal was affected as buildings and whole villages were destroyed by the huge waves.

The exact number of casualties cannot be confirmed,' said a government official, 'but thousands more have been injured.'

The earthquake registered 8.9 on the Richter scale. By yesterday afternoon, over 60,000 dead bodies had been found and much higher figures are being predicted. There are fears that many others will be left homeless.

Aid is going to be sent by many countries and rescue teams from Europe are being flown in tomorrow.

Most of the buildings on the coast are said to be in ruins. The problems were being made worse because lots of hospitals were badly damaged.

The area is not often threatened by tsunamis.

Many people were left homeless

5 Read the sentences below. Why is the 'doer' of the action not given in each sentence? Match the sentences (1–2) with the uses of the passive (a–b).

1 The patient was operated on after the accident.
2 My car has been stolen.

a It's obvious who the 'doer' is.
b We don't know who the 'doer' is.

Find similar examples of the passive in the text.

6 Read these sentences and then choose the correct option to complete the rule.

1 Over 60,000 dead bodies had been found.
2 The area is not often threatened by tsunamis.

We use the passive with '*by* + **noun**' when it *is/isn't* important who or what does something.

Practice

7 What tenses are underlined in the examples below? Identify the uses of the passive from Exercises 5 and 6.

1 The news today <u>will be read</u> by James Cook.
2 Three men <u>are being questioned</u> about last month's bank robbery in Weymouth.
3 According to a report, hundreds of people <u>are attacked</u> in the streets every day.
4 The law about TV stations <u>has been passed</u> in parliament today.
5 The scandal <u>was uncovered</u> by two reporters from *The Washington Post*.

8 Put the verbs into the passive. Use an appropriate tense.

1 He _____ (just offer) a well-paid job with Radio Four.
2 _____ (the Oscar ceremony report) in the news last night?
3 I think cinema _____ (replace) gradually by TV and computers in the next century.
4 This programme became very popular after the main presenter _____ (vote) the most interesting TV personality of the year.
5 _____ (his next book publish) soon?
6 Some films should _____ (not watch) by children and they should only _____ (show) on TV after ten o'clock.
7 Look at those men in dark glasses! I think we _____ (watch).

9 Change these sentences into the passive making the underlined words the subject of the passive sentences. Add '*by* + noun' if necessary.

1 The police fined <u>the driver</u> for speeding.
2 People have sent <u>her</u> lots of birthday cards.
3 The lights went out when they were serving <u>the meal</u>.
4 Journalists asked <u>the prime minister</u> a lot of difficult questions.
5 Nobody has told <u>me</u> what to do.
6 The police were following <u>him</u> until he got home.
7 They didn't ask <u>him</u> about the accident.

10 Rewrite the newspaper report below using the passive where possible.

Example
'More can be brought out alive'

'We can bring more out alive'

Thousands have died in the earthquake in Iran, but as a British rescue team goes in, there is optimism that they can save lives.

Many countries such as the UK, Germany, China, Russia and Japan have sent rescue teams to the city and they still hope they will find survivors. As they arrived, queues of injured people surrounded the medical and rescue workers. Difficult travelling conditions had hampered their journey to the disaster zone.

'We are still optimistic that we can bring more out alive,' said Graham Payne, the director of the 60-strong British team. 'If anyone is trapped, there is a good chance we will find them.'

On the first day, the team used snake-eye cameras, hi-tech listening devices and carbon dioxide detectors to locate survivors.

11 The passive is very common in news broadcasts and newspapers. In pairs, think about what is in the news at the moment. Use the cues below to help you and add your own ideas.

Example
Large parts of France were destroyed by floods.

• area/place/building/destroyed by …
• team/player beaten by …
• person/people killed or injured on …
• robbers, terrorists or famous person arrested …
• conference/exhibition held in …

Now work in small groups. Talk about what's in the news.

12 **Personalisation** Work in groups. Take turns to say passive sentences about what happened or will happen to *you*.

Example
A *I have been selected for the school volleyball team.*
B *My father will be offered a job in Brussels.*
C *My dog was bitten by another dog last night.*

15 The Price of Fame

Before you start

1 Look at the photos and answer the questions.

1 What do you know about these people?
2 Would you like to be famous? Why or why not?

2 Match the Key Words with the definitions (1–6). There is one extra word.

KEY WORDS: Media words

celebrity, fame, fan, mass hysteria, mass media, the press, stress

1 a keen follower
2 a famous person
3 radio, TV and newspapers
4 pressure caused by difficulties in life
5 the state of being well-known
6 journalists and photographers

Listening

3 Read the Strategies.

LISTENING STRATEGIES: Listening for specific information

- Before you listen, make sure you understand what information you need.
- Read any cues, questions, key words and try to guess possible answers to matching, true/false or multiple-choice questions.
- While you are listening, listen for words from the questions or synonyms (e.g. *star* or *celebrity*).
- Don't worry if you don't understand everything. Concentrate on the important words.
- If you are not sure about an answer, make a guess!

Read the sentences below. Use the Strategies and listen to a radio programme about fame. Are the sentences true (T) or false (F)?

1 ☐ The first big 'stars' appeared in the USA in the 1930s.
2 ☐ Rudolph Valentino attracted a lot of excited fans.
3 ☐ Celebrities are more famous nowadays because of the mass media.
4 ☐ Film stars do adverts as part of their film contracts.
5 ☐ Paparazzi are aggressive photographers.
6 ☐ John Lennon was killed in a car crash.
7 ☐ Many famous celebrities have died young.
8 ☐ James Dean starred in three films.

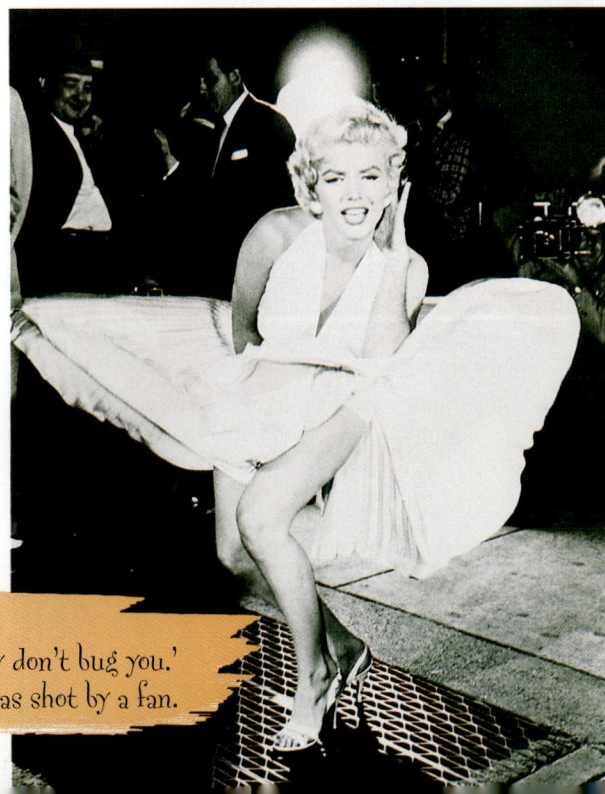

QUOTE…UNQUOTE
'People come and ask you for autographs, but they don't bug you.'
John Lennon(1940–1980), the day before he was shot by a fan.

4 Listen again. List the advantages and disadvantages of fame mentioned in the radio programme. What others can you think of?

5 **Pronunciation** Listen to five sentences from the programme. How many words are there in each sentence? Contractions count as two words.

Example
Tonight we're going to look at fame. → 8 words

6 Listen to the discussion. Who expresses the opinions below, Katy (K), James (J) or both (B)?

1 ☐ The media should respect famous people's privacy.
2 ☐ Famous people shouldn't complain when the press follows them.
3 ☐ The papers are getting worse and worse.
4 ☐ There is too much gossip and sex in the papers nowadays.
5 ☐ There should be some control over the newspapers.

7 Look at the expressions in bold in the Function File. Classify them:

a expressing an opinion
b agreeing
c partly agreeing
d asking for agreement
e disagreeing

FUNCTION FILE

Discussion
1 It's terrible, **isn't it**?
2 **Personally, I think** it's her problem.
3 Oh, **I disagree.**
4 Everyone's got a right to privacy, **don't you think**?
5 **That's true, but** if you sell your story …
6 … you can't really complain, **can you**?
7 Well, **I don't think it's fair.**
8 **You may be right, but** I think she …
9 Well, **in my opinion**, this shows that …
10 **I agree. You're right**, there's …
11 **I totally agree.**
12 **I'm against** too much control.
13 **I'm in favour of** *some* control.

Speaking

8 Read the statements (1–5) below. Decide if you agree or disagree with them. Write notes giving reasons for your opinions.

1 Fame and money bring happiness.
2 The press shouldn't write about the lives of famous people.
3 Famous footballers and pop singers get too much money.
4 The government should tax very rich people a lot more.
5 The government should have more control over newspapers, TV and the Internet.

Example
1 *disagree: Marilyn Monroe – rich/famous – but very unhappy person*

9 Prepare a short presentation for your group. Give your opinions on the statements in Exercise 8.

Example
I don't think fame and money bring happiness. Marilyn Monroe is a good example. She was rich and famous but she was very unhappy.

Vocabulary: Multi-part Verbs (4)

10 Choose the correct alternative for each question.

1 In your family, who is usually the first person to turn *to/on* the TV when you get home? What time is the TV usually turned *off/over* in your home?
2 What programmes make you want to turn *off/over* to another channel?
3 Do you ever turn *away/up* when you're watching something very frightening?
4 Do you ever turn the volume of the TV *up/off* or down? Why?
5 If somebody turns *up/on* at your house, do you turn the TV *over/off* or leave it on?
6 If there is a disagreement in your family about which programme to watch, who in your family do you turn *up/to* for support?

11 Work in pairs. Use the questions to interview your partner.

51

16 Communication Workshops

*H*enry VIII is a historical TV drama in two parts produced by Granada Television. It is set in England during the sixteenth century. The exciting story is based on historical fact – Henry VIII had six wives, executed two of them, and broke with the Catholic Church in order to get a divorce from his first wife, Catherine of Aragon.

In the first episode, shown on TV last Sunday night, Henry meets and falls in love with his second wife, Anne Boleyn. After Anne's failure to give him a son, Henry turns against her and she is executed despite being innocent of any crime.

Ray Winstone plays Henry like a London gangster, an angry man who becomes a cold, calculating killer. Nevertheless, he can also be a caring husband and an affectionate lover. Asumpta Serna is excellent as Queen Catherine who is loyal in spite of Henry's treatment of her. Helena Bonham-Carter plays the brave but devious Anne Boleyn very well. Among the all-star supporting cast, there are some outstanding performances although some of the dialogues sound unnatural.

The filming is imaginative with good action scenes, for example when Henry fights in a tournament. However, some of the scenes are violent and the film is definitely not for children. The costumes are beautiful and the film is shot in some spectacular locations, such as Arundel castle.

To sum up, this episode shows how history can be more exciting than any modern gangster film or soap opera. Don't miss the second episode next Sunday!

Writing

Before you start

1 Look at the photo. Do you know anything about Henry VIII of England? What kind of person do you think he was? Read the review and find out more.

2 Look at the underlined linking words in the text. Which of them are used to contrast ideas?

A Review

Write a review of a film or TV drama series. Follow the stages below. See Writing Help 4 on page 141.

Stage 1
Choose something to watch on TV (e.g. a film, an episode of a series or soap opera). While you are watching, take notes in English about these:

- background to the story; where and when it is set
- main events in the plot
- actors and the characters they play
- location, scenes and costumes

After you have watched:
- write a brief personal comment about it and think about who you would recommend to watch it.

Stage 2
Use your notes to write a review in five paragraphs. Use linking words.

Stage 3
Check your review.

Talkback
Work in groups. Read each other's reviews. Discuss the programmes.

Example *I saw that programme, too, but I didn't like it because …*

Listening

A TV Debate

Listen to a television debate.

1 Listen to a TV debate and complete the sentences with the correct option (a, b or c).

1 The woman thinks that …
  a young people are addicted to TV.
  b TV stops people reading.
  c people don't go out enough.

2 The man thinks that …
  a TV is educational.
  b TV causes many problems.
  c TV is complete rubbish.

3 The woman thinks that …
  a most programmes are educational.
  b there is too much violence on the news.
  c some young people copy TV violence.

4 The man thinks that …
  a people copy violence they read about in the papers.
  b newspapers shouldn't pay criminals.
  c newspapers make too much money.

5 The woman is in favour of …
  a more sport.
  b treatment for Internet addicts.
  c control of the media by the government.

2 Which guest interrupts the other rudely – the man or the woman? Do you remember how he/she interrupts? What words or phrases did he/she use?

Speaking

Before you start

1 Which of the expressions in the Function File are polite and which are rude?

FUNCTION FILE

Interrupting
- Nonsense!
- Excuse me. Can I say something?
- I'm sorry. I'd like to say something.
- You're wrong.
- I'd just like to say ...
- Rubbish!
- Can I interrupt a moment?

2 Pronunciation Listen and repeat the *polite* expressions.

A Discussion based on stimulating material

Discuss the photos and extracts. Follow the stages below.

Stage 1

Read the Strategies.

SPEAKING STRATEGIES: Preparing for discussion based on stimulating material
- Look at the visual material (e.g. photos, headlines, captions, short extracts, adverts, notices, graphs, etc.).
- For each item,
  - **a** think about where it might be from (e.g. a popular newspaper).
  - **b** think about whether it gives you information or opinions.
  - **c** think about how the topic relates to you personally (e.g. How much TV do you or people you know watch?).
  - **d** think about your opinions on the topic (e.g. Do you think violence on TV makes people behave more violently?).
- Think about questions someone might ask you about the material and your possible answers.

Stage 2

Work on your own. Use the Strategies to think about the photos and text.

Stage 3

Work in pairs or groups. Discuss these questions about the media.

- What do you think about the kind of film in the photos?
- What kinds of newspapers are the extracts from? What are they about? Do you read these kinds of newspapers?
- What influence do these kinds of TV programmes and newspapers have in your country?
- Do you think there should be any control of the media?

Talkback

Tell the class one thing you agreed on.

New report blames TV for 'copycat violence'

There is a connection between crimes committed by young offenders and the programmes they watch on television, according to a new government report.

POP STAR'S SECRET LOVER TELLS ALL ...

A Nation of Couch Potatoes

British teenagers and adults are spending more time in front of the TV and on the Internet, a new report revealed today.

Language Problem Solving 4

Causatives: *to have/get something done*

1 Match the people (1-4) with the personal adverts (a-e). There is one extra advert.

> **1** I had my hair done yesterday but you'd never know it now!

> **2** We've had the car serviced at last!

> **3** Next month, I'm going to get my bike repaired.

> **4** My computer's really slow. I need to get the hard disk upgraded.

a **Bill's Bike Repairs** Bikes repaired at rock bottom prices. 11 Corve St. Tel – 01584 879 587

b **Ken's Stylists** "I *always* have my hair cut at *Ken's*," says one of our many satisfied customers. Haircuts with style. 23 High Street. Tel – 01584 873 217

c **Shropshire Computer Services** Specialists in software. Computers repaired and upgraded. Tel – 01584 873 312

d **Temeside Garage** Services while you wait! Very reasonable prices. 9 Temeside Avenue (near the bridge). Tel – 01584 987 456

e **Ready Builders** Get all your small jobs done ! No job is too small. Phone us now: 01584 876 819

2 Complete the sentences from Exercise 1.

> **have/get something done**
>
> I ¹_____ my hair ²_____ yesterday but you'd never know it now!
> We ³_____ the car ⁴_____ at last!
> Next month, I'm going to ⁵_____ my bike ⁶_____.
> I need to ⁷_____ the hard disk ⁸_____ .

Who did/will do the activities:

a the people who are talking?
b someone else/an expert?

Now choose the correct option (a or b) to complete the rule.

> We use **have/get something done** when we want to say that **a** we do something ourselves or **b** we ask someone/an expert to do it for us.

3 Match each sentence with the person (a or b) who would say it.

1 I must translate this contract into English.
2 I must have this contract translated into English.
   a a translator   **b** a businessman
3 I've cleaned all the windows in the hotel.
4 I've had all the windows in the hotel cleaned.
   a a cleaner   **b** the hotel manager
5 I'm going to get a tooth removed.
6 I'm going to remove a tooth.
   a a dentist   **b** a patient

4 Look at these names of services. What can you have done there?

Example
1 *manicurist's* – I can have my nails done there.

1	manicurist's	**4**	dressmaker's
2	dry cleaner's	**5**	optician's
3	shoe repairs	**6**	dentist's

5 Rewrite the sentences using *have/get something done*.

Example
1 *We're going to have/get the roof repaired.*

1 We're going to ask someone to repair the roof.
2 Will you ask someone to paint the kitchen?
3 I've returned from a car-wash.
4 A garage is servicing my motorbike.
5 Where can I find someone who will develop these photos?
6 She's not going to ask anyone to pierce her ears.
7 The builders replaced the broken window.
8 We should ask someone to install the washing machine.

6 In pairs, use the situations (1–7) to ask for and give advice. Use the cues in brackets and the words below.

> jeweller's, plumber, passport office, tailor, ironmonger's, garage, builder

Example
1 **A** *The roof leaks. How can I get it repaired?*
  B *You need to find a good builder.*

1 The roof leaks. (repair)
2 I've got a flat tyre. (pump up)
3 My watch has stopped. (fix)
4 My trousers are too long. (shorten)
5 I've lost my spare key. (cut)
6 I don't have a valid passport. (renew)
7 There is no running water in their house. (connect)

Culture Corner 4

Elton John

1 Read about Elton John. Complete the gaps (1–4) with the sentences (a–e) below. There is one extra sentence.

a It was Lennon's last 'live' performance.
b They had their first hit, *Your Song*, in 1970.
c He won the battle.
d That year, he won his first Grammy award.
e It was the start of a long-lasting partnership.

2 Listen to the song and read the lyrics.

3 Listen again and do the task for each verse.

- **Verse A:** Complete the gaps with verbs.
- **Verse B:** The words in red are wrong! Correct them.
- **Verse C:** Complete the gaps with nouns.
- **Verse D:** Put the lines in the correct order.

Candle in the Wind

A Goodbye, Norma Jean,
Though I never ¹_____ you at all,
You had the grace to hold yourself
While those around you crawled.
They ²_____ out of the woodwork
And they ³_____ into your brain,
They set you on the treadmill
And they ⁴_____ you change your name.

B And it seems to ⁵be you lived your life
Like a candle in the wind,
Never knowing who to ⁶sing to
When the ⁷pain set in.
And I would have liked to have known you
But I was just a kid
Your candle ⁸turned out long before
Your legend ever did.

C ⁹_____ was tough,
The toughest role you ever played.
Hollywood created a ¹⁰_____
And the pain was the price you paid.
Even when you died
The ¹¹_____ still hounded you,
All the ¹²_____ had to say
Was that Marilyn was found in the nude.

D From the young man in the 22nd row
More than just our Marilyn Monroe
Who sees you as something more than sexual
Goodbye Norma Jean

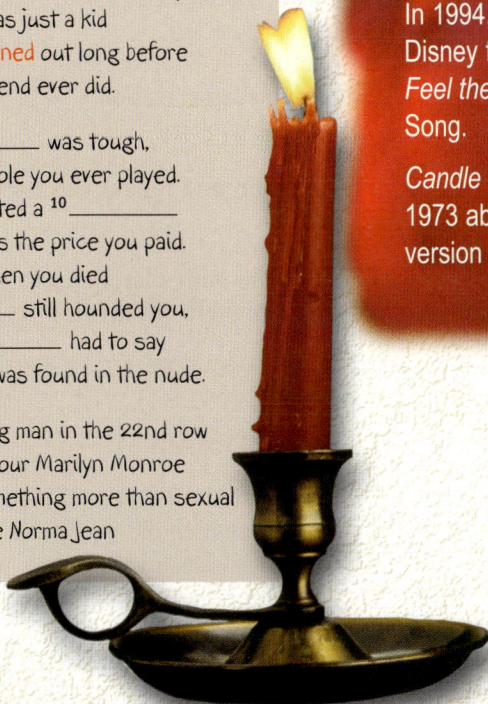

Elton John's real name is Reginald Dwight. He was born in 1947 and started playing the piano when he was four. As a teenager, he played the piano in several groups and then, in 1966, he met Bernie Taupin and started writing music for Bernie's lyrics. ¹_____

²_____ Between 1972 and 1976, Elton John and Bernie Taupin's hit-making machine was virtually unstoppable. *Rocket Man* began a four-year run of sixteen single hits and *Honky Chateau* was the first of seven consecutive number one albums.

Throughout the mid-seventies, Elton's concerts were enormously popular. In 1974, he persuaded John Lennon to join him on stage in New York. ³_____

However, success, fame and endless touring put Elton under a lot of stress. By the late 1980s, he was fighting against cocaine addiction. ⁴_____ In 1992, he established the Elton John AIDS Foundation and decided to donate money from the sales of his singles to AIDS research.

In 1994, Elton wrote some songs with Tim Rice for the Disney film, *The Lion King*. One of their songs, *Can You Feel the Love Tonight?*, won an 'Oscar' for Best Original Song.

Candle in the Wind, is a John/Taupin composition from 1973 about Marilyn Monroe. In 1997, Elton sang a special version of it at Princess Diana's funeral service.

4 Answer these questions about the song.

1 Why didn't the singer ever meet Norma Jean (Marilyn Monroe)?
2 How does the singer feel about her?
3 Why does he describe Marilyn Monroe and Princess Diana as 'candles in the wind'?

5 Your Culture Think of celebrities in your country who had problems with fame. Tell class about them.

Review 4

Grammar

1 Rewrite the sentences in the passive beginning with the words given.

1 The Romans published the first newspaper in 59 BC.
The first newspaper ...
2 Photographers follow the British Royal Family everywhere.
The British Royal Family ...
3 Marconi invented radio communication in 1894.
Radio communication ...
4 They have published *The Times* in London since 1788.
The Times ...
5 Digital technology is changing the media.
The media ...
6 Over eighty million people around the world use the Internet.
The Internet ...
7 Do they show too much violence on television?
Is too much ... ?
8 Channel 4 haven't produced a new drama series for months.
A new drama series ...

🎧 Listen and check your answers from Exercise 1.

🎧 **2** **Pronunciation** Listen again and underline the part of the verb that is stressed.

Example
1 *was published*

3 Complete the sentences using *have* or *get* with these verbs.

fix, pierce, cut, service, repair, photocopy

1 Our fax machine is out of order. We need to
get it repaired .
2 My motorbike has done over 20,000 kilometres.
I'm going to _____.
3 Your hair's much too long. Why don't you _____?
4 Alison gave me those earrings. Now I'll have to _____.
5 The school gave her a certificate. She wants to _____
6 My CD player is broken. Before my birthday party, I've got to _____.

Vocabulary

4 Match the words (1–5) with the definitions (a–e).

1 the popular press   4 a soap opera
2 a chat show   5 current affairs
3 a top-up card

a news about recent events
b a way of paying for mobile phone calls
c a TV drama about the lives of ordinary people
d newspapers usually with gossip about celebrities
e a TV show in which famous people are interviewed

Find three more words from the module. Write a definition and an example sentence for each one.

5 Rewrite the descriptions using compound adjectives.

Example
1 *an eighteen-year-old girl*

1 a girl who is eighteen
2 a boy with long hair
3 a summer holiday of eight weeks
4 a journey of two hours
5 a party that goes on all night
6 jewellery made by hand

Pronunciation: Word Stress

🎧 **6** Mark the main stress in the words below. Then listen and check your answers.

1 advert/advertisement
2 popular/popularity
3 celebrate/celebrity
4 music/musician
5 photograph/photographer
6 organise/organisation
7 publish/publicity

🎧 Listen again and repeat the words.

7 Can you say this proverb? Use the Phonetic Chart in the Mini-dictionary to help you. What does the proverb mean?

/nəʊ njuːz ɪz gʊd njuːz/

Check Your Progress

Look back at the Module Objectives on page 45.
◎ Which activities did you enjoy most?
◎ Which activities did you have problems with?
◎ Which grammar area do you need to practise more?

5 Advertising

Warm-up

1 Look at the adverts (A–C). Which of the Key Words could you use to describe them?

KEY WORDS: Opinion adjectives
amusing, attractive, awful, boring, brilliant, clever, colourful, dull, offensive, ridiculous, serious, sexist, shocking, silly, successful, tasteless, terrible, unusual, weird

What is the message of each advert?

2 Think about these questions.

1 What sort of adverts do you like most?
   a TV adverts **b** radio adverts
   c magazine adverts **d** billboard adverts
2 What sort of adverts do you think are the most effective? Why?
3 Which products usually have the best or worst adverts?
4 What do you think is the best advert on TV at the moment? Why do you like it?

3 Look at the Key Words below. Which expressions show:

a good value? **b** good quality?

KEY WORDS: Advertising Expressions (1)
absolutely delicious, bargain prices, cool, distinctive, durable, fantastic value for money, good flavour, guaranteed, high/top quality, something special, stylish, tasty, totally reliable, unique, waterproof

4 Listen to the adverts (1–5). Match them with the descriptions (a–f). There is one extra description.

a really delicious
b stylish and good value
c the perfect present for a woman
d healthy and natural
e cheap but fashionable
f durable and reliable

A

B

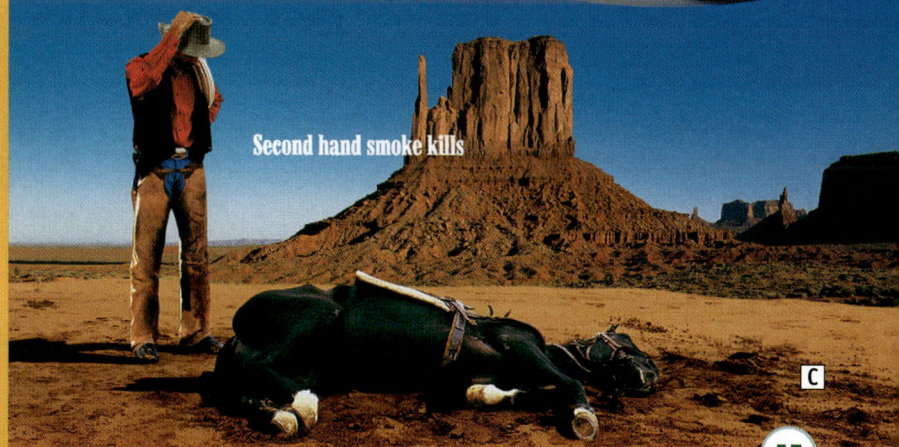

C

17 Persuasion

Before you start

1 Look at the Key Words. Which of these products do you think they refer to?

a a music CD   **b** a holiday   **c** aftershave   **d** a mobile phone

KEY WORDS: Advertising Expressions (2)
compact shape, debut performance, dreamy melodies, exclusive resorts, five-star restaurants, flat screen, full of fun, permanent Internet connection, luxurious suites, masculine scent, natural ingredients, sensual and refreshing

Reading

2 Read the adverts (1–4) and check your answers to Exercise 1.

1

Babel BX99
• Special Offer – €300! •
now only

We have the edge over all other models for price and performance. Our top quality phone with 300-pixel camera will help you capture those important moments. Take photos yourself or download them from the Internet. View them on the flat screen and send them to your friends, with sound if you like! This model gives you a permanent Internet connection so you can download web pages quickly.

The **Babel BX99** has a stylish, compact shape. And don't worry – it's a piece of cake to use!

FREE connection, software and car charger

14-DAY MONEY BACK GUARANTEE!

2

SPECIAL OFFER - €35 for 237ml bottle!

ICEFRESH KEEPS YOU COOL

Our introductory offer for this brand new aftershave, ICEFRESH, is not to be sniffed at! ICEFRESH has a cool, crisp and distinctly masculine scent which will make you even more irresistible. ICEFRESH is both sensual and refreshing. Natural ingredients leave your skin cool, relaxed and fresh – and keep you that way all day.

Suitable for all skins.

Special offer

3

Come Away With Me

This CD is something special. Norah's voice is as smooth as honey and she has a wonderfully lazy way of singing. This CD contains an excellent blend of blues, jazz and country music, sung with simple backing of piano, bass and drums. Three of the songs were written by Miss Jones herself and these all have warm, dreamy melodies. An excellent debut performance.

Norah Jones

Read what the critics say:

'There is real greatness to her voice which can be compared to the legendary jazz singers Billie Holiday and Ella Fitzgerald. And she's only 22!'
Jade Fuller, Music Now.

'She is a breath of fresh air in a world of manufactured music.'
Wayne Small, Xmag.

'This is one of the best albums I've heard for a long time. Buy it – you won't be disappointed.'
Rickie Palmer, CD Review.

3 According to the adverts (1–4), which product:

1 is recommended by other people?
2 has free extras or special savings?
3 is easy to use?
4 has just come out?
5 is the best of its kind?
6 promises to return your money if you are not satisfied?

4 Work in groups. Discuss these questions. Use the Opinion adjectives on page 57.

1 Which are the best and the worst adverts? Why do you think so?
2 Which advert tempted you most? Why?
3 Which adverts give the most practical information? Give examples.
4 Which parts of the adverts do you think are exaggerations?
5 Which advert is the most difficult for you to understand? What makes it difficult?

OUT-OF-THIS-WORLD EXPERIENCES

4

We offer you the best holidays in the world with exclusive resorts in the Caribbean, Mediterranean and Indian Ocean. All our resorts are full of fun. We have tennis, golf, sailing, water skiing, snorkelling, scuba diving and extreme sports like parachuting and hang-gliding. And we give free, professional tuition.

You can choose from a wide range of accommodation, from standard rooms to our luxurious suites. And you can eat anywhere from a simple bar to a five-star restaurant. Our hotel staff will give you a warm welcome and do everything to make your holiday memorable.

We organise travel to and from the resorts and deal with any problems, so you don't have to worry about anything. Just sit back and enjoy yourself!

BOOK NOW FOR AN OUT-OF-THIS-WORLD EXPERIENCE!

Phone
00016 99765
for a
free brochure
or visit our website at
www.outworldexp.co.uk

5 Read the Strategies.

READING STRATEGIES: Dealing with idiomatic expressions

* Look at the words in the idiomatic expression. Remember that the words do not mean exactly what they say.
* Try to imagine the image created by the expression (e.g. *smooth as honey*).
* If you can't work out the meaning like that, find the expression in the text. Read the sentence it is in and those around it. Use the context to make a guess.
* Write down the expression in your notebook with an example and a translation in your own language. Choose an expression that is similar if there is no direct translation.

Vocabulary: Idiomatic Expressions

6 Use the Strategies to match the expressions (1–9) from the adverts with their meanings (a–i).

1 *have the edge over* all other models
2 will help you *capture the moment*
3 *a piece of cake* to use
4 our offer is *not to be sniffed at*
5 her voice is *as smooth as honey*
6 she is *a breath of fresh air*
7 an *out-of-this-world* experience
8 our staff will *give you a warm welcome*
9 just *sit back* and enjoy yourself

a extremely easy
b too good to ignore
c are better than
d new and original
e create a memory
f absolutely amazing
g relax
h be friendly and helpful
i pleasant and easy to listen to

QUOTE ... UNQUOTE
'Advertising is the greatest art form of the twentieth century.'
Marshal McLuhan, Canadian writer (1911–1980)

7 Complete these sentences with expressions from Exercise 6.

1 The exam was _____! Much easier than I expected.
2 Both teams are playing well but I think Arsenal _____ Liverpool and they'll win.
3 I know you don't feel well so just _____ and let me cook dinner.
4 I love going to her house. She always gives you a _____.
5 There is 30% off TVs in the sales this month. That's _____.
6 That new history teacher is a _____. The rest of the department is a bit old and boring.

Speaking

8 Work in pairs. Student A reads about 'Handycom' on page 129 and Student B reads about 'Musicman' on page 130. Then take turns to ask and answer questions to find out:

* what it is/what it does/how it works
* the advantages over other products
* the price

9 Choose a real product or make one up (e.g. CD/DVD/shoes/watch). Think of five good things to say about it.

Example

Total Disaster, by Grunge, is one of the best CDs I've heard recently. It is a really cool mixture of rap and jazz. The saxophone ... .

Tell the class about the product.

18 Classified Ads

Before you start

1 Your Culture Look at the Key Words. Which kinds of classified adverts do you find in newspapers in your country?

KEY WORDS

accommodation, birthday greetings, births, courses and tuition, deaths, for sale/to swap, lonely hearts, lost and found, marriages, wanted

2 Read the adverts below. Which sections in the Key Words would you find them in?

A **Mr Universe in five days** *or your money back!*
Only £100! **Guaranteed** bodybuilding method. **At home – no gym. No exercise needed!** Send cheque payable to Jack Sharp, PO Box 431.

B **Congratulations**, Mandy, on your 21st birthday! With all our love from Mum and Dad, Jon, Nattie and Sean xxx

C *Maggie Marsh* Patient female driving instructor 1st lesson free Tel. 66543 987865

D *Colston-Warren. Robert and Sharon are pleased to announce the birth of their baby boy, Alexander, on 28 January. 3.6 kilos. Thanks to everyone concerned.*

E **Dog Talk** Teach your dog to talk with this unique course. Reply to PO Box 987.

F **FOUND** Grey parrot with red tail. Accrington Road area. V. friendly, good talker. Tel. 01998765 09876.

G **Yamaha 600cc motorbike.** Excellent condition. Two years old. £4,000. Bargain. Tel. Barrie 009876 98765.

H **Are you out there?** Fun-loving, attractive male, mid-20s, looking for female, similar age. Likes cinema, reading and good conversation. Tel. 009876 87654.

3 Read the adverts again. Which of the adverts would you <u>not</u> trust much? Why not?

4 Listen to three dialogues. Match them with three of the adverts (A-H).

Presentation

5 Read the dialogue below. Match the <u>underlined</u> examples (1–10) with the tenses and verb forms (a–e) in the table.

Sue **1** <u>I'm going to take</u> my driving test. I think **2** <u>it might help</u> me get a job.

Pat Have you had any lessons yet?

Sue No, **3** <u>I'm having</u> my first one tomorrow afternoon.

Pat What time?

Sue **4** <u>I finish</u> classes at three o'clock and **5** <u>I'm seeing</u> my instructor afterwards.

Pat Oh, **6** <u>I may come</u> and watch! No, only joking! Who's your instructor?

Sue Someone my mum knows. My mum thinks **7** <u>she'll be</u> good. She's got a hundred per cent pass rate.

Pat You should be all right, then. Pity about the weather. Look at those clouds.

Sue Yeah, **8** <u>it's going to rain</u>, I'm sure.

Pat Listen, I think **9** <u>I'll take</u> this road. It's quicker. And **10** <u>I'll drop you off</u> at the lights. Is that OK?

Sue That's fine.

TENSE / VERB FORM	
a *be going to* + infinitive	
b Present Continuous (future use)	
c Present Simple (future use)	
d *will* + infinitive	
e *may/might* + infinitive	

6 Match the <u>underlined</u> examples (1–10) in Exercise 5 with the following uses (a–g).

a prediction based on experience or intuition
b intention
c prediction based on observing the present situation
d personal arrangement
e official/fixed arrangement that we can't change
f spontaneous decision
g uncertain prediction

7 Which of these sentences with *will* express: a spontaneous decision? b prediction?

1 I'll give you a lift, I promise.
2 I think I'll try this course.
3 I'm sure it'll be really good fun.
4 I just know you'll love it.

8 Which of these sentences is the speaker more certain of something happening in the future?

1 It *may/might* help me get into the rugby team.
2 They *will* make you pay a lot of money.

Practice

9 Complete the sentences using the verbs in brackets with *will* or *be going to*.

1 Sarah is going on holiday tomorrow. I'm sure she _____ (enjoy) it.

2 Chris is coming to my wedding party. I hope he _____ (not bring) anyone with him.

3 Susan is getting quite big now. You can see that she _____ (have) a baby.

4 Don't answer the phone, I _____ (get) it.

5 He eats like a horse and doesn't do any sport. He _____ (not be) selected for the school football team.

6 I have to stay at home tonight – I _____ (study) for my history test.

7 I've heard that Peter and Jane _____ (spend) their honeymoon in Corsica.

10 Put the verbs in brackets into the correct future form.

1 A Have you decided where to go on holiday with your family?
  B We haven't decided yet, but I think we _____ (go) to Italy.

2 A Have you decided where to go on holiday with your family?
  B Yes, we _____ (go) to Italy, we've booked a hotel in Venice.

3 A Did you know that Mrs Brown is in hospital?
  B Really? I _____ (visit) her some time this week.

4 A Did you know that Mrs Brown is in hospital?
  B Yes, I know. I _____ (visit) her next Tuesday.

5 A Did you listen to the weather forecast this morning?
  B No, but just look at the sky. It _____ (be) nice and sunny.

6 A Is it something serious, doctor?
  B No, Mr Jones. Take the pills three times a day and you _____ (feel) better soon.

7 A Are you flying somewhere?
  B Yes, to London. My plane _____ (leave) in an hour. I have to hurry.

8 A Are you sure all the guests will come to the reception?
  B I don't know. Some of them _____ (be) too tired to come.

11 Use the correct form of the verbs in brackets to complete people's reactions (1–5) to these ads.

LOST – On number 75 bus - Thursday. Black leather briefcase with initials 'I.C.' Important manuscript inside. Reward. Tel. 6925 672 456.

1 I _____ (call) right now. I think I saw it last night.

HOLIDAY English
Intensive course, six days a week, five hours a day. 10-30 August.
CALL: 00 122 257 493

2 This looks interesting. And it _____ (start) just after I come back from holiday.

...ENTRES
y also:
...Ware (01920) 460777
...arlow (01279) 641886
..X (01992) 637736

Tai-Chi LESSONS
Chinese instructor.
Small groups. Mon/Thu.
Info: 57 Warwick St., 2-5pm.

3 I think I _____ (go) there on Thursday. I _____ (go) shopping with Mum today.

EMERGENCY REPAIRS
Experienced plumbers and electricians available 24 hours. Tel. 01254 638 9002

Computer for ...
Call 01992 60...

4 I _____ (keep) this ad for my granny. Her electric cooker breaks down all the time so she _____ (need) it soon.

WORD PROCESSING IN 5 DAYS
Learn at home. We provide computers/software. £50 a day.
Tel. 034876 95665

5 That's ridiculous! £50 a day! I've got a computer so I _____ (learn) on my own.

12 Personalisation Think about your plans, make decisions and predictions and write five sentences about the future. Use all the different verb forms from this lesson.

Example

The Spanish football team is going to qualify for the World Cup. I may not pass my driving test. I'm going skiing with my friends in February.

In pairs, share your sentences and react to them.

Example

A *The Spanish football team is going to qualify for the World Cup.*
B *Do you think so? I don't think we'll get past the first round!*
A *I'm going skiing with my friends in February.*
B *I envy you. I can't ski so I'm going to stay at home.*

19 Taking it Back

Vocabulary: Multi-part Verbs (5)

Before you start

1 Read the questionnaire. Match the <u>underlined</u> verbs with the meanings below. Use the Mini-dictionary to help you.

compare products and prices, get rid of, approach, begin, give advice about, phoned, convinced/deceived, study, return, see if something fits

2 Work in pairs. Take turns to give your answers to the questionnaire. Check your partner's answers on page 130. How good a consumer is he/she?

3 Look at the Key Words. Which of the problems could you have with the products below? Use the Mini-dictionary to help you.

computer game, portable CD player, DVD, jeans, shirt, track suit, video

KEY WORDS: Shopping Problems
have buttons missing, fade in the wash, make a funny noise, not big enough in the sleeves, not work properly, not work at all, shrink in the wash, too big/small, too tight around the collar

Are You a Good Consumer?

1 Before you buy something, do you <u>shop around</u> in different places?

a always   b sometimes   c never

2 Are you easily <u>taken in</u> by adverts and the appearances of products?

a always   b sometimes   c never

3 When you buy something, do you ever <u>throw away</u> the receipt?

a always   b sometimes   c never

4 Before you buy clothes, do you <u>try</u> them <u>on</u> first?

a always   b sometimes   c never

5 When you buy a gadget, do you <u>read through</u> the guarantee and conditions?

a always   b sometimes   c never

6 If you have a problem with a product, do you <u>take</u> it <u>back</u> to the shop as soon as possible with the receipt, guarantee and packaging?

a always   b sometimes   c never

7 When you take something back, do you <u>go up to</u> a shop assistant and <u>start off</u> by explaining the problem politely?

a always   b sometimes   c never

8 Have you ever <u>rung up</u> your local consumer protection organisation to <u>help</u> you <u>out with</u> a problem?

a yes   b no   c never

Listening

🎧 **4** **Listen to three dialogues in shops. Match the customers (1–3) with the situations (a–d). There is one extra situation. Which customer …**

a kept the receipt and the box?
b didn't have a receipt?
c asked to see the manager?
d didn't read the instructions carefully?

🎧 **5** **Listen again and complete the Function File.**

<table>
<tr><td rowspan="6" style="writing-mode: vertical-lr;">FUNCTION FILE</td><td colspan="2">**Shopping Problems**</td></tr>
<tr><td>**Customer**</td><td>**Shop Assistant/Shopkeeper**</td></tr>
<tr><td>1_____? I've got a problem with this shirt. It's 2_____ around the collar. And it's not 3_____ in the sleeves, either. There are a couple of buttons 4_____, too.</td><td>Have you got 5_____, love? I'm afraid I can't 6_____ your money without a receipt.</td></tr>
<tr><td>This track suit faded and 7_____ in the first wash. It says on 8_____ that it's machine washable. Well, it's 10_____, I suppose. But thanks anyway.</td><td>I'm 9_____, but we can't refund your money.</td></tr>
<tr><td>The first time I used it, it didn't 12_____. Now it doesn't 13_____.

I think I'll take 16_____.</td><td>What exactly's 11_____ with it? Have you got the receipt and 14_____ it came in? I can either get you 15_____ or I can refund your money. Did you pay by 17_____ or by cash?</td></tr>
</table>

Speaking

6 **Your Culture** Why do you think the shop assistants call customers 'love', 'madam' or 'sir'? Do shop assistants say similar things in your country? What differences are there?

🎧 **7** **Pronunciation** Listen and repeat the expressions from the dialogues.

Speaking

8 Imagine you bought a product and had problems with it. Write notes about it.

Example

- radio/make – Roberts/model – 679/cost – ¤ 35

- headphones do not work, cannot get favourite station

- the radio (✓), the receipt (✓), the box (✗)

9 Work in pairs. Take turns to act out the situations as customer and shop assistant.

Example

A *Good morning. I've got a problem with this radio. It's a Roberts 679 and it cost ¤ 35.*
B *Right, sir. What's wrong with it?*

20 Communication Workshops

UNITED COLORS OF BENETTON.

The Micra. Ask before you borrow it.

YOU CAN WITH A NISSAN

http://www.michaelarehn.de

IL GUSTO
italian boots
colonnaden + hamburg

Listening

Before you start

1 Read the Strategies.

LISTENING STRATEGIES: Matching people with what they say

- Read the opinions. <u>Underline</u> opinion words and other important ones (e.g. Thinks that adverts are sexist.).
- The first time you listen, try to get an idea of each person's opinion.
- Listen for important words that you have <u>underlined</u> *or* paraphrases of them (e.g. adverts that treat women like objects) and mark the answers.
- The second time you listen, check your answers and try to answer the others.

LIGNAGE
The art of ...

A Discussion

Listen to two people discussing adverts.

2 Listen to the discussion and use the Strategies to decide who has these opinions, Phil (P), Liz (L) or both of them (B).

1. ☐ doesn't like the car advert at all.
2. ☐ thinks the car ad is a bit sexist.
3. ☐ thinks that the washing powder ad is funny.
4. ☐ likes humour in advertising.
5. ☐ thinks the government should control advertising.
6. ☐ thinks that toy adverts are bad for children.
7. ☐ likes ads with attractive women in them.
8. ☐ thinks advertising manipulates people.
9. ☐ thinks advertising can be an art form.

Speaking

Before you start

Read the Strategies.

> **SPEAKING STRATEGIES: Giving a short presentation**
> - Give yourself plenty of time to look for materials or information.
> - Draw a flowchart to represent your presentation with useful words and expressions. Don't write full sentences.
>
>   ① *show advert from magazine to class*
>
>   ② *describe it – car advert*
>   - *sports car/in showroom/ metallic blue/expensive*
>   - *model/blond/tight skirt/high boots*
>
>   ③ *my opinion*
>   - *don't like it* • *no info about car*
>   - *sexist/uses women to sell products to men*
>
> - Use your flowchart to practise your presentation. Use words like 'right', 'well' and 'OK' to help give you time.
> - When you are giving your presentation in class, don't rush!

A Class Presentation

Give a short presentation to the class about two adverts.

Stage 1

Either choose two adverts from this lesson or look through magazines at home and find two adverts – one you like and one you don't like.

Stage 2

Draw a flowchart to represent what you are going to say. Be prepared to:

- describe the adverts. • say why you like or don't like them.

Stage 3

Practise giving your presentation at home. Use the expressions in the Function File below. Use the Opinion adjectives on page 57.

> **FUNCTION FILE**
>
> **Giving Opinions**
> Personally, I think it's really imaginative and ...
> In my opinion, this advert makes you think ...
> I'm in favour of government control.../
> I'm (totally) against ...

Talkback

Talk to the class about the adverts you have chosen.

Writing

Before you start

1 **Read the email and match the parts (1–5) with the following:**

- final question • ending • reason for writing
- more questions • initial questions

From: Nicholas Thomas [nthom@rvu.uk]

To...	Activa Customer service
Cc...	
Subject:	product enquiry

(1) I am writing to ask some questions about the 'ACTIVA Pentium 5 laptop' advertised on your website.

(2) First, it says that the ACTIVA is very powerful. Is it powerful enough to play all computer games? The advert also mentions an 'extra fast Internet connection'. What exactly does that mean? Is it fast enough to download programmes easily?

(3) Another question is about size. I need a computer that is not too big to put in my school bag and not too heavy to carry. However, I do not want a keyboard that is so small that I can't use it.

(4) Finally, exactly what do you mean by 'fully guaranteed'? Could you tell me how long it is guaranteed for? Does the guarantee cover accidents or just technical problems?

(5) I look forward to hearing from you.
Yours,
Nicholas Thomas

---

2 **Look at the expressions (a-e) from the email. Which of them are followed by *to* + infinitive?**

a powerful enough **b** fast enough **c** (not) too big
d (not) too heavy **e** so small that

A Written Enquiry

Write an email (120–150 words) asking for information about a product. Follow the stages and use Writing Help 5 on page 142.

Stage 1

Choose an advert and think of questions to ask.

Example
(a radio)
- *batteries – how long do they last?*
- *stations* • *size* • *weight* • *headphones*

Stage 2

Use your notes to write an email asking for information. Use linking words. Then check your email.

Talkback

Work in groups. Read each other's emails. Tell the class which products your group chose.

Language Problem Solving 5

Geographical names

1 Read this profile of Scotland and then complete the table.

Scotland occupies the northern part of Britain, bordered in the south by England, in the East by the North Sea and in the West by the Atlantic Ocean.
The country consists of the mainland and many islands, such as the Hebrides, the Shetlands and the Orkneys.
Tourists come to Scotland from Europe and all over the world. The capital of Scotland, Edinburgh, is a popular tourist centre. Tourists also come to see Scotland's beautiful landscape: the lakes, such as Loch Lomond or Loch Ness, famous for the Loch Ness Monster, and the Grampian Mountains, with their highest peak, Ben Nevis (1343 m). The most important river in Scotland is the Clyde, which flows through Glasgow.
Although Scotland is part of the United Kingdom, it has its own banknotes, a separate educational and legal system and its own parliament.

the	geographical name	example from the text	your own example
	continents		
–	countries	*Scotland*	
✓	countries (exceptions)	*the United Kingdom*	
	cities		
	lakes		
✓	rivers		
	seas and oceans		
	single mountains		
	mountain ranges		
–	single islands	*Britain*	
	groups of islands		

2 Complete the sentences with *the* where necessary.

1 A lot of people have emigrated from _____ Europe to _____ United States.
2 Large parts of _____ Netherlands, including its capital, _____ Hague and other famous cities, such as _____ Amsterdam and _____ Rotterdam, lie below sea level.
3 _____ Mount Kosciuszko is the highest mountain and _____ Lake Eyre is the biggest lake in _____ Australia.
4 _____ Corsica is an island in _____ Mediterranean Sea.
5 _____ Prague, the capital of _____ Czech Republic, is famous for its bridges over _____ Veltava.
6 _____ Andes form the backbone of _____ South America.
7 _____ Canary Islands are a popular summer resort for European tourists.

3 Read the text about Scotland again and write a similar one about your country.

Articles

General or specific

4 Which sentences talk about one/a few elephant(s) and which refer to the whole species?

a The circus called off the show because **the elephants** had all fallen ill.
b **The elephant** is the largest animal in Africa.
c For centuries, **elephants** have been killed for ivory.
d During the safari, we were attacked by **an elephant**.
e When we were at the zoo, **the elephant** was having a bath.

5 Put *a/an*, *the* or nothing in the gaps. In which sentences does the noun refer to the whole group of people, animals or things?

1 _____ whale is the biggest living mammal.
2 We saw _____ whale in the sea park in Florida.
3 Do you find _____ computers useful in your job?
4 _____ computer is the most important invention of the twentieth century.
5 How much was _____ computer you bought last month?

6 Read the sentence and choose the best paraphrase (a or b) for the expression in bold.

The young don't think about old age.

a a specific young person
b young people in general

7 Complete the sentences using *the* and one of these adjectives: *poor, rich, homeless, disabled, unemployed.*

1 Winter is a difficult season for _____ who often die of cold and hunger.
2 Should _____ pay higher taxes to support _____?
3 The government has created new jobs for _____.
4 The school has special facilities for _____, like lifts, wide doors and special toilets.

To the west of England, lies a small, almost secret country called Wales. It is a land of green and grey: green fields, valleys and hills; grey mountains and sky, and grey stone castles.

The mystery of Wales

A

The story of the Welsh people is one of determined resistance to invaders – the Romans, the Saxons, the Vikings, the Normans and finally the English. After the fall of the Roman Empire in 410 AD, barbarian Angles and Saxons invaded Britain. Legendary kings and princes, like King Arthur, won important victories against the Saxons but gradually these original 'Britons' were pushed west into the hills and mountains of Wales. Welsh princes fought hard against the English but Wales was finally conquered. In 1301 Edward I gave his son the title of Prince of Wales and in 1536 Wales was united with England.

B

Despite the conquest, this small nation of three million people has maintained its unique culture and strong national identity, particularly through its language. Welsh, a Celtic language very different from English, is one of the oldest languages in Europe. However, in the nineteenth century and first half of the twentieth century, the Welsh language declined. The British government made English the official language and English was the only language allowed in schools. The number of Welsh speakers went down from 80% to under 20% of the population. Since the 1960s, though, there has been a revival. Welsh, along with English, is an official language and is spoken by half a million people. It is taught in schools, it is spoken in the Welsh Assembly, Wales' own regional 'parliament' and there is a Welsh TV channel.

C

A tradition of storytelling, poetry and singing began in the castles of the Welsh princes in the Middle Ages and continues today. Every year, *eisteddfods* are held around the country. An *eisteddfod* is a meeting of poets and singers who take part in competitions. As well as literature in the Welsh language, Wales has produced poets in English such as Dylan Thomas and R.S. Thomas. Famous actors include Richard Burton, Anthony Hopkins and Catherine Zeta-Jones. Wales is a musical nation and choirs are important. Nowadays, when the national rugby team plays in the capital, Cardiff, 80,000 voices can be heard singing the Welsh hymn, 'Bread of Heaven'.

D

The flag of Wales, with its red dragon, is one of the oldest in the world. It was brought to Britain by the Romans. The patron saint of Wales is St David who converted Wales to Christianity and established the Welsh church. The leek, a vegetable, is another national symbol. St David ordered his soldiers to wear them on their helmets before the Welsh went into battle against the Saxons.

1 What do you know about Wales? Choose a, b or c.

1 The population is ...
   a 3 million.   b 13 million.
   c 30 million.
2 The capital is ...
   a Cardiff.   b Belfast.
   c Edinburgh.
3 The official languages is/are ...
   a English.   b Welsh.
   c English and Welsh.
4 The national symbols are ...
   a a dragon and a leek.
   b a lion and a rose.
   c a castle and a tree.

2 Read the article and check your answers.

3 Read the article again. Match the sections (A–D) with these headings. There's one extra heading.

• Symbols of Wales   • Welsh History
• Welsh Sport   • The Welsh Language
• Welsh Culture

4 Why do you think Wales is called an 'almost secret' country?

Comparing Cultures

Prepare for a class discussion. Work in groups. Find out some key information about your country's history and its culture. Decide who is going to make notes about each area:

• early history   • difficult times
• language   • traditions
• national symbols

Each group takes turns to present the information. What are the similarities and differences between your country and Wales?

Review 5

Grammar

1 Complete the sentences with the correct future form of the verbs in brackets.

1. I've decided. This year I _____ (study) a lot harder than I did last year!
2. The train _____ (leave) London at 8.15 next Tuesday morning. It _____ (arrive) in Edinburgh at 14.30.
3. Thanks, I'd love something. I _____ (have) a cup of tea, please. And I _____ (have) a chocolate biscuit, if that's okay.
4. I know the chances are small. But, who knows, I _____ (win) ¤ 1 million on next week's lottery.
5. Watch out! Behind you! That dog _____ (bite) you!
6. This year we _____ (go) to Greece on holiday. We _____ (stay) in a villa on one of the smaller islands.
7. I think Arsenal _____ (win) the league this year. I mean, they've got a really good team, haven't they?
8. Yes, Dad, I _____ (come) back before midnight. I promise.
9. Personally, I don't think she _____ (win) a gold medal. What do you think?

2 Complete all the answers in the quiz with *the* where necessary. Then choose the correct answers.

1. What is the longest river in Britain?
   a _____ Thames b _____ Clyde c _____ Severn
2. What is the highest mountain in Britain?
   a _____ Ben Nevis b _____ Snowdon
   c _____ Scafell
3. What is the biggest lake in Britain?
   a _____ Loch Ness b _____ Lake Windermere
   c _____ Loch Lomond
4. Which group of islands form the southernmost part of Britain?
   a _____ Hebrides b _____ Channel Islands
   c _____ Scilly Islands
5. What is the name of the sea between Wales and Ireland?
   a _____ North Sea b _____ Welsh Sea
   c _____ Irish Sea
6. What is the biggest wild mammal in the British Isles?
   a _____ fox b _____ red deer c _____ roe deer
7. What is the biggest bird in the British Isles?
   a _____ golden eagle b _____ imperial eagle
   c _____ black vulture
8. What group of British people watches the most hours of television?
   a _____ young b _____ middle-aged
   c _____ elderly

🎧 **Now listen and check your answers.**

Vocabulary

3 Choose the correct words in *italics* to complete the sentences.

1. That machine *does/produces/makes* a funny noise.
2. This blouse is made of *top/first/absolute* quality material.
3. You can have a *cheap/basic/standard* room or a *luxury/exclusive/quality* suite.
4. The Italians are very friendly. They give you a *hot/warm/cool* welcome when you go to their houses.

4 **Multi-part verbs** Complete the sentences below.

1. I was taken _____ by the brochure. The holiday wasn't what I expected.
2. If it doesn't work properly, why don't you take it _____?
3. Before the exam, I read _____ all my notes.
4. She's a real squirrel and never throws anything _____!

Pronunciation: Vowel Sounds (2)

5 Look at the <u>underlined</u> sounds below. Say them to yourself.

1. ea: h<u>ea</u>lthy/h<u>ea</u>rt/pl<u>ea</u>sed/h<u>ea</u>r/w<u>ea</u>r/h<u>ea</u>rd
2. ai: <u>ai</u>r/barg<u>ai</u>n/r<u>ai</u>n
3. ia: brilli<u>a</u>nt/reli<u>a</u>ble/marri<u>a</u>ge
4. ie: fr<u>ie</u>nd/bel<u>ie</u>ve
5. ei: rec<u>ei</u>pt/<u>ei</u>ther
6. ou: col<u>ou</u>rful/c<u>ou</u>rse/f<u>ou</u>nd/c<u>ou</u>ple
7. ue: val<u>ue</u>/uniq<u>ue</u>/g<u>ue</u>ss/
8. ua: q<u>ua</u>lity/g<u>ua</u>rantee/sens<u>ua</u>l/grad<u>ua</u>lly/lang<u>ua</u>ge
9. ui: s<u>ui</u>table/s<u>ui</u>te/t<u>ui</u>tion/b<u>ui</u>lding

🎧 **Listen to the sounds and the words. Then listen again and repeat them.**

Look through modules 1–4 for more examples of the sounds above.

6 Can you say this proverb? Use the Phonetic Chart in the Mini-dictionary to help you. What does the proverb mean?

/nevə dʒʌdʒ ə bʊk baɪ ɪts kʌvə/

Check Your Progress

Look back at the Module Objectives on page 57.
◎ Which activities did you enjoy most?
◎ Which activities did you have problems with?
◎ Which grammar area do you need to practise more?

▶▶ Now read the story *The Third Man*, Literature Spot 2, page 134.

6 People

In this module you will...

- **read** diary extracts and a description
- **listen to** descriptions of people, a radio programme, dialogues and a song
- **talk about** people and relationships; **practise** describing people
- **write** a description of a person
- **learn about** modal verbs for speculation and modals in the past

Warm-up

1 Add these words to the correct group in the Key Words.

beard, blond, curly, elderly, long, overweight, slim, wavy, wrinkles

KEY WORDS: Appearance
Hair: bald, dark/fair/red/grey, fringe, plaits, ponytail, shoulder-length
Age: in her/his (early/mid/late) teens/twenties/thirties, middle-aged
Face: chin, eyebrows, forehead, freckles, lips, moustache, shape: narrow/thin/long
General: good-looking, dark/light complexion, short, tall, well-built

Add more words to the list.

2 Use the Key Words and write four or five sentences describing the physical appearance of someone famous (e.g. Nicole Kidman).

Example
She is in her thirties and is very tall and good-looking. She's got blond hair ...

Work in pairs. Read your partner's sentences. Can you guess the person?

3 Listen to the descriptions. Which two people in the big photo are the police looking for?

4 Work in pairs. Take turns to describe people in the photos. Your partner guesses who it is.

Example
She's got quite a long face with a wide mouth and quite small eyes. She's also got long blond hair and glasses.

69

21 Generations

Before you start

1 Look at the photos in this lesson and discuss these questions:

1 How are the people dressed?
2 What do the clothes tell us about the people?
3 Which clothes do you like most? What kinds of clothes do you like wearing?

2 Your Culture What differences are there between your generation and your parents' generation? Think about these things:

- tastes in music/clothes/films
- interests/hobbies • attitudes to life

Do you ever disagree with your parents about any of the things above?

THURSDAY 13	DECEMBER

JENNY GAVE US A GOOD LAUGH LAST NIGHT. IT WAS THE SCHOOL DISCO AND SHE AND SADIE HAVE BEEN WHISPERING IN CORNERS ABOUT IT FOR WEEKS. WHEN IT WAS TIME FOR HER TO LEAVE, JENNY CAME DOWNSTAIRS WEARING A VERY ORDINARY – SUSPICIOUSLY ORDINARY – SKIRT AND T-SHIRT.

CLUTCHED IN HER HAND, HALF-HIDDEN BEHIND HER BACK, WAS A BULGING CARRIER BAG. I ASKED HER WHAT WAS IN THE BAG AND SHE WENT BRIGHT RED.

'JUST ME BOOTS,' SHE MUTTERED. 'IN CASE IT RAINS.' HONESTLY, I COULD HAVE FALLEN OFF MY CHAIR BUT I KEPT A STRAIGHT FACE AND ASKED TO SEE. INSIDE WERE SOME AWFUL BLACK RAGS (SKIRT, TOP AND AN OLD MAN'S WAISTCOAT, BY THE LOOK OF IT). UNDERNEATH IT ALL WERE THE DOC MARTEN'S WE BOUGHT HER FOR LAST YEAR'S WALKING HOLIDAY. SHE WAS OBVIOUSLY INTENDING TO CHANGE SOMEWHERE ELSE AND TRANSFORM HERSELF INTO ONE OF THOSE HIDEOUS GOTHIC CREATURES. PRESUMABLY SADIE OR CATHERINE HAD THE MAKE-UP AND HAIR GLUE WAITING. I ACTED SURPRISED AND SAID IF IT WAS ONLY BLACK CLOTHES SHE WAS TRYING TO HIDE, IT WASN'T WORTH THE BOTHER.

JENNY WENT OFF WITH A SMUG SMILE ... AND MIKE AND I SETTLED DOWN TO A QUIET EVENING WITHOUT HER STEREO BLASTING THROUGH THE PLACE.

I THINK JENNY FORGOT ABOUT THE TIME IT WOULD TAKE TO RESTORE HERSELF TO 'NORMAL' BECAUSE SHE WAS HALF AN HOUR LATE BACK AND EVEN THEN SHE LOOKED LIKE A BATTERED PANDA. ANYWAY, I GAVE HER THE USUAL LECTURE ABOUT BEING LATE BUT IT WAS HARD NOT TO LAUGH.

---

13 Thu

December

The school disco last night was FANTASTIC, once I got there. Mum spotted my bag. I had to show her my clothes ... but then Mum acted like she was a real cool parent. If she could have seen me after we left Cathy's ...!! Cathy lent me her make-up, and Sadie got our hair just right.

The old fogey at the door didn't want to let us in – he's somebody's parent. Almost makes mine look trendy.

The best bit of all was that David Slater was really knocked out by the gear – asked whether we went for that look all the time. I said only on special occasions and he laughed. Then he asked me for a DANCE!

To be truthful, it was not all that romantic ... and we didn't actually touch. But with the music so loud we had to get quite close to shout in each other's ear! I was very hopeful but he had to leave early for some reason. Still, at least he didn't dance with anyone else. I'm in with a chance, surely (?).

He's got to go to his grandparents for Christmas, too. I just knew we would have a lot in common. Anyway, he's going to give me a call after Christmas. A DATE?

I was late back from the disco – it took me ages to get that stuff out of my hair. Mum talked about 'responsibility' and 'concern for others' as usual but who cares? David Slater had noticed me!

[A]

[B]

(From *Not Dressed Like That, You Don't* by Yvonne Coppard)

Reading

3 Read the diaries of a girl (A) and her mother (B) on page 70. Answer these questions.

1 Where did Jenny get changed for the school disco?
2 What kind of clothes did she wear there?
3 Why was she late after the disco?
4 Who did she go to the disco with?
5 Why did her parents have a quiet night?

4 Read the Strategies.

> **READING STRATEGIES: Inferring or 'reading between the lines'**
> - Read the question carefully and find the relevant part(s) of the text.
> - Identify the most important words related to the question.
> - Think about the relationships between characters and use your knowledge of the world to make guesses.

Now use the Strategies to decide if the statements are true (T) or false (F).

Text A

1 ☐ Jenny thinks other parents are even less cool than hers.
2 ☐ David Slater was surprised by the clothes Jenny was wearing.
3 ☐ David and Jenny had a romantic dance together.
4 ☐ Jenny is spending Christmas with her grandparents.
5 ☐ She was not happy after the disco because her mother gave her a lecture.
6 ☐ She hopes David wants to go out with her.

Text B

7 ☐ Before the disco, Jenny and Sadie had talked a lot about their clothes for it.
8 ☐ Jenny got embarrassed because she was not telling the truth.
9 ☐ Her mother was angry when she saw the clothes.
10 ☐ Jenny was pleased because she thought that her mother did not know how she was going to dress.
11 ☐ Jenny's mother did not know what Jenny looked like at the disco.
12 ☐ Her mother thought that Jenny looked funny when she came back.

5 What do you think will happen later in the story? Tell the class.

Vocabulary: Opposites

6 You can often make opposites of adjectives using a prefix.

Examples
*usual/**un**usual, honest/**dis**honest, dependent/**in**dependent, possible/**im**possible*

Use the prefixes to make opposites of the adjectives in *italics*. Use the Mini-dictionary to help you.

Peter is very *organised* and *reliable*. He is also *sociable*, *sensitive* and *tolerant*. He seems *interested* in and *aware* of other people's feelings and is often *kind*. When you ask him for something, he is always *sympathetic* and *helpful*. He is also very *patient* with children. I think he must be very *satisfied* with his life.

Speaking

7 Were the statements (1–7) made by a parent or a teenager?

1 'That looks awful! You look like a tramp.'
2 'I forgot about the time and the bus was late.'
3 'Why didn't you ask me first?'
4 'I've got to study for my exams and I can look after the dog.'
5 'Anyway, my friends are allowed to stay out later.'
6 'All my friends have got one.'
7 'Your father really wants you to come.'

8 Match the statements (1–7) above with the situations (a–c) below.

a the son/daughter goes out with friends and comes home very late at the weekend
b the parents are going on a family holiday but the son/daughter wants to stay at home
c the son/daughter gets an unusual haircut and begins wearing different clothes

Think of more reasons to support the parent's or the teenager's point of view.

Example
c (parent) They don't allow them at school.

9 Work in pairs. Take turns to be a parent and the son or daughter. Act out the situations in Exercise 8.

22 People Watching

Before you start

1 Work in pairs. How curious or 'nosey' are you? Discuss these questions.

1 Do you like watching people? Do you imagine things about their lives? What?
2 When you see groups of people, do you try to work out the relationships between them?
3 Do you ever listen to other people's conversations?
4 Do you like to watch what your neighbours are doing? Why?

2 Read the conversation about the people in the photos. Try to complete the gaps.

A Hey, look at that yacht.
B They must be seriously ¹_____.
A Yes. Do you recognise them? They could be ²_____.
B Or they may have won the lottery! And look! There's a girl swimming near them.
A She might know them.
B I don't think so. She's a long way from the ³_____.
A She may not realise that. She might be snorkelling.
B One thing's for sure, she can't be ⁴_____ about swimming back. Or she might not know about the ⁵_____!
A Can you see that guy over there? He's horribly sunburnt!
B Wow! He must have been in the sun all day.
A Mm. He might have fallen ⁶_____.
B Well, he can't have put any sun cream on, that's for sure.
A Look. Someone's taking some photos of us!
B What a nerve!

🎧 **Listen and check your guesses.**

Presentation

3 Read the dialogue again. Complete the gaps (1–11) with the modal verbs: *must, may, may not, might, might not, can't, could*.

They ¹_____ **be** seriously rich.
They ²_____ **be** famous.
They ³_____ **have won** the lottery.
She ⁴_____ **know** them.
She ⁵_____ **realise** that.
She ⁶_____ **be** snorkelling.
She ⁷_____ **be** worried about swimming back.
She ⁸_____ **know** about the sharks!
He ⁹_____ **have been** in the sun all day.
He ¹⁰_____ **have fallen** asleep.
He ¹¹_____ **have put** any sun cream on.

4 What meaning (a, b or c) do _all_ the sentences in Exercise 3 express:

a decision?   b advice?   c speculation?

5 Copy and complete the table. Which of the modal verbs in Exercise 3 express the following?

a strong conviction that something is/was true	*must*
a strong conviction that something is/was <u>not</u> true	
a possibility that something is/was true	
a possibility that something is/was <u>not</u> true	

6 Look at the sentences (1–3) and decide what they are talking about (a, b or c).

1 She might **know** them.
2 She might **be snorkelling**.
3 He might **have fallen** asleep.

a past event
b unlimited present time
c something happening now

Practice

7 **Choose the best paraphrase (a or b) for each sentence.**

1 I'm sure that they forgot about our wedding.
   a They can't have forgotten about our wedding.
   b They must have forgotten about our wedding.
2 It's possible that John is not a rich businessman.
   a John may not be a rich businessman.
   b John can't be a rich businessman.
3 It's possible that Europe will become one state.
   a Europe might become one state.
   b Europe could have become one state.
4 I think Lisa is learning Italian.
   a Lisa could learn Italian.
   b Lisa could be learning Italian.

8 **Complete the gaps in the sentences with the modal verbs.**

must, may, may not, might, might not, could, can't

1 She goes out every evening. She _____ have a family.
2 He looks depressed. He _____ be having some problems.
3 This woman looks like a politician. She _____ work for the government.
4 He's got a very nice sun tan. He _____ be working in an office all day.
5 Her clothes are all very expensive. She _____ be earning a lot of money.
6 He often goes abroad. He _____ be working for the Secret Service.

9 **Rewrite the sentences using modal verbs without changing the meaning.**

1 I'm sure she's relaxing in her room.
   She _____ in her room.
2 Perhaps the plane arrived late and that's why they're not here.
   The plane _____ late, and that's why they're not here.
3 I don't believe you failed the exam.
   You _____ the exam.
4 It's possible that Sam doesn't like classical music.
   Sam _____ classical music.
5 I'm sure John is not forty-five yet.
   John _____ forty-five yet.
6 It's possible that he's living in Paris now.
   He _____ in Paris now.
7 It's obvious they lied to me about their love affair.
   They _____ to me about their love affair.
8 It's quite likely that Bill didn't win the competition.
   Bill _____ the competition.

10 **Look at the photos (A–C) below and try to speculate about the people's present and past. Compare your ideas with a partner.**

Example

C *She must be a kind person. She can't have a lot of money. She could be lonely. Her children may have left home. She might buy her clothes in charity shops.*

11 **Personalisation Look at your classmates and make speculations about what they did in the past, what they are doing now, what they feel, etc.**

Example

Guiseppe looks sad. He may have quarrelled with his girlfriend.
Carla must be thinking about the test – she looks nervous.
Massimo could be hungry because he's looking at the hamburger advert outside.

A

B

C

23 Personality

Spiral

Square

Oval

Diamond shaped

Triangular

Rectangular

Round

Before you start

Vocabulary: Multi-part Verbs (6)

1 Match the verbs below with the multi-part verbs in *italics* in the sentences.

stop trying, depress, have a good relationship with, continue doing something, criticise, tolerate, meet, start doing (a hobby or a sport)

1 Geoff never lets things *get* him *down*.
2 Alice doesn't *give up* easily and always *gets on with* her work in class.
3 My mum *gets on with* most people and she loves to *get together* with her friends.
4 Tom is good at art and would like to *take up* photography.
5 Charlie is always *getting at* me.
6 Mary *puts up with* a lot of criticism.

2 Choose the Key Words that describe each person in Exercise 1.

KEY WORDS: Personality Adjectives (1)
bad-tempered, cheerful, confident, creative, critical, disorganised, dynamic, generous, hard-working, helpful, honest, insensitive, materialistic, moody, outgoing, patient, persistent, positive, reliable, selfish, shy, sociable, stubborn, sympathetic, tolerant

Example
Geoff is very cheerful.

3 Describe yourself. Be honest! Use the multi-part verbs and two or three Key Words to write about yourself.

Example
I'm shy. I get on with people I know but I don't like meeting new people.

Listening

4 Choose one of the chocolates. Then listen to the radio programme. Do you agree with the description of your personality?

5 Read the Strategies.

Listening Strategies: True/False Questions
• Before you listen, read the statements. Where you can, try to make guesses about what is true or false.
• Underline important words (e.g. opinion adjectives or facts and numbers) in the statements.
• While listening, listen for these words or synonyms of them (e.g. attractive/good-looking).
• When you listen a second time, check your answers

Listen to the descriptions of a girl. Use the Strategies to decide if the statements are true (T) or false (F).

1 ☐ Lucy sometimes changes the colour of her hair.
2 ☐ She is as good-looking as a model.
3 ☐ One of her favourite hobbies is walking.
4 ☐ She's a person that her friends can rely on.
5 ☐ She could work harder at school if she wanted.
6 ☐ The best time of the day for her is the morning.
7 ☐ She is very organised and tidy.
8 ☐ She is a friendly, outgoing person.

6 Listen to the descriptions again and complete the Function File.

FUNCTION FILE

Describing People

Appearance:
What does she **1**_____?
She's usually got **2**_____ hair. And she sometimes **3**_____ in a pony tail.
Everyone says she **4**_____ a model!

Interests:
What does she like?
She likes **5**_____ to music, rock music – she's always **6**_____ her Walkman on!

Personality:
What is she **7**_____?
She's got a lovely **8**_____, you know.
She sometimes **9**_____ a bit disorganised, but really she's totally **10**_____.
And she's **11**_____ helping other students.
She always **12**_____ her best.
She can be a bit **13**_____ in the mornings.
She's always **14**_____ and will always do **15**_____ to help.

Speculation:
A nice girl. Her parents **16**_____ be proud of her.

7 Which of the statements (1–3) are true of all three sentences (a–c)?

a She's always thinking.
b She's always helping others.
c She's always forgetting her arrangements.

1 The speaker expresses strong feelings (positive or negative).
2 She does these things very often.
3 She's doing these things now.

8 Now use the cues to write sentences using *always* and the Present Continuous.

Example
1 *She's always forgetting things.*

1 forget things (she)
2 criticise people (he)
3 buy presents (my mum)
4 lose my keys (I)
5 borrow my pencil (they)

What things are you always doing? Tell the class.

Example
I'm always getting lost.

Speaking

9 Write notes about someone you know.

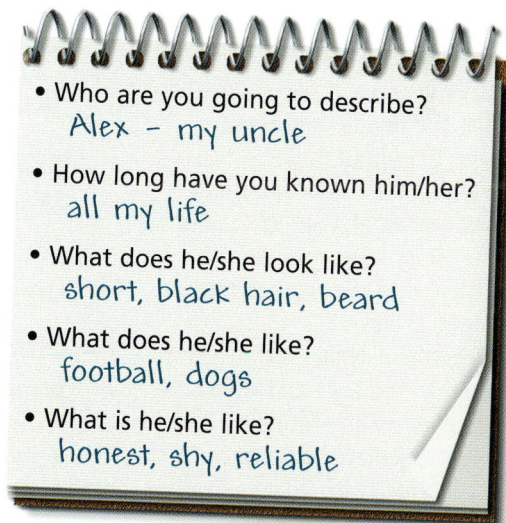

- Who are you going to describe?
  Alex – my uncle
- How long have you known him/her?
  all my life
- What does he/she look like?
  short, black hair, beard
- What does he/she like?
  football, dogs
- What is he/she like?
  honest, shy, reliable

10 Work in pairs. Ask and answer the questions in Exercise 9.

Example
A *Who are you going to describe?*
B *My uncle. He's called Alex.*
A *Mm ... and what's he like?*

QUOTE ... UNQUOTE
'*Being* a personality is not the same as *having* a personality.'
Alan Coren, British writer (1938 –)

24 Communication Workshops

Speaking

Before you start

1 Read the Strategies.

Speaking Strategies: Speculating About Photos

- Describe the people and the places in the photos.
- Speculate about the people: how old they are; what they do; where they are from; what they are like as people; what the relationship is between them.
- Speculate about what has happened in the past and what could happen in the future.
- When you speculate about the photos, interact with your partner (e.g. The boy looks kind, don't you think?).
- Discuss your opinions of the people's clothes and decide if you would like to meet them.

2 What else could you speculate about when you discuss photos?

Example
where they are, their moods

Discussing a Photo

Discuss the photos.
Follow the stages below.

Stage 1
Use the Strategies to prepare for the discussion.

Stage 2
Work in pairs. Discuss the photos.
- Who are the people?
- What is their relationship?
- How do you think they feel about each other?
- Where are they? What are they doing?
- What do you think they are talking about?
- Which of the people would you like to meet? Why?

Talkback
Form a group with another pair. Compare the results of your discussions.

Example
A *We think they must be going out together.*
B *We don't agree. We think that they must have just met.*

Listening

Before you start

1 Work in pairs. Think of ten people from history who you think were geniuses.

2 Which categories do they fit in?

- artistic   • scientific
- mathematical   • philosophical
- political   • military   • sporting

A Radio Programme

Listen to a programme about geniuses.

3 Listen to the programme. Which of these people are <u>not</u> mentioned?

- Shakespeare
- Leonardo da Vinci
- Chopin
- Michelangelo
- Einstein
- Copernicus
- Aristotle
- Churchill
- Bach
- the Brontë sisters
- Newton   • Strauss   • Mozart

Chopin

4 Listen again and match the sentences (1–10) with the people: Dr Hofmeyer (H), Carlo Rossi (R), or both (B).

1 ☐ Thinks that a lot of geniuses show their brilliance during childhood.

2 ☐ There are quite a few examples of children who are musical geniuses.

3 ☐ Says that some geniuses were not very good at school.

4 ☐ Makes a joke about his/her schooldays.

5 ☐ Says that most geniuses come from ordinary families.

6 ☐ Gives examples of families of geniuses.

7 ☐ Talks about the Brontë sisters.

8 ☐ Points out that many geniuses die young.

9 ☐ Makes a joke about being a genius.

10 ☐ Gets impatient with the other person.

Writing

Before you start

1 Read the description, My Grandmother. Which paragraphs (1–3) are these topics in?

- appearance   • character • relationships • likes and dislikes
- background

2 Which of the <u>underlined</u> linking expressions in the description give examples?

My Grandmother

[1] My grandmother is called Alice. She is sixty-one and she lives with my grandfather in a flat in the centre of town. It's an old flat and it's quite small. She works in a chemist's – she has worked in the same shop for twenty years. It's hard to imagine the shop without her. She doesn't have any hobbies and doesn't play sport at her age <u>but</u> she loves children and animals, <u>especially</u> dogs. She used to have a collie called Tuka but it died a few years ago. I sometimes meet her in town for a coffee or snack. She hates junk food, <u>such as</u> hamburgers. She never watches TV, except films. Her favourite films are romantic comedies.

[2] Alice has got short, white hair and clear, blue eyes. She is quite short and a bit thin. She always wears lots of make-up, <u>especially</u> lipstick and you can smell her perfume when she kisses you! She is a very cheerful woman. In fact, she's always smiling. Her smile is what people remember about her. She's <u>also</u> very generous and helpful.

[3] My grandmother is very popular with her neighbours, maybe <u>because</u> she is so helpful. <u>For example</u>, she often babysits for people in her street. Grandad says she spends more time with neighbours than with him! They often argue, <u>particularly</u> about politics but after 40 years of marriage, I'm sure they love each other really!

Describing a Person

Write a description of a person you know and like. Follow the stages below and refer to Writing Help 6 on page 142.

Stage 1

Decide who you are going to write about – someone in your family, a friend or a famous person.

Stage 2

Write some notes in the form of a diagram.

Stage 3

Write three paragraphs. Use linking words. Check your description for mistakes.

APPEARANCE
• white hair • lots of make-up
• clear, blue eyes • short • thin

CHARACTER
• cheerful – always smiling
• generous • helpful

MY GRANDMOTHER

RELATIONSHIPS
• popular with neighbours
• often babysits
• argues with Grandad

LIKES
• talking, esp. gossip
• animals, esp. dogs
• loves children

DISLIKES
• TV (except films) • junk food

Talkback

In groups, read your descriptions. Who would be the most interesting person to meet?

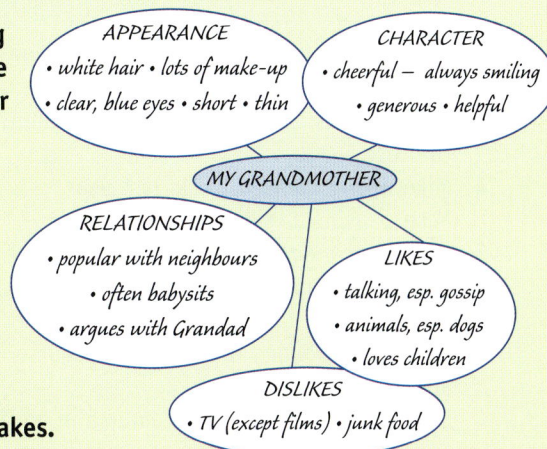

Language Problem Solving 6 Modals in the past

had to, didn't have to, could(n't), be able to

1 Read the text and look at the modal expressions (1–7) in blue. Match them with the meanings (a–g) below.

Before I went to school, I was a happy and carefree child. I **1didn't have to** do any homework or sit in a chair for hours every day. I just **2had to** stay with my granny. I **3could** do what I wanted and she never complained about my behaviour. The only thing I **4couldn't** do was to leave the garden on my own. I learned a lot of things from my granny. By the time I was five, I **5could** sing and play the piano a little. However, before I went to school, I **6couldn't** draw or paint very well because my granny wasn't very keen on art. But she was a great sports fan. We went on cycling trips and played games. One summer, she took me to see the World Cup and we **7were able to** watch Diego Maradona play against Germany.

a managed to (past achievement)
b was obliged to (obligation in the past)
c wasn't obliged to (lack of obligation in the past)
d had the ability to (ability in the past)
e didn't have the ability to (lack of ability in the past)
f was allowed to (permission in the past)
g wasn't allowed to (lack of permission in the past)

2 Rephrase the words in *italics* using the modal expressions from Exercise 1. Make sure the pairs of sentences have the same meaning.

1 My dad *didn't know how to* drive until he was 30.
   My dad _____ drive until he was 30.
2 They *were obliged to* reply to the invitation within ten days.
   They _____ reply to the invitation within ten days.
3 The students *were allowed to* talk to one another after the test.
   The students _____ talk to one another after the test.
4 Mike *wasn't allowed to* ski last year.
   Mike _____ ski last year.
5 *Did* you *manage to* get the tickets to the match?
   _____ you _____ get the tickets to the match?
6 She *wasn't obliged to* pay for her course in advance.
   She _____ pay for her course in advance.

3 Complete the sentences with *had to, didn't have to, could, couldn't, was/were able to.*

1 When I was a child, I _____ clean or wash the dishes – my parents did it.
2 During the war, people _____ eat very simple food.
3 My granny didn't speak Italian but she _____ communicate with our guests in French.
4 Jenny _____ use computers at all until she did a computer course.
5 Before the telephone was invented, people _____ write letters.
6 Einstein _____ speak until he was four but he _____ count very quickly.
7 Captain Scott and his team _____ reach the Pole but they didn't manage to return.
8 By the twenties, women _____ wear long skirts any longer – shorts and short dresses became acceptable.
9 Victor Frankenstein knew that he _____ destroy the monster he had created but he _____ catch him.
10 My maths teacher was not very strict – we _____ use our notes in tests.

4 Think about how ordinary people lived in Europe in the Middle Ages. Use the cues and modal expressions from the lesson to write sentences.

Example
They couldn't travel fast from one place to another.

- travel fast from one place to another
- take a hot shower every morning
- cure illnesses such as pneumonia
- worry about the greenhouse effect
- travel on foot or on horseback
- build very big churches
- work from 9 to 5
- perform medical operations

5 Think about your childhood. Write sentences about your abilities, obligations and achievements when you were seven years old. Use modal expressions from this lesson.

6 Work in pairs. Share your childhood memories.

Example
A *When I was seven, I couldn't speak English. Could you?*
B *I could say a few words.*

BOB DYLAN

A Bob Dylan was born in 1941. He started singing in New York clubs in the early 1960s and made his first album in 1962. In the USA at that time, many poor people and minorities like black people had no civil rights. Dylan's early protest songs, such as *Blowing in the Wind* and *The Times They Are A-Changin'*, became associated with the civil rights movement for social change.

B During the mid-1960s, he was influenced by rock music. He began playing electric guitar and his concerts were extremely loud. Also, his lyrics became more complex in songs such as *Like a Rolling Stone* and *Visions of Johanna*.

C Bob Dylan has made over forty albums and his songs have covered a wide variety of musical styles. Also, he has been on tour more or less continuously since 1989 – something his fans refer to as the 'Never-Ending Tour'.

Dylan in the 1960s

1 Read about Bob Dylan. Match the paragraphs (A–C) with the headings (1–4). There is one extra heading.

1 Changing Style   3 The Voice of Protest
2 Best selling record   4 Life on the Road

Do you know anything else about the USA in the 1960s? Tell the class.

2 Read the song lyrics. Use the Mini-dictionary to help you with new verbs or expressions. Try to guess the gapped words. Think about the rhymes in each verse.

Example
1 *grown (roam)*

Now listen and check your guesses.

3 Match the statements (1–5) with the verses (A–E).

1 Journalists and writers should observe society carefully.
2 People should realise that society is changing if they want to survive.
3 Parents cannot impose their values on their children any more.
4 The old, unfair social structure is already disappearing.
5 Politicians should pay attention to the demand for social change.

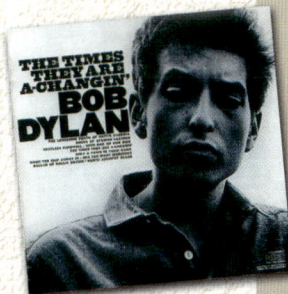

4 Your Culture What protest songs do you have in your country? What would you like to hear a protest song about nowadays? Tell the class.

The Times They Are A-Changin'

A Come gather round people wherever you roam,
And admit that the waters around you have 1 _____,
And accept it that soon you'll be drenched to the bone.
If your time to you is worth saving,
Then you better start swimming or you'll sink like a
2 _____,
For the times they are a-changin'.

B Come writers and critics who prophesy with your pen
And keep your eyes wide the chance won't come
3 _____,
And don't speak too soon for the wheel's still in spin,
And there's no telling who that it's naming.
For the loser now will be later to 4 _____,
For the times they are a-changin'.

C Come senators, congressmen, please heed the call
Don't stand in the doorway, don't block up the 5 _____
For he that gets hurt will be he who has stalled.
There's a battle outside and it is raging.
It'll soon shake your windows and rattle your 6 _____,
For the times they are a-changin'.

D Come mothers and fathers throughout the land,
And don't criticize what you can't 7 _____,
Your sons and your daughters are beyond your command
Your old road is rapidly ageing.
Please get out of the new one if you can't lend your
8 _____,

E For the times they are a-changin'.

The line it is drawn, the curse it is cast,
The slow one now will later be 9 _____
As the present now will later be 10 _____,
The order is rapidly fading.
And the first one now will later be 11 _____
For the times they are a-changin'.

79

Review 6

Grammar

1 Complete the sentences using *must*, *may* or *can't*.

1 They have got two houses and three cars. They _____ be rich.
2 I don't know what nationality he is. He _____ be Belgian.
3 Everyone has got their umbrellas up. It _____ be raining.
4 Fiona is very brown. She _____ have just got back from holiday.
5 I've no idea where she is. She _____ be out shopping.
6 I can't find my pen and I last had it this morning. I _____ have left it at school.
7 His light is on. He _____ have gone to sleep yet.
8 The letter's not here. She _____ have taken it.

2 Work in pairs. Speculate about the following situations using *must*, *might*, *may* or *can't* in the present or the past.

Example
1 **A** *He must be a good player.*
   B *Or he might have been lucky.*

1 He scored three goals in one match.
2 Paul hasn't come to school today.
3 Miriam knows a lot about dinosaurs.
4 He's crashed into a bus.
5 Kate's crying.

3 Complete the sentences with *had to*, *didn't have to*, *could*, *couldn't*, or *was/were able to*.

1 We _____ pay to get in – it was free!
2 It rained heavily but we _____ shelter in a shop doorway.
3 Before emails, people _____ send letters by post.
4 Our car broke down but we _____ push it to a garage.
5 I _____ get up early because it was a holiday.
6 My brother is very bright; he _____ read when he was four.
7 It was a very formal occasion; I _____ wear a suit and tie.
8 I _____ get to school because of the heavy snow.
9 My English wasn't perfect but I _____ negotiate the price of the hotel room.
10 When I was a student in Spain, I _____ wear summer clothes for most of the year.

Vocabulary

4 Copy the table and write opposites of these adjectives in the correct column.

kind, possible, aware, dependent, honest, interested, organised, reliable, satisfied, sensitive, sociable, tolerant, patient, usual

un ...	in ...	dis ...	im ...
unkind			

5 Multi-part verbs Complete the sentences with *at*, *down*, *on*, *together*, *up* or *with*.

1 This miserable weather is getting me _____.
2 I gave _____ trying because it was too difficult.
3 The teacher asked us to get _____ _____ our work.
4 I don't know how you can put _____ _____ all this noise.
5 We'll have to get _____ some time.
6 We don't get _____ _____ our neighbours.
7 My big brother is always getting _____ me.

Pronunciation: Difficult Sounds

6 Look at the Phonetic Chart in the Mini-dictionary. Which words in the following sentences have these sounds?

/θ/, /ð/, /tʃ/, /ʃ/, /dʒ/, /ʒ/

1 Marriage will be more popular this century – that's my prediction.
2 The teacher with short hair is in his thirties.
3 Both of them then watched television together.
4 I think she's a sympathetic, cheerful and generous young girl.
5 It's unusual to like both maths and literature.
6 I think you should go to China this January.

🎧 Now listen and check your answers. Then listen again and repeat the sentences.

7 Can you say this proverb? Use the Phonetic Chart in the Mini-dictionary to help you. What does the proverb mean?

/æbsəns meɪks ðə hɑːt grəʊ fɒndə/

Check Your Progress

Look back at the Module Objectives on page 69.
◎ Which activities did you enjoy most?
◎ Which activities did you have problems with?
◎ Which grammar areas do you need to practise more?

7 Learning

The Thinker
by Rodin

In this module you will...

- **read** magazine articles, an essay and an education factfile
- **talk about** learning and school experiences; **practise** asking for information
- **listen to** people talking about memory, schools and a phone call
- **write** a 'for and against' essay
- **learn** more **about** conditional sentences and verbs followed by an *-ing* form or infinitive

Warm-up

1 Game **Work in pairs. Look at the words in the box for one minute. Then close your books and write down all the words you can remember together.**

> sandcastle, embarrassing, zero gravity, mobile phone, hip hop, weird, imitation, jealous boyfriend, photo, kayak, mandolin, paper airplanes, message, harp, statue, stunts, the web, enormous, sword fighting, show business, the Internet, guitar

2 Read the Strategies. Which did you use to remember the words in Exercise 1?

MEMORY STRATEGIES

- Read the list of words in silence a few times.
- Repeat the words aloud. Begin with one word, then two, then three and so on.
- Think of items visually (e.g. *a paper airplane*).
- Make connections between words (e.g. *mobile phone, message, the Internet*).
- Classify words grammatically (e.g. *embarrassing, enormous, weird* = adjectives).
- Classify words alphabetically (e.g. *sandcastle, show business, statue*).

School of Athens in
Ancient Greece by Raphael

3 Listen to four students talking about how they remember words. Match the students (1–4) with the strategies (a–d).

1 Johan 2 Basia 3 Pablo 4 Hilmi

a analytical – thinks about the structure of words.
b visual – writes or draws; connects words with pictures.
c self-testing – does personal tests or asks someone at home to give a test.
d oral – says words aloud; makes connections between words.

4 Choose three things that you are good at remembering.
numbers: phone numbers, dates, scores, prices
sounds: voices, melodies, bird songs
images: what people wear; details of rooms and furniture
places: names, directions
smells: places, food

Work in pairs. Tell your partner about yourself and give examples.

Example
I'm good at remembering dates in history.

25 Get Learning!

Before you start

1 Look at the photos and answer the questions.

1 Where are the people? Who do you think they are?
2 What are the people doing? Why do you think they are doing it?
3 Which activity would you find the most difficult to learn? Why?

2 Which of these things have you used to help you learn English? Which others would you like to try?

books, cassettes or CDs, classes, computer games, computer programs, the Internet, lectures, mobile phones, radio or television programmes, videos or DVDs

B
Offbeat Web Courses

The web is a great place to learn new skills. However, there are some strange choices! Let me introduce you to the weird world of online classes.

My terrible sandcastle-building skills have always been very embarrassing for my kids and me. But now, thanks to www.sandcastlecentral.com, I can make brilliant sandcastles with towers and bridges!

If you can't dance, then you should visit www.bustamove.com. This website can get you dancing to hip hop or salsa in no time. Small, animated figures take you through the various dance steps, with different levels from beginners to advanced.

A
M-Learning Revolution

Teachers are used to asking students to turn off their mobile phones but soon they could be a major classroom aid for teaching and learning.

'Having spent years getting young people to put their mobiles away, we'll actually be asking students to get them out,' predicts Sally Paggetti, a teacher in Richmond. Currently, three schools in the Richmond area are taking part in a revolutionary m-learning project in which students will use their mobile phones. 'I think students have been very motivated by the project and were quick to learn how to use the new phones,' said Ms Paggetti.

The UK has a high number of mobile phones, with about 80% of homes owning one or more. More phones nowadays have links to the Internet and can do picture messaging. They are also a lot smaller than computers so you can take them anywhere.

Students can use the phones to get access to learning materials. 'And for language classes, there are amazing possibilities. Students can see and speak to people in a school in France or Germany,' says Ms Paggetti. 'I've also used mobiles on school trips – students make calls and send pictures back to friends working at school.'

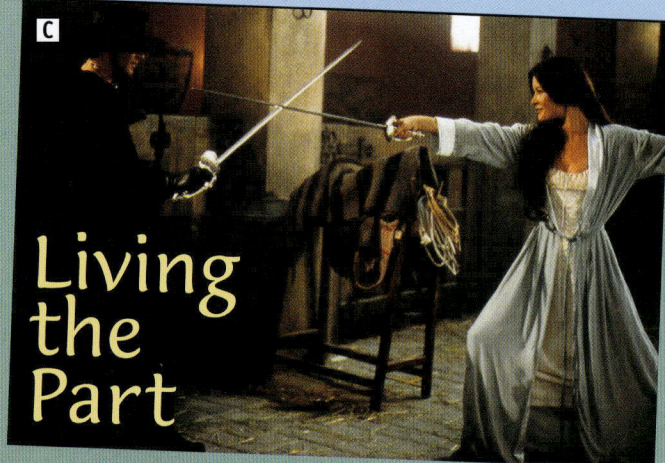

C
Living the Part

More and more top Hollywood actors are taking up 'method-acting'. This means that they live the part they are going to play and even take classes in order to learn special skills.

Robert de Niro was one of the first actors to learn a musical instrument when he learnt to play the saxophone for his part in *New York, New York*. Since then, actors like Nicolas Cage, Meryl Streep and Sean Penn have learnt the mandolin, the harp and the jazz guitar respectively.

Other actors have learnt how to look after themselves. Keanu Reeves spent six months studying martial arts for *The Matrix*, while Catherine Zeta-Jones and Antonio Banderas had to learn sword fighting for *The Mask of Zorro*. Brad Pitt learnt how to box for two of his films – so jealous boyfriends should be no problem for him now!

Some actors have learnt more specialist skills. For his part in *The Horse Whisperer*, Robert Redford learnt how to train horses by whispering into their ears. And the actors in *Apollo 13* made the effort to learn to move in zero gravity.

All these skills must surely make their performances more convincing. Imagine having a party with Redford whispering to horses in one corner, Cage playing the mandolin in another, as Zeta-Jones fights with Banderas in the garden. There's no business like show business!

And if you <u>get</u> excited at the thought of flying an airplane, you can <u>take lessons</u> at www.firstflight.com. The advert says 'Start learning to fly today for $49.99!' – it can't be *that* easy! Apparently, you learn what to do during the takeoff, flight and landing – and how to <u>take action</u> in an emergency.

As well as all this, you can learn to make fantastic paper airplanes at www.bestpaperairplanes.com, make a kayak with Steve Baxter at www.olympus.net/personal/sbaxter or become a 'balloon scientist' at www.BalloonHQ.com.

So what are you waiting for? Log on and learn something!

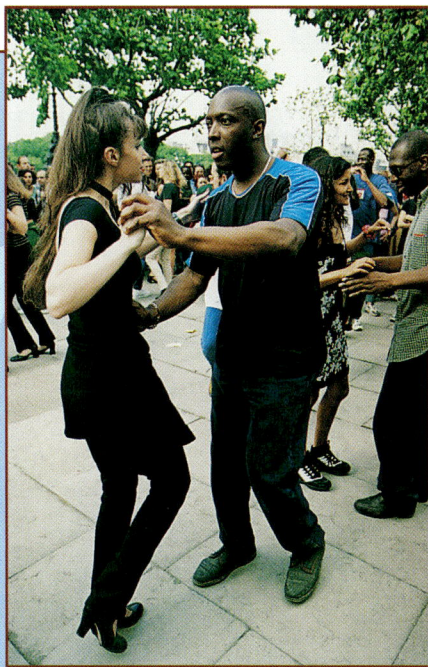

Reading

3 Work in groups of three. Each student reads a different text – A, B or C. Answer these questions about your text.

1 Who and/or what is the text about?
2 What can the people learn?
3 What ways of learning from Exercise 2 are mentioned?

4 Tell the other students in your group about the article you read.

Example
Well, it's about mobile phones. It's about three schools in Britain where …

While you are listening, think of a question to ask about the other articles. What is the most interesting information for you?

5 Read the Strategies.

READING STRATEGIES: Facts and opinions
- Facts give information which is definitely true (e.g. Three schools are taking part in a project).
- Opinions often contain adjectives that show what a person thinks about something (e.g. *fantastic, boring*).
- Opinions are often expressed by speculating. Look out for verbs like *should be, can't be, could be* and *must be* and expressions like *I think, I suppose* or *personally, apparently*.

6 Now read all the texts. Use the Strategies to find one fact and one opinion in each one.

7 Answer these questions.

1 What opinions are given about …
   a using mobile phones in school? b learning on the Internet?
   c method acting?
2 What, in your opinion, are the pros and cons of each way of learning?
3 What examples of humour can you find in texts B and C?

Vocabulary: *get, have, make, take*

8 Find the <u>underlined</u> expressions in the texts (A–C). Match them with these meanings. Use the Minidictionary to help you.

become, build, carry, do something, learn, help you to do something, organising, make someone do something, connect to, participate in, reach, start to do, telephone, try hard

Speaking

9 Work in pairs. Ask and answer questions. You can choose more than one answer or give another alternative.

1 What would you like to learn to do?
   a dance salsa
   b fly a plane
   c play a musical instrument
   d do martial arts
2 What would you like to learn to make?
   a clothes b exotic meals
   c furniture d jewellery
3 Why are you learning English?
   a to get better at it
   b to get a better job
   c to get school qualifications
   d to get to know people from other countries
4 Which two of these things do you think are most useful for learning a language?
   a to have a good memory
   b to have patience
   c to make an effort
   d to be interested in it
5 How do you learn languages best?
   a taking part in class activities
   b doing exercises at home
   c doing games and listening to songs
   d having regular tests
6 What problems do you have speaking in English?
   a I sometimes get nervous.
   b I make a lot of mistakes.
   c I take a long time to say things.
   d I can't remember the right words.

10 Tell the class two things about your partner.

GRAMMAR FOCUS:

26 Teachers

Before you start

1 Work in pairs. Discuss the questions below.

1 Who was your favourite teacher at primary school?
2 What can you remember about him/her?
3 Why did you like him/her?

2 Read the texts and answer these questions.

Text A

1 At school, Graham says he was …
   a hard-working but shy.   **b** uncooperative and lazy.   **c** not clever but enthusiastic.
2 Graham liked Mr Jenkins because he was …
   a funny.   **b** enthusiastic.   **c** well-prepared.
3 Graham thinks Mr Jenkins helped with his …
   a astronomy.   **b** confidence.   **c** determination.

Text B

4 Mr Jenkins thought Graham was …
   a very intelligent but lazy.
   b good in all subjects.
   c very difficult to teach.
5 Mr Jenkins often feels …
   a unhappy.   **b** proud.   **c** worthwhile.
6 Mr Jenkins says teachers nowadays have to deal with …
   a lack of equipment.   **b** large classes.
   c small classes.

Presentation

3 Read the conditional sentences in blue in the texts (A and B). Say if they are Zero Conditional, First Conditional or Second Conditional. Match them with their meanings.

a a rule, something that's always true
b a piece of advice
c a future situation that is unlikely to happen
d a future situation that is possible
e a present situation that is impossible
f an event that is possible if it's not stopped by something

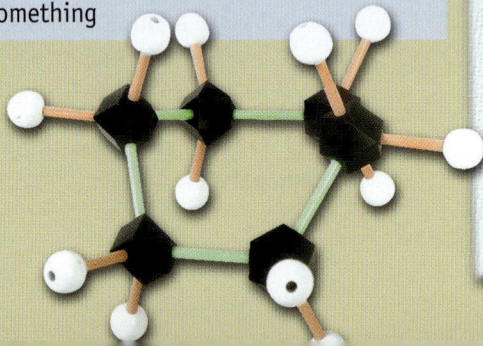

A

MY INSPIRATION

Graham Lawrence, 29, science author and TV presenter, went to Overton Comprehensive, 1986–94.

I haven't seen Mr Jenkins since I left school but he was my inspiration. I wasn't very good at most school subjects. I didn't make an effort, especially in history and languages. If I'd taken part in my French lessons, I might actually have learnt some French. And I wouldn't have had to take evening classes! Now I tell my own kids: 'If I were you, I'd try to learn as much as you can. It might be useful in future!'

Anyway, I remember that when I went into Mr Jenkins's science class, I became interested in a subject for the first time. Mr Jenkins was full of enthusiasm and he got everybody interested. He used to demonstrate things with lots of practical examples. One day he took us outside and we built a rocket and actually launched it! His lessons were great fun.

I wasn't a particularly willing and cooperative student at school, probably because I was lazy and lacked confidence but Mr Jenkins made me feel that I could do things. I was interested in astronomy and he asked me to give a presentation to the class. That was really the first time I ever tried to explain science to an audience. If I hadn't had that experience, I honestly don't think I would have become a TV presenter. You know, you can't stand in front of millions of people unless you have confidence.

When I'm preparing a programme, I often think about how Mr Jenkins would have done it. Now I know he's still at the school, I think I'll get in touch with him if I need some new ideas!

What would I have done if I hadn't had a science teacher like Mr Jenkins? It's difficult to say but all I know is that if he hadn't taught me, my life would probably have been very different.

I don't think any school would risk having me as a full time teacher but if I got an interesting offer I could do some science teaching myself.

B

MY PUPIL

Brian Jenkins, science teacher at Overton Comprehensive

When Graham came into my class he was a bit 'difficult'. But when he got interested, it all changed. He was extremely bright and if he'd studied, he could have done much better in all his other subjects. I've seen him a couple of times on TV and I say to my wife, 'Oh look, I used to teach him!' Students like Graham certainly make my job worthwhile. It's difficult teaching nowadays – there are more discipline problems and not enough money. Unless you are a dedicated teacher, you won't stay in teaching long. Class sizes have gone up and it's difficult doing lessons in laboratories with big groups. But if you're a teacher, you have to cope with all sorts of problems.

Anyway, I love teaching. I think I'd be very unhappy if I did some other kind of job. It's a great feeling when you know you've taught something well. It also makes me proud when I see my pupils doing well, like Graham. I feel that I've achieved something.

Third Conditional

4 Complete the conditional sentences from the texts with *would, could, might, have, had* or *hadn't*.

1 If I'd taken part in my French lessons, I _____ have learnt some French.
2 If I hadn't had that experience, I honestly don't think I _____ have become a TV presenter.
3 What would I _____ done if I hadn't had a science teacher like Mr Jenkins?
4 If he _____ taught me, my life would have been very different.
5 If he _____ studied, he _____ have done much better.

5 Read this Third Conditional sentence from the text and answer the questions.

If **I'd taken part** in my French lessons, I **might** actually **have learnt** some French.

• What time is Graham talking about: past, present or future?
• What really happened: Did he take part in his French lessons? Did he manage to learn French at school?

6 Complete this pattern of the Third Conditional.

If + _____, would/wouldn't/could/couldn't/ might/might not + _____ + 3rd form of the verb

Practice

7 Use the cues to complete the conditional sentences.

1 If I were you, _____ (I/go to university).
2 If I read too long, _____ (my eyes/usually/go red).
3 _____ (you/not be able/go sailing with us) if you get a holiday job in the summer.
4 If you spoke English and French, _____ (you/can work at the Council of Europe).
5 _____ (you/not get the job) unless you have a driving licence.
6 If I go to bed early, _____ (I/normally/get up early too).
7 _____ (he/study/abroad) if he got a grant.
8 If the weather doesn't change, _____ (we/not climb to the top).

8 Which of the conditional sentences is correct in each context?

1 Jimmy didn't revise and failed the test.
   a If Jimmy hadn't revised, he would have failed.
   b If Jimmy had revised, he wouldn't have failed.
   c If Jimmy revised, he wouldn't fail.

2 Mark studied history and became a history teacher.
   a Mark wouldn't become a history teacher if he didn't study history.
   b Mark wouldn't have become a history teacher if he hadn't studied history.
   c Mark would have become a history teacher if he had studied history.
3 The weather was good so we went out.
   a If the weather hadn't been good, we wouldn't have gone out.
   b If the weather had been good, we would have gone out.
   c If the weather was good, we would go out.

9 Complete these Third Conditional sentences with the verbs in brackets in their correct forms.

1 If the exam _____ (not be) so difficult, I _____ (pass).
2 If he _____ (work) a little harder, he _____ (win) a scholarship to study abroad.
3 I _____ (not help) him with his maths if he _____ (not promise) to help me with my French.
4 If they _____ (not study) computing, they _____ (not get) such good jobs.
5 If I _____ (learn) Russian at school, I _____ (understand) what they were saying.
6 I _____ (not need) a holiday job if I _____ (win) a scholarship.
7 Where _____ (you study) if you _____ (have) a choice?

10 Rewrite these sentences as conditionals.

1 I went to school in Mexico, where I learnt Spanish.
2 I didn't do any sport at school and I wasn't very fit when I graduated.
3 There were fewer school subjects in the past so pupils didn't have to learn so much.
4 My teachers were fantastic so I loved going to school.
5 The teachers didn't give us a lot of tests so we weren't afraid to go to school.

11 **Personalisation** Finish these sentences. Then, in pairs, discuss your answers with your partner.

1 If my family were millionaires, _____.
2 If I had been born in 1900, _____.
3 Unless I finish university, _____.
4 If I was thirty now, _____.
5 If I had gone to a primary school abroad, _____.
6 If I was of the opposite sex, _____.

27 Schools

Listening

2 **Read the Strategies.**

> **LISTENING STRATEGIES: Multiple-choice questions**
> - Read the questions and alternative answers.
> - Try to eliminate any unlikely answers and try to predict possible answers from your general knowledge.
> - Decide what type of information you are listening for (e.g. adjectives, numbers, frequency or quantity words).
> - Remember, the words in the recording may not be the same as the words in the question. Try to think of synonyms of important words.
> - The first time you listen, try to get the general idea and mark any answers that are clearly correct.
> - The second time, focus on the answers you are not sure of.
> - If it is a test and you don't know the answer, always guess!

3 **Listen to five people talking about the schools they went to. Use the Strategies to answer the questions.**

1 David usually saw his family …
  a at weekends. **b** once a month. **c** during the holidays.
2 David says his teachers were …
  a strict and unhelpful. **b** strict but helpful. **c** strict but fair.
3 Robert's school had …
  a no sports facilities. **b** hardly any sports facilities.
  c good sports facilities.
4 They probably closed Robert's school because …
  a the teaching was bad. **b** it was very old.
  c it was in the town centre.
5 Mary was good at …
  a computer studies. **b** sport. **c** science.
6 One thing Mary didn't like was …
  a the colour of the uniform. **b** the size of the school.
  c the after-school clubs.
7 Barbara says she …
  a had strict teachers. **b** didn't have a timetable.
  c didn't learn anything.
8 Barbara says the rules and punishment system was …
  a very strict. **b** surprisingly successful. **c** completely unfair.
9 James didn't have any friends at first because …
  a he didn't live near the school. **b** he didn't like sport.
  c he was very shy.
10 James felt proud because …
  a he went to secondary school on his own. **b** he made lots of friends. **c** he helped design the school's first web page.

Which of the schools mentioned can you see in the photos (A and B)?

4 **Listen again and make notes on the main things each speaker talks about. Then write a question for each one.**

Example
What days did David not have to wear a uniform?

Before you start

1 **Copy and complete the table with the Key Words.**

> **KEY WORDS: Schools**
> assessment, choir, homework, library, private school, rules, school trips, science laboratories, state school

Types of school	boarding school
Facilities	gymnasium, swimming pool
Activities	chess club, drama club
Discipline	punishments
Learning	timetable, subjects

5 Work in groups. Take turns to ask your questions.

6 Your Culture Answer these questions.

1 What are the similarities between the schools in Exercise 3 and your school?

2 Which school do you think is the best, your school or one of the schools in Exercise 3? Why?

7 Listen to two students discussing two schools. Match the opinions (1–9) with the replies (a–i) in the Function File.

> **FUNCTION FILE**
>
> ### Disagreeing and contradicting politely
>
> **1** I think it would be great.
> **2** You'd fall behind with your studies.
> **3** She must have learnt something at school.
> **4** I'm sure most students would just do nothing.
> **5** That must be awful.
> **6** That's probably better, isn't it?
> **7** I think we have too much homework.
> **8** We have to do some work at home.
> **9** That's awful.
>
> **a** I don't agree. **f** Not necessarily.
> **b** Not really. **g** I suppose so, but …
> **c** I don't think so. **h** Don't exaggerate.
> **d** Perhaps, but … **i** No, it isn't.
> **e** I'm not so sure.

8 Pronunciation Listen and repeat the expressions.

Speaking

9 Game Think about the advantages and disadvantages of these things.

- boarding schools • school rules and punishments
- homework • exams

Now work in pairs. Talk about the things above. Try to contradict everything your partner says! Use the expressions from the Function File with the correct intonation.

Example

A *I think boarding schools are bad because it's better to be with your family.*

B *I don't think so. They teach you to be independent.*

A *Perhaps, but …*

10 Now tell the class your real opinions about schools.

> QUOTE … UNQUOTE
> 'Education is what remains when we have forgotten all we have been taught.'
> Lord Halifax (1633–95)

Vocabulary: Multi-part Verbs (7)

11 Read the sentences (1–9) from the dialogues in this lesson and complete them with the correct form of the multi-part verbs below.

> be into, catch up with, fall behind, get on with, get together, go into, go on to, go over, put off, set up, take up

B

1 If you _____ with your work, they'd _____ it with you.

2 They'd help you _____ your work at weekends.

3 If you _____ your work, you were OK.

4 At weekends, we used to _____ and _____ town.

5 I _____ swimming – there was a club after school.

6 When I first started, I _____ studying for weeks!

7 In the end, I _____ do computer studies at university.

8 Most kids _____ football and I wasn't interested in sport.

9 We _____ the school's first web page.

Now listen and check your answers.

12 Work in pairs or groups. Take turns to say sentences about life in your school. Use the multi-part verbs from Exercise 11.

28 Communication Workshops

Listening

Before you start

1 Look at the photo. Would you like to study English abroad? Why or why not?

A Phone Call

Listen to a phone call requesting information.

🎧 **2** A girl is phoning a language school to find out about summer courses for her foreign friend. Listen to the phone call and complete the information in the brochure.

Hereford House ⭐ *the place to learn English!*

Summer Courses
* We offer **1**_____-week courses in July and August.
* Our maximum class size is **2**_____ students.
* Qualified and experienced teachers give **3**_____ lessons a day.
* We have excellent facilities; a computer room, a **4**_____ and a self-study centre.
* We can arrange accommodation with a local **5**_____ or you can stay in the school in your own **6**_____ room.

After-school activities
* Afternoon activities include swimming, **7**_____ and beach sports.
* Cultural and sightseeing trips to **8**_____.
* Nightlife includes discotheques and **9**_____ on the beach.
* Prices: from **10**£_____.

For more information: 0807 949 948   www.hhouse.co.uk

---

3 Would you like to go to the school? Why or why not?

Speaking

Before you start

🎧 **1** Read the extracts (1–10) from the phone call in the Function File and choose the correct alternative. Then listen and check your answers.

FUNCTION FILE

Asking for information
1 *I'd like/I want* some information about summer courses, please.
2 *How long/How big* are the courses?
3 Could you *inform/tell* me about the lessons?
4 Could you *say/tell* me about the facilities?
5 Where *exactly is/is exactly* the school?
6 *How/What* about accommodation?
7 What kind of *after-school/post-school* activities are there?
8 Do you organise any *journeys/trips*?
9 How much do the courses *charge/cost*?
10 *Could/Can't* you send me a brochure and application form, please?

2 Read the Strategies. Can you think of any other ways of helping people understand you?

SPEAKING STRATEGIES: Dealing with misunderstanding
* If other people don't understand, try to explain by using other words (e.g. *What I mean is that ...*).
* If you didn't hear, ask the person to repeat it, (e.g. *I'm sorry, could you say that again?*).
* If you don't understand something you think is important, ask the other person to explain (e.g. *I'm sorry, but what exactly do you mean?*)

Asking for and giving information

Roleplay phone calls. Follow the stages below.

Stage 1

Work in pairs. Student A reads the information about a language school in Ireland on page 129. Student B reads about one in the States on page 131.

Stage 2

Act out telephone conversations asking for and giving information. Use the expressions from the Function File above.

Talkback

Tell your partner one good thing and one bad thing about his/her school. Would you consider going on a summer course there? Why or why not?

Writing

Before you start

1 Read the essay and match these headings with the paragraphs (A–D).

- your conclusions
- arguments against the title
- introduction
- arguments for the title

2 Which of the <u>underlined</u> linking words:

- contrast ideas? • list ideas? • summarise?
- give examples?

A 'For and Against' Essay

Choose one of the titles below and write an essay giving your opinions. Follow the stages and see Writing Help 7 on page 143.

- There should be no compulsory school subjects. Students should be allowed to choose the subjects they want to study.
- Schools don't prepare young people for life in the real world.
- There should be more discipline in schools.

Stage 1

Write some notes 'for' and 'against' the title.

Example (for the first title)

Pros
students don't work hard if they're not interested in the subject

Cons
some students might only choose 'easy' subjects

Stage 2

Make a rough plan. Organise your notes into four paragraphs.

- introduction
- arguments against the title
- arguments for the title
- your conclusions

Stage 3

Write your essay. Use linking words. Then check your essay.

Talkback

In groups, read each other's essays. Do you agree with the others?

Exams are a fair way of testing students. Do you agree?

A Every year thousands of students take important exams which can decide their future. <u>For example</u>, students have to pass exams with satisfactory grades in order to get a place in a university. <u>However</u>, are exams a fair way of judging a student's ability?

B <u>On the one hand</u>, exams seem fair. The questions are the same for all students. <u>Also</u>, the exams are marked according to a strict scheme and usually by more than one examiner. <u>Furthermore</u>, students do the exams at the same time and under the same conditions.

C <u>On the other hand</u>, there are some drawbacks with exams. <u>Despite</u> some students deserving to pass, they might be so nervous on the big day that they make a mess of the exam. <u>Moreover</u>, there may be other reasons, <u>such as</u> illness, which affect a student's performance in an exam. An alternative to exams would be a system of continuous assessment of course work by teachers during the year <u>although</u> this would mean more regular testing and more work for teachers. There would be a greater opportunity for students to copy work, <u>too</u>.

D <u>To sum up</u>, exams are not the ideal way of testing students and the idea of assessing students' work over a longer period is becoming more popular. In my opinion, the best system would be a mixture of the two – 50% exams and 50% course work.

Language Problem Solving 7
Verbs followed by an -ing form or infinitive

1 Read the text. What are the strategies you use to learn English?

'I **enjoy** learning vocabulary by listening to songs in English. I **don't mind** listening to songs several times and writing the words down. I often **need** to look up words in the dictionary and sometimes, when I get stuck, I ask my teacher. She **has offered** to work with me on a song if I don't have the lyrics. We listen to the song together and if I **fail** to get the word or line, she **helps** me to understand it. She often **makes** me listen to one bit a few times. She only **refuses** to listen to hip hop. If you **want** to do the same as me, I **suggest** listening to singers like David Gray and Norah Jones because you can actually hear the words. I don't **advise** you to listen to heavy metal because the lyrics often don't mean much and you **risk** learning incorrect grammar forms!'

2 Copy and complete the table with the verbs in blue. Some of the verbs fit in more than one line. Use your Mini-dictionary to check all the possible verb patterns.

verb + to + infinitive	*Want to do something*
Verb + object + to + infinitive	*Want someone to do something*
Verb + object + infinitive	
verb + -ing form	

Now put these verbs in the table. Use the Mini-dictionary to help you.

admit   afford   agree   arrange   ask   avoid
can't stand   choose   consider   decide   deny
expect   give up   learn   let   love   manage
plan   practise   promise   tend

3 Complete the text with the correct form of the verbs in brackets.

If you are planning ¹_____ (come) to Scotland as a tourist, you have plenty of interesting places to choose from. People who enjoy ²_____ (hike) should consider ³_____ (go) to the mountains in the north of Scotland. You don't have to book accommodation in advance as you will certainly manage ⁴_____ (find) a local person who will offer ⁵_____ (put) you up at a very reasonable price in their B+B.

If you love ⁶_____ (sail) and you don't mind ⁷_____ (be) cold and wet, you can go to the lakes in the North. You can either choose ⁸_____ (stay) in a cottage or go camping and practise ⁹_____ (cook) your meals on an open fire next to a lake.

The Scotish coast tends ¹⁰_____ (be) colder than the sunny Mediterranean beaches but many people claim it's more beautiful. If you can't stand ¹¹_____ (stay) in a crowded town or can't afford ¹²_____ (pay) for a luxurious hotel, arrange ¹³_____ (stay) in one of the many small coastal villages. You certainly won't risk ¹⁴_____ (meet) too many people if you decide ¹⁵_____ (go) for a long walk along the beach.

4 Tick the possible answers. There may be more than one correct answer.

1 We discussed it for a long time and in the end he _____ to sponsor the festival.
   a agreed   **b** offered   **c** gave up
2 When I _____ going to the cinema, he said he preferred the theatre.
   a asked   **b** refused   **c** suggested
3 If you live abroad for some time, you _____ losing your old friends at home.
   a risk   **b** let   **c** fail
4 In 1995, we _____ to get an interview with the Queen Mother.
   a gave up   **b** managed   **c** failed
5 I think you should _____ studying medicine. You would be an excellent doctor.
   a decide   **b** consider   **c** agree
6 The theatre was so small that they _____ to let any more people in.
   a denied   **b** refused   **c** didn't want
7 She is so poor now that she had to _____ eating out and buying expensive clothes.
   a give up   **b** afford   **c** consider
8 If you want to be a manager, you should _____ to deal with people tactfully but firmly.
   a practise   **b** learn   **c** admit

5 Complete the sentences using the correct form of a verb to say something true about yourself.

1 I avoid _____
2 I can't stand _____
3 I love _____
4 I enjoy _____
5 I don't mind _____
6 I can't afford _____

6 Use six of the verbs below to describe some of the things that happened to you this week. Use the Mini-dictionary to check the verb pattern.

Example
*Yesterday I decided to **give up eating** sweets.*

admit   afford   agree   avoid   consider   decide
deny   fail   give up   hope   learn   let   manage
offer   plan   practise   promise   put off   refuse
risk   suggest

Culture Corner 7

In England and Wales, 93% of schools are free state schools and 7% are private schools. Confusingly, some private independent schools are called 'public' schools! The most famous is probably Eton. Scotland has its own education system.

In the US, 90% of schools are free state schools. Most of the private schools were set up by religious groups.

Education is compulsory from five to sixteen years of age. There are three main stages: primary (Years 1–6); secondary (Years 7–11); and optional 'sixth form' (two or three years of pre-university study). State secondary schools are mainly 'comprehensive' schools, which means pupils don't have to pass a special exam to go there. In some areas, though, local authorities operate a 'selective' system.

There is no national system but most states have compulsory education from five to sixteen. There are twelve 'grades'; elementary school (1st–8th grade); high school (9th–12th grade). Some states have 'junior high' schools (7th–9th grade).

England and Wales have a national curriculum (Scotland has its own) and pupils have to study core subjects like maths, English and science. At fourteen, students can study optional subjects. At sixteen, pupils specialise and choose three or four subjects.

There is no national curriculum but in most states, core subjects are compulsory. Students can also choose options or 'electives'. Some of the most popular of these are performing arts, cooking and driver's education.

Pupils do tests in core subjects from the age of seven. At sixteen, they do exams called GCSE (General Certificate of Secondary Education) in a variety of subjects. If pupils stay on at school, they take 'A' or 'A/S' level exams in their specialised subjects as part of the university entrance procedure.

Education in the UK and the USA

Most schools have exams after each of the higher grades. Then, after 12th grade, pupils take exams to get their high school diploma.

About 40% of pupils go on to higher education. Virtually all British universities are public and each university demands certain 'A' level grades. If students are successful and there are places available, they can choose which university to go to. The government only gives a few grants so most students borrow money from a bank which they have to pay back when they leave university.

Over 60% of students go on to higher education; two-year colleges for vocational training; four-year colleges and universities for academic degrees. State universities are run by the individual state and charge quite low tuition fees. There are also private universities. The most prestigious and expensive are Harvard, Yale and Princeton.

The setting up of a national curriculum has probably raised standards in most areas but some people say that there is too much testing. Pupils have to do an average of 87 official tests during their time at school! Some inner-city schools also have serious problems of discipline and violence.

In the 1980s, US students were getting low scores in reading, writing and basic maths. Since then, scores have improved but are still lower than in many other developed countries. Another serious problem is violence and guns in schools and there have been several shootings. The situation has improved with the use of ID cards, cameras and metal detectors to stop pupils bringing guns to class.

1 Read about schools in the UK and the USA. Which of these things are mentioned?

subjects, universities, teachers, exams, fees, violence, uniforms

2 Find three similarities and three differences between the British and American education systems.

3 What are the nearest British equivalents of these American words?

• elective • elementary school • grade
• high school diploma

4 Where would you prefer to study? Why?

Comparing Cultures

Prepare for a discussion comparing the education systems in the UK and the USA with the system in your country.

Work in groups. Use the information in the text to write notes about the system in your country.

• Talk about the differences between systems.
• Explain the advantages and disadvantages of each system.
• Say how your education system can be improved.

Review 7

Grammar

1 Read this story and write Third Conditional sentences about John Smith's day.

Example

If Spot hadn't barked, John wouldn't have woken up in the middle of the night.

John Smith worked in a bank in London and lived with his dog, Spot. One night, Spot started barking in the middle of the night. John woke up and he couldn't get back to sleep. The next thing John knew, it was eight o'clock – he had overslept! He got dressed quickly and ran to the station. When he got there, he saw a train and jumped on it – but it was going the wrong way! He got off at the next station and didn't get to London until 9.15. He called a taxi but it got stuck in a traffic jam. When he got to work, he realised he hadn't got his wallet with him. He had to borrow ten pounds from his boss, who was quite angry. An hour later, he had lost four million pounds on the currency market. When his boss came to talk to him, she found him asleep in front of his computer. Of course, John lost his job.

2 Complete the text with the correct form of the verbs in brackets.

Magda, Maria and Sophia met on a summer school in England. One night, they wanted **1**_____ (go) dancing so they decided **2**_____ (go) into town and agreed **3**_____ (meet) in the centre. They couldn't afford **4**_____ (go) to an expensive club and were hoping **5**_____ (find) somewhere cheap. An English friend suggested **6**_____ (go) to the 'Elektrik' club. They walked there to save money but hadn't planned **7**_____ (get) lost! Finally, they managed **8**_____ (find) it. Inside, they avoided **9**_____ (talk) to any suspicious characters. They enjoyed **10**_____ (dance) all night. It was brilliant. They also met some boys who promised **11**_____ (see) them again. One of the boys offered **12**_____ (give) them a lift home in his car but Maria said they'd arranged **13**_____ (get) a taxi. They didn't mind **14**_____ (share) a taxi because it was safer.

Vocabulary

3 Choose the correct verb in *italics* to complete the sentences.

1 I am *taking/getting* lessons to *get/have* my driving licence.
2 She *made/got* quite angry and decided to *make/take* immediate action.
3 I *had/made* an effort and passed my exams.
4 If we can *get/make* the head teacher to agree, we're going to *have/make* a concert at the end of the year.
5 I was late because I couldn't *get/make* my computer to work.
6 I always try to *make/take* part in speaking activities in English.
7 She *had/made* a phone call to the university to find out what books to *get/have* for the new term.

4 **Multi-part verbs** Complete the sentences with a suitable word.

1 I must catch up _____ my work this weekend.
2 We get _____ well with our English teacher.
3 He went _____ to be a successful TV presenter.
4 Can you go _____ that explanation again?
5 I'd like to take _____ cookery.

Pronunciation: Vowel Sounds (3)

5 Find these sounds and the example words in the Phonetic Chart in the Mini-dictionary.

here/ɪə/, there/eə/, note/əʊ/

Now <u>underline</u> the sounds above in these sentences.

1 Where is your homework?
2 I hope you realise this is serious.
3 My ideal school would be near a park.
4 He spoke carefully and explained things clearly.
5 She noticed her own name on the envelope.

🎧 Listen and repeat the sentences.

6 Can you say this proverb? Use the Phonetic Chart in the Mini-dictionary to help you. What does the proverb mean?

/dəʊnt pʊt ɔːl jɔː egz ɪn wʌn bɑːskɪt/

Check Your Progress

Look back at the Module Objectives on page 81.
◎ Which activities did you enjoy the most?
◎ Which activities did you have problems with?
◎ Which grammar area do you need to practise more?

▸ Now read the story *Thomas Edison's Shaggy Dog*, Literature Spot 3, page 136.

8 Careers

In this module you will...

- **read** magazine articles, a report and a formal letter
- **listen to** dialogues, radio programmes, an interview and a song
- **talk about** careers, jobs and wages; **practise** doing interviews
- **write** a curriculum vitae and a letter of application
- **learn about** reported statements and reported verb patterns

Warm-up

1 Look at the photos (A–D) and the Key Words. What jobs are the people doing? What sort of person would be suitable for these jobs? Why? Use the Mini-dictionary to help you.

KEY WORDS: Personality adjectives (2)
brave, careful, creative, confident, dynamic, emotional, flexible, generous, hard-working, helpful, logical, motivated, organised, patient, practical, reliable, sensitive, sympathetic, tolerant

Example
I think a film director needs to be creative and confident.

2 Listen to five situations. Match them with the jobs. There is one extra job.

- doctor • hotel receptionist • journalist
- plumber • shop assistant • travel agent

3 Work in pairs. Look at the Key Words below. How many jobs related to the career areas can you think of in two minutes?

Example
art – artist, painter, sculptor

KEY WORDS: Careers
art, business, construction, design, engineering, farming, fashion, information technology, law, literature, the media, medicine, science, sport, travel and tourism

4 Think about your personality and choose a job you'd like to do. Tell the class.

Example
I'm good with animals and I'm a practical person. I'd really like to be a vet.

5 Complete the sentences with these words in the correct form.

career, job, profession, work

1 She's got a good _____ in a bank.
2 Tidying my bedroom was hard _____!
3 Law, medicine and teaching are all respected _____.
4 He had a successful _____ as a journalist.

93

29 Odd Jobs

Before you start

1 Look at the illustrations (1–4). What jobs do you think the people are doing?

Reading

2 Read the text quickly and check your guesses for Exercise 1.

3 Read the Strategies.

READING STRATEGIES: Headings and paragraphs

- Read each paragraph carefully. Underline important words and write down the topic(s) of each paragraph (e.g. *1 odd jobs*).
- Look at the headings. In newspaper articles, these often contain idiomatic expressions which play on the double meanings of words. Try to work out the meaning of them (see Reading Strategies Lesson 17 on page 59).
- Read the paragraphs again and match headings and paragraphs. Look for words from the headings or synonyms of them (e.g. *odd jobs/strange jobs*).
- Check that the extra topic does not match any of the paragraphs.

Use the Strategies from Lesson 17 page 59 to match the headings (1–9) with the explanations (a–i).

1 Musical Chairs
2 Sticky Situation
3 A Real Charmer
4 Workaholics
5 Spoilt for Choice
6 Desperate Measures
7 Pushy People
8 Calming Influences
9 Specialists

a Someone who makes everyone like them
b Aggressive people
c To have too many options
d A party game involving music and chairs
e People who work too much
f Experts in specific jobs
g A difficult situation
h Do something extreme
i Someone or something that calms you down

Which of the headings (1–9) above are idiomatic expressions?

4 Use the Strategies in Exercise 3 to match the headings (1–9) with the paragraphs (A–H). There is one extra topic.

A *How many jobs can you think of? Twenty? Thirty? No doubt the list includes doctor, lawyer, teacher, mechanic, plumber, and so on. The most dedicated career adviser could perhaps name a hundred. But there are over 500,000 jobs in existence to choose from! So, if you want to do well, how can you decide the best way to make a living? This week, Paul Hamilton takes a light-hearted look at some very ODD JOBS!*

B King Alfonso XIII of Spain was going deaf so he employed an 'Anthem Man'. His only job was to give a signal to the king when the national anthem was being played so that he would know when to stand up and when to sit down!

C If you cannot find a tuneless monarch to be your employer, the railways offer jobs of all sorts. In Japan, 'Passenger Pushers' are employed full time by the railway companies in Tokyo. During the rush hour, when hundreds of people are trying to get on the metro, they do their best to squeeze everyone into trains so that the doors will close properly.

D Another technological advance that led to job creation on the railways was the invention of chewing gum in 1928. When they finished their gum, many passengers just dropped it on the floor of the station and management at New York's Grand Central Station had to do something about it. In the end, they employed a professional gum remover who had a lot of work to do – he collected, on average, over three kilos of the sticky menace per day. I suppose you could say he got attached to his job!

E Escalators have provided inspiration for other rewarding careers. When the first moving staircase was installed at Harrods Department Store in London in 1898, it made many people scared. Shop assistants were put at the top of the escalator with instructions to give brandy and smelling salts to customers! And in 1911, when Earls Court

5 Read the text again and answer these questions.

1 Why are 'Passenger Pushers' necessary on the metro in Japan?
2 Why does the writer describe chewing gum as a 'menace'?
3 Why did Harrods employ special shop assistants on the escalator?
4 Why were sewage works a problem in Berkshire?
5 Why was Miss King successful?

underground station installed its first escalators, many people were worried about their safety. London Transport had a great idea; they employed a man with a wooden leg. His job was to walk up and down the escalators all day to show passengers how safe they were.

[F] In 1982, dozens of neighbours in a village in Berkshire made complaints about the smell from the nearby sewage works. So twelve people were employed to sniff the air outside their homes to estimate the smell. The Amsterdam police have a similarly specialised task force

called the 'grachtenvissers'. Their sole duty is to help motorists whose cars have got stuck in canals! This trend towards specialisation has grown dramatically in the last few years but it is not an entirely recent phenomenon. In medieval Japanese armies, special soldiers did the gruesome job of counting up the number of decapitated heads after each battle!

[G] In America, Miss Edith King was given an unusual job in the army. She was employed by the US War Department in 1905 with the task of finding soldiers who had run away from the army. She collected $50 for each deserter. Her only weapon was flirtation. If the runaway soldiers thought they were going to have a good time, they were making a big mistake – she led over five hundred into court. She must have had real charm!

[H] Being unemployed often makes people think of unique ways to make money. Take Jim Parker from Sacramento. Last year he got the sack from his job in a high-tech company and has found it impossible to get full-time work. In desperation, he became self-employed and is now trying hard to sell advertising space. If the price is right, he intends to tattoo an advert – on his forehead! He has already turned down an offer of $75,000.

6 'Odd jobs' mean both strange jobs and small jobs (e.g. washing someone's car). Have you ever done any odd jobs? Tell the class.

Example
I've done baby-sitting a few times. I got paid ... .

Vocabulary: Collocations

7 Use the table below to classify these words from the text that often go together.

offer (someone) a job, close (something) properly, turn down (an/the/their) offer, make (a/your/his) living, do well, get stuck, get the sack, try hard, find (it/something) impossible, become self-employed, provide inspiration, grow dramatically

VERB + NOUN	VERB + ADVERB	VERB + ADJECTIVE
offer a job		

8 Complete the sentences with collocations from Exercise 7 in their correct form.

1 My grandfather _____ as a miner for forty years.
2 I was _____ as a waiter in a fast-food restaurant but I _____ because I can't stand the smell of hamburgers!
3 I _____ to understand the instructions of my new digital camera and had to ask a friend to help me.
4 The number of cars in our city has _____ in the last few years.
5 That suitcase is broken and now it doesn't _____ .

9 Complete the vocabulary networks with these words from the text:

well, a living, your best, something about it, work, somebody scared, a complaint, a job, a (big) mistake, people think, money

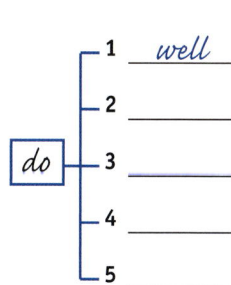

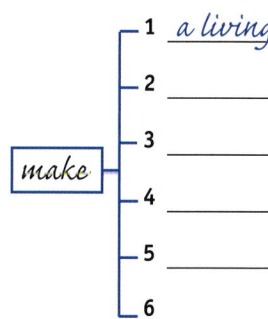

do: 1 *well* 2 3 4 5

make: 1 *a living* 2 3 4 5 6

Add more expressions to the networks.

Speaking

10 Game Play in groups. Take turns to think of a strange job. The others ask up to twenty questions to guess the job. You can only answer 'Yes' or 'No'.

Examples
Do you work outdoors? Do you wear a uniform? Do you have to travel?

GRAMMAR FOCUS:

30 Dangerous Jobs

A

B

C

Before you start

1 Look at the photos (A–C) and answer the questions.

1 Who are the people and what are they doing?
2 Why are the jobs dangerous?
3 Would you like to do any of these jobs? Why? Why not?

2 Work in pairs. Look at the Key Words. What do you think are the five most dangerous jobs? Put them in order.

KEY WORDS: Jobs

architect, cashier, construction worker, electrician, farm worker, fire fighter, fisherman, forestry worker, journalist, lorry driver, miner, pilot, police officer, politician, soldier, taxi driver, window cleaner

Now turn to page 131 and check your list. Which information surprised you?

3 Listen and complete the interview.

How would you describe Sandra's personality?

Most of us have safe nine-to-five jobs. We interviewed someone whose job is very different. Sandra Gimenez, **1**_____ *, is a detective in the New York Police Department.*

Q Why did you decide to be a police officer?

A My family comes from the Bronx so I know the problems caused by crime. I once saw a mugging in my neighbourhood and my older **2**_____ had problems with drugs. I didn't want to just sit there and do nothing. So I joined the NYPD.

Q What do you do now?

A Well, now I'm working in **3**_____. But I have only been here since last year. We've had some difficult cases. We're working on a big case now but I can't tell you about it.

Q Have you ever been in any danger?

A Yes. Last **4**_____, we were looking for a suspect near a gas station. We saw an individual fitting the description. When we tried to arrest him, he pulled a gun on us. I had to shoot but I didn't hurt him badly. Yesterday, I received a bravery award for it.

Q Do you like your job?

A The **5**_____ in the department are great and I like my work. In this job, no day is the same, you know. But it's stressful and my family worries about me all the time. Today I spoke to my mom about it. I'm going to stop doing it after I get married **6**_____ – I won't feel the same about taking risks. If we have children, I'll try to get a different job in the department. ■

4 Read the journalist's report of the interview. Find five factual differences.

Sandra said that her family came from the Bronx so she knew the problems caused by crime. She told me that she had seen two muggings and her older brother had had problems with drugs. She said she hadn't wanted to just sit there and do nothing so she had joined the NYPD. When I asked about her present job, she replied that at that time she was working in homicide but that she had only been there since the year before. She said they had had some difficult cases and were working on a big one then but she couldn't tell me about it. I asked her if she had ever been in any danger. She then admitted that a dangerous incident had happened the month before. She said that they had been looking for a suspect near a factory and had seen an individual fitting the description. She told me that when they had tried to arrest him, he had pulled a knife on them. She confessed that she had had to shoot him but she had not hurt him badly. She said that the day before she had received a bravery award for it. Finally, Sandra talked about her future. She told me she liked her job but that it was stressful and that her family worried about her all the time. That day she had spoken to her father about her job. She said she was going to stop doing it after she got married the following year – she wouldn't feel the same about taking risks. She said that if they had children she would try to get a different job in a shop.

Presentation

5 Look at the sentences from the interview and find the same information in the report. Complete the table with sentences from the report and the names of the tenses.

INTERVIEW	TENSE/VERB FORM
'My family **comes** from the Bronx.'	Present Simple
►► Sandra said that her family **came** from the Bronx	Past Simple
'We'**ve had** some difficult cases.'	
►►	
'We'**re working** on a big case.'	
►►	
'I **didn't want** to sit there and do nothing, so I **joined** the NYPD.'	
►►	
'We **were looking** for a suspect.'	
►► They **had been looking** for a suspect.	Past Perfect Continuous
'I'**m going to stop** doing it after I get married."'	
►►	
'I **won't feel** the same about taking risks.'	
►►	
'If we **have** children, I'll **try** to get a different job.'	
►►	

Study the changes in verb forms when the reporting verb is in the past tense. What changes in pronouns can you see in the reported statements?

6 These time and place expressions were used in the interview. Find their equivalents in the report.

• here • now • last year • last month • yesterday • today • next year

Example
here → *there*; now → *at that time/then*

7 Notice that after *say* we can use *that* but it's not necessary.

She said (that) they had been looking for a suspect.
She said she was going to stop doing it.

How is *that* translated into your language?

Practice

8 Read the reported statements and choose the correct option (a or b).

1 He said he would work abroad.
   a He worked abroad at the time of the interview.
   b He was planning to work abroad in the future.
2 He said he had bought a new car.
   a He had the car at the time of the interview.
   b He wanted to buy the car after the interview.
3 He said he was doing a course.
   a He was preparing to do a course in the future.
   b He was in the middle of a course at the time of the interview.

9 Read this report of an interview and write the woman's original words. What job does she do?

Example *I have to be very fit and slim for my job.*

She said she had to be very fit and slim for her job. She admitted that she was actually almost fifteen kilos underweight. She said she had been employed by a few leading fashion magazines. She told us she had worked for two designers during the previous year's shows in Paris but she preferred to work with photographers. She said she was going to stay in the job for the next few years but she announced that she was planning to get married soon and hoped to have a big family. She also told us that she would probably start her own fashion studio some time in the future.

10 Report the sentences of a famous TV chef, Gordon Blue. Remember to change tenses, pronouns and time expressions.

1 'I won two cooking competitions last year.'
   He said _____.
2 'I have never cooked anything Japanese.'
   He admitted that _____.
3 'Yesterday, I prepared lunch for the prime minister.'
   He said _____.
4 'My job is as creative as an artist's.'
   He claimed _____.
5 'I'm working on a new recipe for tomato soup at the moment.'
   He added _____.
6 'I'm sure the soup will be delicious.'
   He said _____.
7 'The BBC are going to start showing my cookery programme next month.'
   He announced _____.
8 'My own restaurant is opening today and I invite all of you for a free meal.'
   He said _____.

11 **Personalisation** Recall something interesting or important that you heard someone say recently and report it to the class.

Example
In the news they said that the president was going to resign.

31 Getting a Job

Vocabulary: Multi-part Verbs (8)

Before you start

1 Match these verbs with the underlined multi-part verbs in 'Advice for interviews'.

think of, talk clearly, invent, relax, arrive, make yourself comfortable, make a list, pretend, communicate, observe everything in a place, talk a lot about, put on good clothes, find information, write

Advice for interviews

1. <u>Dress up</u> for the interview to <u>get across</u> a responsible attitude.
2. <u>Calm down</u> before the interview by having a coffee.
3. Think about the job and <u>write down</u> your strengths and weaknesses.
4. <u>Look</u> things <u>up</u> about the company on the Internet.
5. <u>Turn up</u> at the interview a couple of minutes early.
6. <u>Settle down</u> in your chair and <u>look around</u> the room.
7. <u>Take down</u> notes during the interview.
8. <u>Make up</u> information about yourself.
9. <u>Make out</u> you understand something when you don't.
10. <u>Go on about</u> your personal life.
11. <u>Speak up</u> and express yourself clearly.
12. <u>Come up with</u> a couple of questions about the job.

2 Read the 'Advise for interviews' again and make a list of things *not* to do in an interview.

Example
Don't calm down by having a coffee. Calm down by going for a walk.

3 Look at the photo of the interview for a holiday job above. How well do you think Oliver is doing in the interview? Why?

Listening

4 Listen to the interview. Do you think Oliver got the job? Why or why not?

5 Listen again and complete the Function File.

FUNCTION FILE

Job Interview

Interviewer: I ^{1}_____ you're in your last year at school.
Oliver: Yes, I'm doing my ^{2}_____ this summer. I ^{3}_____ to go to university to study ...
Interviewer: Why do you ^{4}_____ to work with us at Camp Elizabeth?
Oliver: Well, your company has a good ^{5}_____. ... I ^{6}_____ working with children.
Interviewer: What ^{7}_____ do you have?
Oliver: I ^{8}_____ with the youth club at school. I ^{9}_____ sports events and trips.
Interviewer: What ^{10}_____ do you think are important for this kind of job?
Oliver: I'm ^{11}_____ what do you mean exactly?
You ^{12}_____ must have patience. And another ^{13}_____ thing is enthusiasm.
Interviewer : Are there any questions you ^{14}_____ like to ask me?
Oliver: Yes, ^{15}_____ one thing. ^{16}_____ you tell me what kind of accommodation there is?
Interviewer: I'll be getting ^{17}_____ with people next week.
Oliver: Thank you very much. Goodbye.

6 Pronunciation Listen to people asking the interviewer to repeat or explain something. Which of them are polite and which are not?

Listen and repeat the polite questions.

Speaking

7 Work in pairs. One of you is the interviewer and the other is the candidate for these jobs:

- working in a snack bar   • working as a tour guide

Use the notes to prepare for the interviews.

> **Interviewer:** Decide on the pay, hours worked and what kind of person you want to employ. Think of questions to ask about: education, languages, work experience, relevant personal qualities, hobbies/interests
>
> **Candidate:** Think of information about yourself or invent information about: education – your school, your best subjects, languages you speak, work experience, personal qualities, hobbies and interests. Think of a question to ask the interviewer, e.g. about pay and hours

8 Act out your interviews. Use expressions from the Function File. The interviewer decides if the candidate gets the job.

9 Tell the class about your interviews. Did the candidates get the jobs? Why or why not?

10 Your Culture Discuss these questions with your group or the class.

1 Do many students get holiday jobs in your country? What sort of jobs?
2 Do they prepare you for interviews in your school? Is this a good idea? Why or why not?

QUOTE ... UNQUOTE
Advice for the young 'Find out what you like doing best and get someone to pay you for doing it.'
Katherine Whitehorn, British journalist. (1926 –)

Listening

11 Read the Strategies.

> **LISTENING STRATEGIES: Taking notes**
> - Listen once to get the general idea. Write down the main topics mentioned (e.g. *declining industries*).
> - Make a table or information network with the main headings.
> - Listen again and write down important information related to the main topics.
> - Only write down key words and use abbreviations (e.g. *IT – information technology, prof. serv. – professional services*).

How do you take notes when listening to English? Tell the class.

12 Listen to a radio programme about job trends. List these topics in the order they are discussed.

- declining industries   • information technology
- changes in working life   • future jobs
- skills needed

Topic	Information/Example
1 *declining industries*	*e.g. coal mining*
2	
3	
4	
5	

13 Listen again. Use the Strategies in Exercise 11. Write information or examples about each topic in the table above.

14 Work in pairs. Use your notes to tell each other the information you found out.

Example
They said that the declining industries were ... .

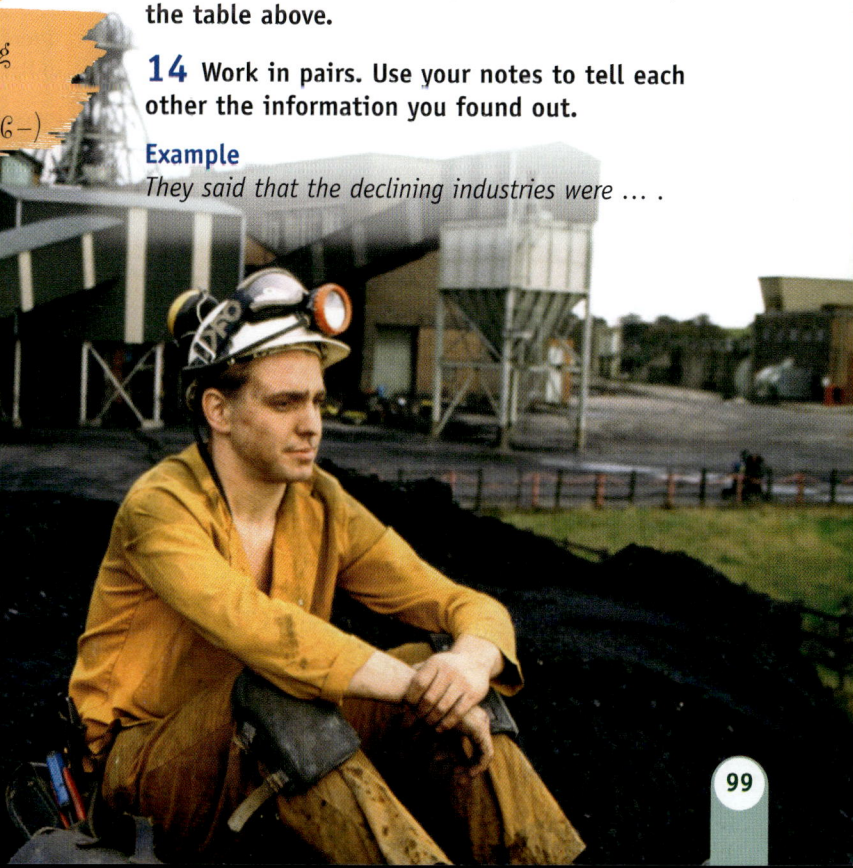

32 Communication Workshops

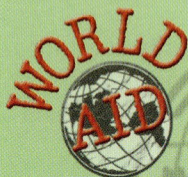

WORLD AID is looking for volunteers to work in our camp in Bangladesh:

- to participate in our flood control and tree-planting operations
- to help look after small children
- to teach basic maths to primary children
- to work on a survey of local wildlife

Write to us saying what kind of work you are interested in. Give details about yourself, say why you are interested and suitable for the work. Successful applicants will receive free transportation, accommodation and board.

A CV and a Letter of Application

Write a CV and a letter applying for work on a volunteer programme. Follow the stages below. See Writing Help 8 on page 143.

Stage 1

Decide which of the jobs in the World Aid advert you are interested in and write a simple CV. Use the headings from the CV below and complete information about yourself, giving relevant dates.

Stage 2

Then write notes about why you want the job, your personal qualities and why you would be good at that kind of work.

Stage 3

Use your notes and CV to write the letter. Check your letter for mistakes.

Talkback

Work in groups. Read each other's CVs and letters. Would you select your classmates for the job? Why or why not?

Writing

Before you start

1 Read the advertisement, the CV and the letter. Do you think Maureen's application will be successful? Why or why not?

2 Match the parts of the letter (1–5) with the topics (a–e).

a formal ending   **b** personal qualities   **c** why good for the job
d reasons for interest   **e** reason for writing

3 Look at the underlined linking words in the letter. Do they express addition or reason?

CURRICULUM VITAE

Personal Information
Name: Maureen Taylor
Date of Birth: 21.03.87
Nationality: British
Address: 87 Orchard Rise, Bishops Castle SY9 7H

Education and Qualifications
Secondary school: Newcastle
'A' levels: English Literature (A), Maths (B), Economics (D)

Experience
2003 – present: Voluntary work Teaching English to Immigrants – St Paul's Church, Bishops Castle.

Other Skills
Driving licence; First Aid Certificate (First Class)

Interests
Reading, cinema, cooking, swimming.

Dear Sir/Madam,

1 I am writing to apply for the position of volunteer worker which I saw advertised in The Guardian last week. I would be interested in teaching maths to primary children in your camp in Bangladesh. I enclose a copy of my CV.

2 I would like to work for you because I am very interested in teaching. I would also like to learn about a different culture as I feel that intercultural understanding is extremely important.

3 I am a hard-working and committed person. For the last three years, I have done voluntary work visiting elderly people in my local area. I have also taught immigrant children so I feel confident I can get on well with people from other cultural backgrounds.

4 I think I could be a good primary teacher of maths due to my teaching experience and since I have Maths 'A' level. In addition, I hold a certificate in first aid, which might be useful.

5 I look forward to hearing from you.

Yours faithfully,

Maureen Taylor

Maureen Taylor (Ms)

Listening

Before you start

1 Work in pairs. Try to guess the answers to the questions below about the EU countries.

1   Which two of these EU countries have the highest cost of living?
    a Denmark   **b** France   **c** Hungary
    d Poland   **e** Sweden
2   Which two countries above have the lowest cost of living?
3   Which two of these EU countries have the highest average wages?
    a Denmark   **b** Germany   **c** Hungary
    d the UK   **e** Poland
4   Which two countries above are near the bottom of the wages table?
5   Which of these jobs is the highest paid?
    a doctor   **b** factory worker
    c farm worker   **d** hotel worker
    e manager
6   Which of the jobs above has the lowest salary?

A Radio Programme

Listen to a radio programme about standards of living.

2 Listen to the radio programme and check your guesses for Exercise 1.

3 Listen again and complete this information.

1   The prices survey did not include
    _____ .
2   A basket of shopping in Copenhagen costs over _____ as much as the same basket in Warsaw.
3   The survey looked at wages in _____ different jobs.
4   Professionals include doctors,
    _____ and _____ .
5   Women are paid between _____ and _____ percent less than men.
6   Female managers receive about
    _____ of a male manager's salary.

4 **Your Culture** What do you think the best and worst paid jobs are in your country? What differences are there in pay between men and women?

Speaking

Before you start

1 Read the Strategies.

SPEAKING STRATEGIES: Interacting in discussions

- Don't dominate the discussion.
- When you want to say something, wait for your partner to pause.
- If you have to interrupt, use polite expressions.
- Involve the other person by asking his/her opinions (e.g. *What do you think about …?*).

2 Look back at the Function Files in Lessons 7, 15, 16 and 27. List some expressions for interacting:

1   involving people   3   disagreeing/contradicting politely
2   agreeing   4   interrupting politely

Examples
1   *… don't you think?*
2   *That's true.*
3   *I suppose so, but …*
4   *I'd just like to say…*

A Discussion

Discuss jobs and wages. Follow the stages.

underpaid?

Stage 1

Look at the list of jobs. Choose two which you think *should* be the best paid and the lowest paid. Explain your reasons.

computer programmer, doctor, farmer, fashion model, fire fighter, miner, nurse, police officer, professional footballer, scientist, street cleaner, teacher

Think of these things about the jobs you have chosen:

- the qualifications, skills and personal qualities needed
- the pay and conditions of the job now
- the importance of the job for society
- what pay and conditions the job should have.

overpaid?

Stage 2

Work in pairs. Use the Strategies to discuss your opinions.

- agree or disagree with your partner
- agree on two best-paid jobs and two lowest-paid jobs

Talkback

Work in pairs. Present your conclusions to the class. Give reasons for your decisions.

Language Problem Solving 8

1 Read the text and complete the expressions below with *say* or *tell*.

In a press conference yesterday, Michael Boyd, one of the best Hollywood stuntmen, said that he was going to retire. He said he had thoroughly enjoyed working with the most famous actors and directors in the world. He told the press that his career had been very successful but his personal life had suffered a lot. He said he was planning to spend more time with his family and told his agent not to try to change his decision.

1	_____ (that) ... .
2	_____ someone (that) ... .
3	_____ someone (not) to do something ... .

2 Put *said* or *told* in the gaps.

One day, Michael **1**_____ his wife, Mary, that he had taken a job in a new James Bond film. Mary **2**_____ she didn't want him to get hurt but Michael **3**_____ he would be careful. A few days later, Mary, who was a James Bond fan, **4**_____ Michael she wanted to go with him to London, where they were shooting some of the scenes. He **5**_____ that he would ask the director but Mary **6**_____ she was sure he would agree. When they were already on location, the director saw Mary and **7**_____ her to quickly put on her evening dress and get into the car. He mistook her for a stuntwoman!

3 Read the text and copy and complete the table with the verbs in blue. Use the Mini-dictionary to help you.

In an interview he **agreed** to give us yesterday, Michael Boyd **announced** that he was going to retire. He **admitted** that he loved his job but **complained** that some of the stunts were getting too dangerous to perform. He **refused** to talk about his private life and **denied** buying a small island in the Pacific. He talked a lot about all the films he had taken part in and **regretted** rejecting an offer to perform stunts for Clint Eastwood in one of his later films. Michael **advised** all young stuntmen and women to avoid taking unnecessary risks and **begged** directors not to put stunt people's lives at risk. When we **asked** him to talk about his plans for the future, Michael **claimed** he was going to help his fellow stuntmen who could not work any more. He **promised** to set up a foundation whose main aim would be to help handicapped actors and stunt people. He had already **ordered** his bank to transfer $50,000 to the foundation's account.

... (that) + sentence	
... (not) to do something	
... someone (not) to do something	
... doing something	

4 Read the report of the interview in Exercise 3 again and write the original words.

Example
1 *OK, I'll give you an interview.*

5 Report what Michael Boyd said to the press.

1 'No, I won't let you take photos of my family.'
He refused _____.
2 'No, that's not true, I have never worked in a sci-fi production.'
He denied _____.
3 'Please, don't ask me about my private life.'
He begged _____.
4 'That's true, they didn't use me for the latest James Bond film.'
He admitted _____.
5 'It's a pity I didn't go to an actors' school.'
He regretted _____.
6 'If I was a young actor, I'd choose my parts very carefully.'
He advised young actors _____.
7 'OK, if you insist, I'll take part in one more film.'
He agreed _____.
8 'I'd like you to write something about my many disabled colleagues.'
He asked _____.
9 'I've been injured many times.'
He claimed _____.

6 Report the conversation between Sylvia and her mother. Use the reporting verbs in brackets.

Mother You realise this is a dangerous job, don't you? (warn)
Sylvia Of course it's dangerous but I love risk and excitement. (admit, explain)
Mother Please, think about it again. Why don't you look for a job at a bank? (beg, advise)
Sylvia Oh, no. I'm not going to sit behind a desk for nine hours every day! (refuse)
Mother Oh dear, why do you always have to be different? (complain)

Culture Corner 8

Will Young

1 Look at the photo and answer the questions.

1 Do you know the singer in the photo? Do you know any of his songs?
2 What sort of lifestyle do you think the singer in the photo has?
3 Would you like to work in the music business? Why or why not?
4 What sort of job would you like to do? Would you like to be famous?

2 Read about the pop music business. Are these statements true (T) or false (F)?

1 ☐ Pop Idol selects ten thousand talented singers.
2 ☐ Will Young became extremely rich overnight.
3 ☐ Some British universities give degrees in pop music.
4 ☐ There are not many jobs as pop stars.
5 ☐ Pop music is big business in the UK.

3 Your Culture What programmes in your country are similar to Pop Idol? Do you like them? Why or why not? Can you study pop music at university?

The Pop Music Business

Trying to become a pop star has never been more fashionable. Over ten million people watched the first edition of 'Pop Idol' in 2002 and the programme is still popular. The TV show is about a group of young hopefuls who want to become Britain's newest pop star. In the first competition, ten thousand participants started out at the beginning but there was only one winner at the end. Overnight, Will Young became a famous star with a recording contract with a big record company and was on his way to becoming a fabulously rich young man.

But winning 'Pop Idol' is not the only way to become a pop star in Britain. Universities and colleges in the UK now offer courses in pop music. Students on these courses receive specialist training which can provide a way in to the music business. An example course is the degree programme in pop music with music technology at Derby University.

Even though very few of the university students may actually become pop stars, there are plenty of opportunities for young people to earn a very good living behind the scenes as session musicians, composers and technicians. Simon Lewis, programme leader for performance technology, said this year's first group of graduates have all found good jobs in Britain's booming pop and entertainment field.

For more information about pop music courses offered in the UK, go to the Education UK website at www.educationuk.org

🎧 **4** Listen to the song and complete the gaps.

So you want to be a rock and roll star?

So you want to be a rock and roll star?
Then listen now to what I've got to say.
Just get an electric **1** _____
And take some time
And learn how to play.
And when your **2** _____ combed right,
And your pants fit tight
It's gonna be all right.
Then it's time to go downtown
Where the agent man won't let you down.
Sell your **3** _____ to the company
Who are waiting there to sell plastic ware*.
And in a week or two
If you make the **4** _____
The girls'll tear you apart.
The price you paid for your riches and **5** _____,
Was it a strange game?
You're a little insane.
The **6** _____ that came, and the public acclaim,
Don't forget who you are,
You're a rock and roll star.

(*records, cassettes and CDs)

Words and music by R. McGuinn and C. Hillman

5 Put the stages of a rock star's career in the correct order, according to the song.

a Sign a recording contract.
b Learn how to play an instrument.
c Become disillusioned with fame.
d Decide on an 'image'.
e Sell lots of albums.

Review 8

Grammar

1 Rewrite the sentences using reported speech.

Example
1 *The teacher asked Mary to close the window.*

1 'Close the window, please, Mary,' asked the teacher.
2 'I've never used that program before,' she said.
3 'Could you give me a lift to the station, please?' she asked me.
4 'I live in Wales,' he said, 'because I got tired of living in London.'
5 'Sam is working for a small company in Manchester,' said Jenny.
6 'I took the day off work yesterday because I had a temperature. But now I feel a lot better,' said Frank.
7 'Give me time to think about it,' she asked me.
8 'I've been working all day, so I'll come swimming with you if it doesn't rain,' he told me.
9 'I won't go unless you join me,' Pete told Kathy.
10 'Get out of the car immediately,' the police officer ordered the man.

2 Write three things that your parents, teachers or friends have said to you in the last few days.

Example
Yesterday, my sister told me she had borrowed one of my CDs.

Read out one of your sentences to the class.

3 Complete the sentences with these verbs.

announced, asked, begged, explained, ordered, said, told

1 The careers adviser _____ me I should study economics.
2 Everyone listened while they _____ the election results.
3 When I _____ him about the argument, he _____ that it was none of my business.
4 The police officer _____ us to move along.
5 I _____ to the teacher why I hadn't done my homework.
6 I _____ my parents to let me go to the club but they refused.

Vocabulary

4 Complete the sentences with the correct forms of *do*, *make*, *have* and *get*.

1 Do you *have* any ideas how to _____ some money this summer?
2 It rained so much that our car _____ stuck in the mud.

3 He always _____ his best in exams.
4 He's so ambitious. I knew he'd _____ well.
5 She _____ a good living from selling hand-made jewellery.
6 I didn't use to like dogs, but I've _____ quite attached to our neighbours' labrador.
7 I'd like to _____ something like voluntary work before I go to university.
8 Last week, they _____ a mistake with my pay again so I _____ an official complaint.
9 He _____ the sack for being late so often.

5 Multi-part verbs Choose the correct alternative in *italics* to complete the sentences.

1 We had to take *down/out/up* notes during the lesson.
2 I looked *out/at/up* the population of China in the encyclopedia.
3 We found out that he had made *off/out/up* the whole story!
4 I came *off/over/up* with a great idea.
5 I can't hear you very well. Can you speak *out/up/over*?
6 I wrote *down/up/over* nearly everything the lecturer said.

6 Complete the sentences with *job(s)* or *work*.

1 There will be thousands more _____ in the IT sector in the next few years.
2 I have got a lot of _____ to do at the moment.
3 In the summer, I've got a holiday _____ working in a café.
4 I would like to get some _____ experience in a lawyer's office.
5 There is no such thing as a _____ for life nowadays.
6 I did a few odd _____ for my uncle at the weekend.

Pronunciation: -*ed* endings

🎧 **7 Listen and write down the full sentences.**

🎧 **Listen again and repeat the sentences quickly.**

8 Can you say this proverb? Use the Phonetic Chart in the Mini-dictionary to help you. What does the proverb mean?

/taɪm ɪz mʌnɪ/

Check Your Progress

Look back at the Module Objectives on page 93.
◉ Which activities did you enjoy most?
◉ Which activities did you have problems with?
◉ Which grammar area do you need to revise?

9 Culture Shock

In this module you will...

- **read** an autobiographical extract, an interview and personal letters
- **talk about** different cultures and manners; **practise** being polite
- **listen to** different accents, an interview and everyday situations
- **write** a personal letter
- **learn about** reported questions and linking words

Warm-up

1 Look at the places in the photos and answer the questions.

1 Which of the Key Words do you associate with each country?
2 Would you like to go to any of these places? Why or why not?

KEY WORDS

Food: barbecues, fish and chips, hamburgers, hot dogs, kangaroo steaks, roast beef
Places: Big Ben, the Empire State Building, Sydney Opera House, the Great Barrier Reef, the Grand Canyon, Buckingham Palace, Uluru (Ayers Rock), Stonehenge, the Statue of Liberty
Sport: American football, baseball, basketball, cricket, football (soccer), golf, rugby, surfing

2 Listen to three people. Which country is each person from?

3 Listen to the people again. Write notes on what they say about:

- the weather - food - free time
- holidays - sport

4 Your Culture Work in pairs. Make a list of things to define the culture and lifestyle of your country to a foreigner.

Example

1 We spend a lot of time walking in the parks and hills.
2 Yachting has recently become very popular because of Ellen McArthur.
3 famous places – Torquay is the English riviera

Tell the class the things you both decided.

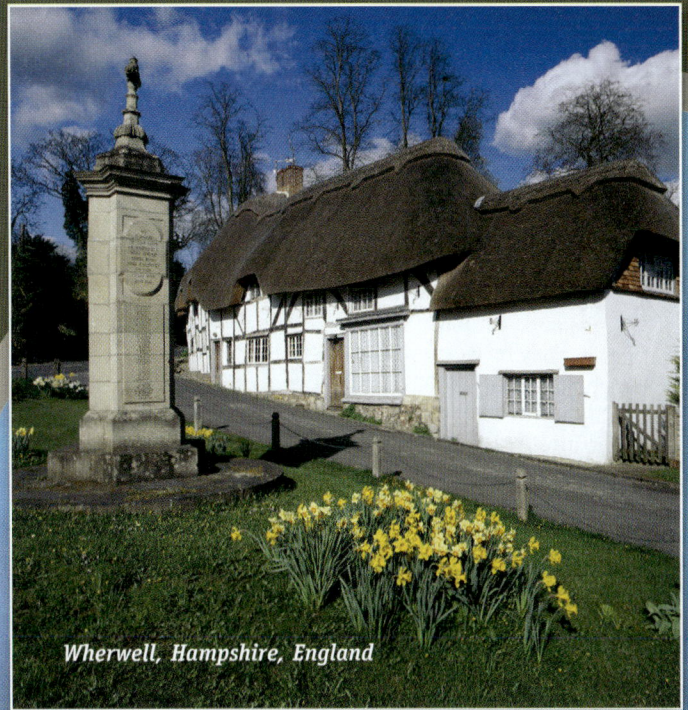

Wherwell, Hampshire, England

The Northern Territory, Australia

New York, USA

105

33 Lost in Translation

A Every day I learn new words, new expressions. I pick them up from school exercises, from conversations, from the books I take out of Vancouver's <u>well-lit</u>, <u>cheerful</u> public library. There are some turns of
5 phrase to which I develop strange allergies. 'You're welcome', for example … I can hardly bring myself to say it – I suppose because it implies that there's something to be thanked for, which in Polish would be <u>impolite</u> …
10   Then, there are words to which I take an <u>irrational</u> liking, for their sound or just because I'm pleased to have deduced their meaning. Mainly they're words I learn from books, like 'enigmatic' or 'insolent' – words that have a
15 <u>literary</u> value, that only exist as signs on the page.
   But mostly, the problem is that … the words I learn now don't stand for things in the same unquestioned way they did in my native tongue. 'River' in Polish was a <u>vital</u> sound, energised with
20 the essence of riverhood, of my rivers, of my being immersed in rivers. 'River' in English is <u>cold</u>. It has no accumulated associations for me.
   When my friend Penny tells me that she's <u>envious</u> or happy or disappointed, I try
25 laboriously not to translate from the English to the Polish but from the word back to its source, to the feeling from which it springs. Already, in that moment of strain, spontaneity of response is lost. And anyway, the translation doesn't work. I don't know how Penny feels when she talks about envy …

> Ewa Hoffman emigrated with her family from Poland to Canada in 1959 and described the experience in her book, *Lost in Translation* (1989). She studied at Yale and Harvard in the USA and was an editor for the *New York Times*.

B Mrs Lieberman is among several Polish ladies who have been in Canada long enough to consider themselves well versed in native ways and who seem to
5 find me <u>deficient</u> in some quite <u>fundamental</u> respects. Since in Poland I was considered a <u>pretty</u> young girl, this requires a basic revision of my self-image. But there's no doubt about it;
10 after the passage across the Atlantic, I've emerged as less <u>attractive</u>, less <u>graceful</u>, less <u>desirable</u>. In fact, I can see in these women's eyes that I'm a somewhat <u>pitiful</u> specimen – pale, with thick
15 eyebrows and without any bounce in my hair, dressed in clothes that have nothing to do with the <u>current</u> fashions. … One of them spends a day with me, plucking my eyebrows and trying
20 <u>various</u> shades of lipstick on my face. 'If you were my daughter, you'd soon look like a princess.'

Before you start

1 If you went to live in North America what would you find most difficult to get used to there?

- the food
- the weather
- free time and sports
- the TV
- clothes and fashion
- the people
- the language

2 Your Culture Work in pairs. Discuss these questions.

1 Are there any words or phrases in English that sound strange to you? Give examples.
2 Are there any words in English which you like because of their sound? Tell the class.
3 What words in your language have very strong associations for you?
4 What English words would you find difficult to translate exactly into your language? And vice versa?

C   The car is full of my new friends, or at least the crowd that has more or less accepted me … They're as <u>lively</u> as a group of puppies … . It's Saturday night, or rather 'Saturday Night', and party spirits are <u>obligatory</u>. We're on our way to the local White Spot, an early Canadian version of McDonald's, where we'll engage in
5 the <u>barbarous</u> – as far as I'm concerned – rite of the 'drive-in'. This activity of sitting in your car in a large parking lot and having sloppy, big hamburgers brought to you on a tray, accompanied by <u>greasy</u> french fries bounding out of their cardboard containers … seems to fill these peers of mine with <u>warm</u>, monkeyish, groupy comfort. It fills me with a <u>finicky</u> distaste …
10   'Come on, foreign student, cheer up,' one of the boys sporting a <u>flowery</u> Hawaiian shirt and a crew cut tells me, poking me in the ribs good-naturedly. 'What's the matter, don't you like it here?'

(From *Lost in Translation* by Ewa Hoffman.)

Reading

3 Read extract A. How would Ewa Hoffman answer the questions in Exercise 2.

4 Read extracts B and C. What else does Ewa find difficult to get used to in Canada?

5 Read the Strategies.

READING STRATEGIES: Dealing with difficult words

- Circle difficult words or expressions which you think are important.
- Use the form (e.g. adjective/noun) and the context to guess the meaning.
- If you are not sure, check your guess in the Mini-dictionary. Translate the word/expression into your own language. There may not be an exact equivalent.
- Remember, creative writers sometimes make up words (e.g. *monkeyish*, *groupy*).
- Check your translations with a partner and then with your teacher.

Work in pairs. Use the Strategies to work out the meaning (a, b or c) of these words and expressions from the texts.

1 turns of phrase (A, line 4)
 a expressions **b** illnesses **c** proverbs
2 stand for (A, line 17)
 a pronounce **b** represent **c** spell
3 strain (A, line 27)
 a great effort **b** great emotion **c** great sadness
4 well versed in (B, line 3)
 a annoyed with **b** experienced in **c** tolerant of
5 plucking (B, line 19)
 a combing **b** painting **c** removing
6 spirits (C, line 3)
 a clothes **b** drinks **c** moods
7 rite (C, line 5)
 a custom **b** hobby **c** test
8 peers of mine (C, line 8)
 a foreigners **b** people of my age **c** strangers
9 sporting (C, line 10)
 a hiding **b** holding **c** wearing
10 crew cut (C, line 11)
 a short hairstyle **b** short jacket **c** short trousers

Which of the words did you need to use the Mini-dictionary for?

6 Work in pairs. Translate the words and expressions in Exercise 5 into your language. Compare your translations with the rest of the class. Which words were difficult to translate?

7 Now read the extracts again. Are these statements true (T) or false (F)?

1 ☐ Ewa doesn't like using some English expressions because they sound rude to her.
2 ☐ Some words in English sound empty of meaning to her.
3 ☐ She finds it difficult to communicate naturally because she tries to translate.
4 ☐ She feels unattractive because Canadian fashions are different from those at home.
5 ☐ The women try to help Ewa because they think she is not very good-looking.
6 ☐ She thinks her Canadian friends are rather childish.
7 ☐ She hides the fact that she isn't enjoying herself.

8 Have you ever met a person from a very different culture? Have you ever been abroad? Did you experience 'culture shock' like Ewa? What was difficult or strange for you?

Vocabulary: Connotation

9 Find the words underlined in the texts and translate them into your language. Have they got positive (+), negative (−) or neutral (/) associations for you?

Example *well-lit (+)*

Which adjectives were most difficult to translate?

Speaking

10 Work in groups of three. Use the words below to start a chain of associations. One person writes down the words.

- hamburger • river • lipstick • home

Example
hamburger ... fast food ... Saturday night ... cinema ... popcorn ...

Read out your word chains to the rest of the class. Are there any surprising or amusing associations?

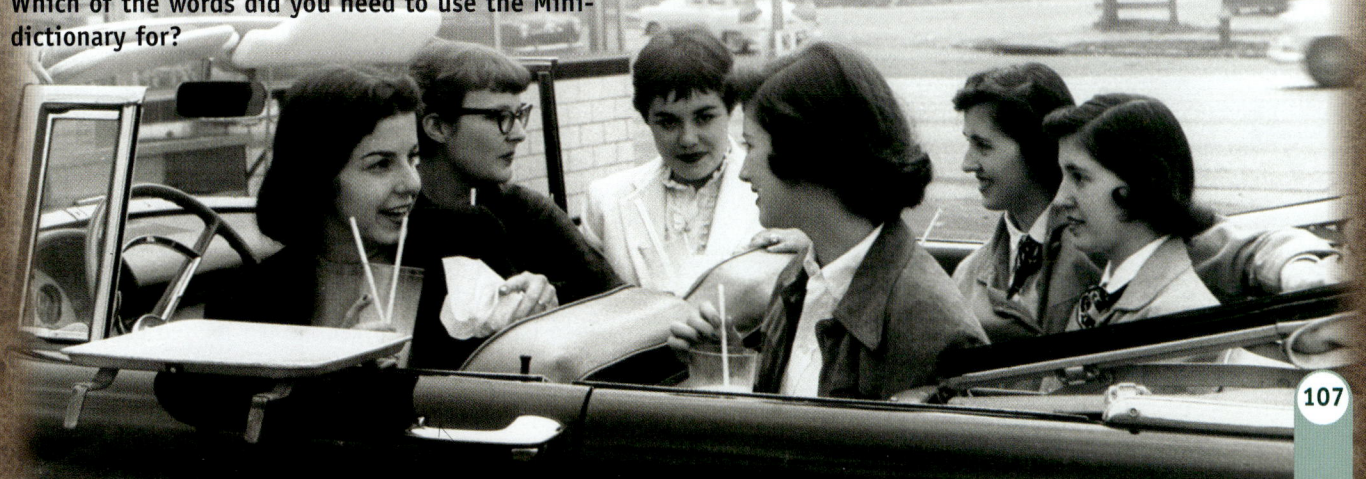

34 Living Abroad

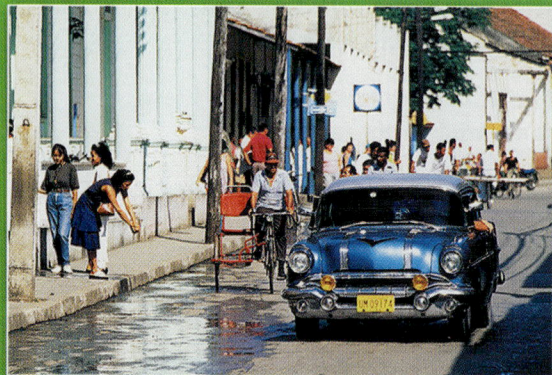

● Cubans Escape
on a Tide of Guinness ●

The sleepy Irish town of Ennis has become home for a growing group of Cuban immigrants. We interviewed one of them, José Luis, who hopes to be granted political asylum in Ireland.

● What is your job?
I'm a **1**_____ . *We're all professionals.*

● Have any of you got money problems?
No, we're not economic refugees.

● Why did you come here?
Because we hope to get **2**_____ *asylum.*

● Are you going to make Ireland your home?
No, we're not. We all want to move on.

● Where do you want to go?
I'd like to live in **3**_____.

● Did you find life difficult here when you first arrived?
Yes, we couldn't understand the Irish accent. And it wasn't easy getting used to the weather – it rains all the time!

● Were the people friendly?
Yes, most of them. Some people thought we were taking their jobs and houses. But generally people were very friendly.

● How long have you been here?
I arrived about a **4**_____ *ago.*

● Is Ireland very different from Cuba?
Yes, the food's totally different! And people's attitudes. People here are less relaxed than in Cuba. They're in more of a hurry. But I like their sense of humour!

● Has the town changed since you arrived?
Well, now there's 'merengue' music in the **5**_____ *at the weekend as well as Irish jigs. And they now serve spicy Cuban food as well!*

● Do you miss Cuba?
Yes, of course. That will always be my real home.

● Do you think you will ever go back?
One day, maybe. I hope so.

Before you start

1 Describe the photos of Ireland and Cuba. Then answer the questions.

1 What differences do you think there are between the two countries?
2 Which place would you like to visit on holiday?

2 Listen to the interview with José Luis on the left. Complete the gaps.

3 Report how José Luis suffered from 'culture shock' when he first arrived in Ireland.

4 Read the conversation between José Luis and an Irish friend after the interview.

Friend What did she want to know?
José Luis She asked me what my job was and if any of us had got money problems. She wanted to know why we had come here and whether we were going to make Ireland our home.
Friend You were talking a long time.
José Luis Yes, she's going to write an article about us. She also asked me if we'd found life difficult when we first arrived. And she wanted to know if the people had been friendly when we first arrived.
Friend You said 'yes', of course!
José Luis Of course I did! Then the journalist asked me how long I had been here and if Ireland was very different from Cuba.
Friend Silly question, really!
José Luis Yes, but when she asked me whether the town had changed since we'd arrived here, I told her about the music and the new pub food.
Friend Anything else?
José Luis Yes, she asked me if I missed Cuba and if I thought I would ever go back.

Presentation

5 Complete the table with the reported form of the interviewer's questions.

JOURNALIST'S QUESTION	JOSÉ LUIS REPORTING THE QUESTION
What is your job?	*she asked me what my job was.*
Why did you come here?	
Are you going to make Ireland your home?	
Were the people friendly?	
How long have you been here?	
Is Ireland very different from Cuba?	
Do you miss Cuba?	

6 Compare the direct and reported questions in the table. What differences do you notice?

Complete the rules by choosing the correct word in *italics* and filling in the gaps.

To report a question:
a when there is a question word, we *include/don't include* it.
b when there is no question word, we add _____ or _____.
c if the reporting verb is in the past tense, we *change/don't change* the tense in the question.
d we use the same word order as in a *question/statement*.

7 Compare how different people report the same question. Notice how the pronouns change.

Journalist	*Do **you** miss Cuba?*
Journalist	I asked **him** if **he** missed Cuba.
José Luis	She asked **me** if **I** missed Cuba.
Friend	Did she really ask **you** if **you** missed Cuba?

Practice

8 Match the questions (1–6) with reported questions (a–e). One of the reported questions can be matched with two direct questions.

1 Where do you work?
2 Where are you working?
3 Where have you worked?
4 Where did you work?
5 Where will you work?
6 Where can you work?

a She asked where I could work.
b She asked where I had worked.
c She asked where I was working.
d She asked where I would work.
e She asked where I worked.

9 Complete the reported questions below. Pay attention to the tense of the reporting verb.

1 'Was Cuba discovered by Columbus?'
   She asked me _____.
2 'Do Canadians have a king or a queen?'
   He wasn't sure _____.
3 'Which side of the road do you drive on in Italy?'
   He doesn't know _____.
4 'When did France stop being a monarchy?'
   He asked me _____.
5 'What do the English eat for breakfast?'
   She wanted to know _____.
6 'When will the next American president be elected?'
   We don't know _____.
7 'Is reggae African music?'
   He wondered _____.
8 'Who are 'Kiwis' and 'Aussies'?'
   She wants to know _____.

Try to answer the questions.

10 Read this report of questions asked by a foreign student who is coming to study in England. Write the original questions.

'First she asked me if the climate was hot or cold and if it rained a lot. Then she wanted to know if she could bring her cat with her into the country and what means of transport was best for coming here. She also asked how much money she needed per month and if she would be allowed to work legally. She asked if we had had many exchange students before and where they had lived. Finally she wondered if the food was different from Spanish food.'

Answer the student's questions.

11 Imagine you are going to interview a foreigner who is living in your country. Prepare questions you would like to ask. Use the interview in Exercise 2 to help you.

Example
What do you like about living here?

What might a foreigner say about your country?

12 Now work in pairs. Use your questions to interview each other.

Example
A *What do you like about living here?*
B *I love the food!*

Report what you learnt to the class.

Example
I asked Lisa what she liked about living here and she said she loved the food.

35 Mind Your Manners

Before you start

1 Your Culture Work in pairs. Answer the questions below.

1 What do you do when you meet someone your age for the first time socially?
   a kiss them more than once
   b kiss them once   **c** shake hands
   d do nothing and say 'hello'
2 What do you do when you meet an old friend in the street?
   a kiss them on the cheeks   **b** kiss them on the lips   **c** hug them
   d do nothing and say 'hello'
3 What do you do when you meet an older person in a formal situation?
   a shake hands   **b** do nothing and say 'hello'   **c** kiss them on the cheeks   **d** kiss them on the lips

A

2 Look at the photos (A–C). What are the people doing? Which photo could be of people from your country?

3 How would you classify people from these cultures?

• Italy • Japan • Britain
• the United States • Argentina

a show a lot of emotion (*affective cultures*)
b act in a very reserved way (*neutral cultures*)
c are in between a and b (*mixed neutral/affective cultures*)

Listen to the radio programme and check your guesses.

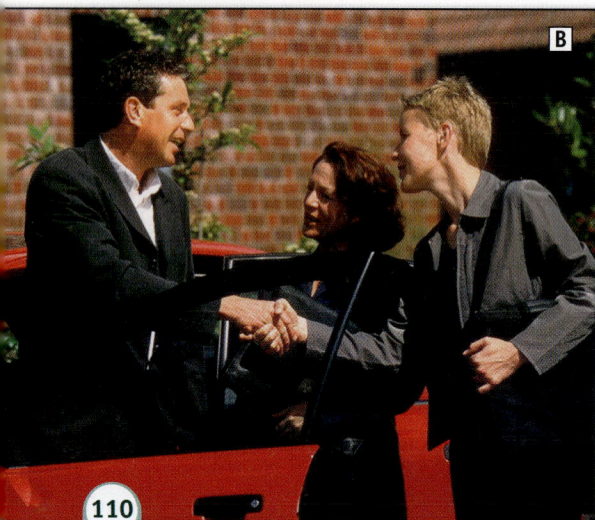

B

Listening

4 Listen to *Culture Matters* again. Complete the table with percentages and *always, often, usually, sometimes, rarely, never*.

	ITALIANS	BRITISH	JAPANESE	AMERICANS
show anger in formal situations	%	%	%	%
use a lot of gestures				
look directly at people				
interrupt or speak at the same time				
say 'please' and 'thank you' a lot				

Work in pairs. Complete the table for people from your country.

5 Listen to Cristina in four situations. Match her dialogues (1–4) with who she is talking to (a–d) and the topic of conversation (e–h).

1 She is talking to _____ about _____.
2 She is talking to _____ about _____.
3 She is talking to _____ about _____.
4 She is talking to _____ about _____.

a a neighbour   **e** a lift to school
b a stranger   **f** a CD she borrowed
c a friend   **g** the salt
d a couple of friends **h** weekend plans

C

6 Match the expressions (1–8) in the Function File with the uses (a–h).

a to make a request to someone you don't know very well
b to reply to someone's thanks
c to apologise to a friend
d to ask for something politely
e to attract someone's attention politely
f to refuse an invitation politely
g to thank someone politely for doing something for you
h to ask to talk to someone

FUNCTION FILE

Being polite
1 Excuse me?
2 Could you pass the salt, please?
3 You're welcome.
4 I'd rather not, thanks.
5 Do you think I could have a word with you?
6 Would you mind giving me a lift to school?
7 Thanks a lot. That's very kind of you.
8 Oh, I've forgotten it! I'm really sorry.

7 Pronunciation Listen and repeat the expressions from the Function File. Pay attention to the intonation.

8 Listen to the dialogues again. This time Cristina sounds rude. Why?

Example
Dialogue 1 → b

a She is too 'direct'.
b She doesn't say 'please' or 'thank you'.
c She shows no interest.
d She interrupts someone.

Speaking

9 Read the Strategies.

SPEAKING STRATEGIES: Preparing for roleplays
• Decide how formal or informal the situation is.
• Think about your role (e.g. age of person, relationship).
• Choose some suitable expressions from the Function File.
• Before you start, practise saying the expressions with polite intonation.

Work in pairs. Use the Strategies to prepare for the roleplays (1–6) and then act out the situations.

Student A
1 You are on a train. Ask someone you don't know to close the window.
2 You are with your friend. Decide what to do at the weekend.
3 You see your middle-aged neighbour in the street. Ask him/her to post a letter for you.
4 You borrowed your friend's magazine last week.
5 You are in a restaurant. Ask the waiter/waitress to give you the menu.
6 You are an English teacher.

Student B
1 You are reading a book on a train. You don't know anybody.
2 You are with a friend. Decide what to do at the weekend. You start.
3 You are middle-aged. You are just going out of your house.
4 Ask your friend to return a magazine he/she borrowed last week.
5 You are a waiter/waitress.
6 Ask your English teacher if you can give in your essay late.

Vocabulary: Multi-part Verbs (9)

10 Complete the verbs in the dialogue below with these words:

up with, on, back, off, up (x2)

A Hey, *Anne*? Are you going *into the centre*?
B Well, actually I'm going **1**_____ *home*. I'm in a bit of a hurry.
A Do you think you could you drop me **2**_____ *near the post office*?
B OK, but hurry **3**_____. I've got to pick **4**_____ *my sister in twenty minutes*.
A Great! Hang **5**_____ a second. I'll just get *my bag*.
B I'm going to the *car park*. Catch **6**_____ me there!

Listen and check your answers.

11 Work in pairs. Practise the dialogue from Exercise 10. Change the information in *italics*.

QUOTE ... UNQUOTE
'Modern man is educated to understand foreign languages and misunderstand foreigners.'
G.K Chesterton, English writer (1874–1936)

36 Communication Workshops

Listening

Before you start

1 Work in pairs. Describe a photo on the spread.

1 What do you think the people are talking about?
2 Have you ever been in a situation like this? What happened?

2 Read the Strategies.

> **LISTENING STRATEGIES: Identifying style**
> - Informal style is more direct. Listen for contractions and informal or slang expressions (e.g. *yeah, sure, OK, thanks, great*).
> - Formal style usually contains longer sentences and polite words and expressions (e.g. *would you mind ..., please, thank you, do you think you could ...*).

Look at the photos (A–D). In which of the situations would you expect to hear formal language?

Everyday situations

Listen to everyday dialogues.

3 Tomek is studying English at a language school in London. Listen and match the dialogues (1–6) with these situations (a–g). There is one extra situation.

a arranging to go out	e at the doctor's
b renting a room	f at the dinner table
c at the bank	g asking for meaning
d asking for directions	

4 Listen again and answer these questions.

1 Which dialogues are formal and which are informal?
2 Which two dialogues start formally and continue informally?
3 When does Tomek unintentionally sound rude? What does he say? What *should* he say?

What is the correct way to formally address an older person that you know?

- Mr/Mrs • Sir/Madam • Paul/Carol
- Mr Jones/Mrs Jones/Ms Jones

Speaking

Roleplays

Imagine you are at a language school in the UK. Act out possible situations. Follow the stages below.

Stage 1

Look at the situations (1–8) and decide how formal or informal they are. Prepare some things to say and practise saying them politely.

1 You meet your landlord/landlady for the first time. Ask some questions about renting a room, e.g. about visitors, keys, laundry.
2 You are having dinner on your first night. Ask the landlord/landlady to pass you something.
3 You go to the bank to change money.
4 You broke something in the house. Apologise to your landlord/landlady.
5 Ask your landlord/lady for a favour, e.g. for help with your homework.
6 Arrange to do something at the weekend with a friend.
7 Ask someone in the street for directions to a place.
8 Ask a friend from your language school to do you a favour, e.g. lend you some money.

Stage 2

Work in pairs. Act out the situations. Take turns to be the other people.

Talkback

Assess your partner for politeness.

very polite/quite polite/not very polite

Writing

Before you start

1 Read Suzanne's reply to Sonia. What questions do you think Sonia asked?

2 Match the headings below with the paragraphs (1–4) in Suzanne's reply.

- finishing off • introduction (chat/questions) • plans for the trip
- some advice

3 Look at the underlined linking words in the letter. Match them with these words.

anybody, anything, anytime, anywhere

Dear Sonia,

1 Thanks for your letter. I'm glad Lara still remembers me! I'm fine, though since I got back from staying with you in Brussels, I've been really busy. You know what it's like when you've got exams coming up, don't you?

2 Anyway, I'll try to answer your questions about the trip. Get mum and Dad <u>whatever</u> you like. They love sweet things, so some Belgian chocolates would be great. You really don't have to get me anything. It's difficult to say what sort of clothes to bring because the weather is so unpredictable these days. I'd bring summer clothes but with a couple of jumpers.

3 We're really looking forward to your visit to London. We can go <u>wherever</u> you want but I think you'd like the Science museum and the Tower of London. I've also got a few ideas for our nightlife! One more thing – we're on the Internet now, so you can email <u>whoever</u> you want at home <u>whenever</u> you feel like it.

4 Well, I really must go now as I've got my aerobics class. I'm really looking forward to seeing you. Send me your flight details when you know them.

Lots of love,

Suzanne x

4 Complete the sentences with *whenever, whoever, wherever* or *whatever.*

1 _____ is on the phone, I don't want to speak to them.
2 The party starts at nine, so come _____ you want after that.
3 Come in. Sit _____ you like.
4 _____ you do, don't ask him about the exam.

A Personal Letter (2)

Write a letter to an exchange partner. Follow the stages and use Writing Help 9 on page 144.

Stage 1

Imagine the person you are writing to. Think about the advice you want to give him/her. Include:

- ideas for presents
- the kinds of places you will show him/her in your area
- the kinds of activities you will do
- the kind of clothes that would be suitable for these activities

Stage 2

Organise your notes into four paragraphs like Suzanne's letter and then write your letter. Use linking words.

Stage 3

Check your letter.

Talkback

In groups, read each other's letters. Is there any advice that you don't agree with? Tell the others.

Language Problem Solving 9   Linking words

1 Read the text. Which advice do you find most useful?

You will find cultures different from your own wherever you go in the world. Although other cultures and ways of life might seem strange at first, they can be fascinating if you approach them with an open
5 mind.

Before you travel anywhere, learn a bit about the place you are going to. As soon as you show interest and some knowledge about their country, people will respond much better to you. Even though you do not
10 speak their language, knowing a few words like 'please' or 'thank you' will be appreciated. Do not expect everyone to speak English – take a phrasebook so that you can try communicating.

Then, after arriving in the country, the most
15 important thing is to keep your eyes open. First, observe how people behave, what they do when they meet each other. As well as that, you can watch local TV. Even if you do not understand a word, you will learn something. In many countries you can also buy
20 a local newspaper in order to see what you can understand. Because most languages have international words, you will probably be able to find out something.

Above all, be adventurous. Try out local specialities
25 like fried ants (from Colombia) even if they might appear a bit strange. Actually, despite their appearance, they are delicious! Do not just stick to the tourist areas but go exploring in local areas unless they are known to be dangerous. Go shopping
30 in local shops where you will meet local people and eat out in local restaurants. However, first check that the food is safe.

Finally, when in another country, respect people's culture and its differences from yours. Remember that
35 you are their guest.

2 Match the groups of linking words (a–f) from the text with their functions (1–6).

1 Explaining causes
2 Giving reasons
3 Giving conditions
4 Contrasting
5 Giving more information
6 Sequencing actions/events

a finally, when, before, as soon as, then, after, first
b however, but, despite, although, even though
c unless, if, even if, when
d where, wherever
e because
f in order to, so that

3 Complete the sentences (1–6) with possible linking words.

although   after   before   when   as soon as
but   because   despite   even though
in order to   so that

1 _____ his injury, he continued playing.
2 _____ he heard the news, he left the country.
3 He smiled _____ he was in pain.
4 _____ causing the accident, he wasn't interrogated.
5 He phoned _____ complain about the service.
6 He came early _____ we could discuss everything before class.

4 Rewrite the sentences as one sentence using the linking words in brackets.

1 The weather was horrible. We decided to go camping. (despite)
2 I suppose the tickets for Sting's concert have been sold out. I will try to get inside. (even if)
3 I'll find a job. I'll rent a flat. (as soon as)
4 I spoke very slowly. All the foreigners could understand me. (so that)
5 I take an English dictionary. I go anywhere. (wherever)
6 I learn languages. I want to communicate with people from different countries. (because)

5 Rewrite the sentences with the same meaning using the linking words provided.

1 He played the match despite his illness.
Although …
2 I never travel by plane if I don't have to.
Unless …
3 The rain stopped before the match began.
After …
4 He didn't have a lot of money but he managed to start his own business.
Even though …
5 He climbed the Empire State Building because he wanted to be famous.
In order to …

6 Complete the sentences in a logical way.

1 People have pets in order to …
2 I drink a lot of coffee although …
3 I get angry when …
4 Children often cry because …
5 Dogs don't bite unless …
6 Most people work so that …
7 A lot of people watch soap operas even though …
8 Film stars earn a lot of money even if …

AUSTRALIA

1 Look at the pictures. What do you know about Australia?

2 Work in pairs. Student A turns to page 129, Student B turns to page 131. Read the factfiles about Australia. Then take turns to ask questions to complete the information in your factfile.

3 Do you think these statements about Aborigines are true (T) or false (F)? Read the text and find out.

1. ☐ Aborigines originally came from India.
2. ☐ They were farmers.
3. ☐ There is no written Aboriginal language.
4. ☐ Europeans destroyed their traditional way of life.

🎧 4 Listen to someone talking about Australia and make notes about:

- outdoor activities
- sports • animals
- farming and industry
- immigration

Now compare your notes with another student's.

5 Would you like to visit or live in Australia? Why or why not?

Comparing Cultures

Prepare a short presentation about another country to give to the class.

- Choose a country you're interested in.
- Choose different areas to find out about, e.g. climate, the environment, famous people, important industries, popular sports and activities, population, wildlife.
- Decide what order you are going to talk about the things and then give your presentation to the class.
- While you are listening to other presentations, think of one question to ask.

Aborigines

Aborigines probably came to Australia from Indonesia 50,000 years ago. The oldest skeleton is about 38,000 years old and was found with traces of ceremonial paint. Originally, Aborigines were nomads and didn't have a sense of land ownership, although tribes returned to particular places to bury their dead. Some places, like Uluru, were sacred because they were associated with 'Dreamtime', the time when the earth was formed.

Aborigine legends, songs and dances tell of powerful spirits who created the land and people during the Dreamtime. There was no written Aboriginal language and most of the 600 tribes spoke different dialects. However, the tradition of the Dreamtime united the people. Rock paintings showing this creation period can be found all over the country.

The arrival of Europeans gradually brought an end to the traditional Aboriginal way of life. Today, most Aborigines live in cities and towns and only a few continue the old nomadic way of life.

In recent years, white Australians have become more sensitive to the Aborigines' situation and there is a growing appreciation of their culture.

Review 9

Grammar

1 Report the following questions.

1 'Where does your exchange partner live?' asked Stan.
Stan asked me _____.
2 'Does she often write to you?' asked Martha.
Martha asked me _____.
3 'Are you going to go in the summer?' asked Tom.
Tom asked me _____.
4 'Will you send me a postcard?' asked Louise.
Louise asked me _____.
5 'What time does the plane leave?' asked Bernard.
Bernard asked me _____.
6 'How long is the flight?' asked Miriam.
Miriam asked me _____.

2 Game Work in groups. Play this grammar game.

- Student A whispers a question to Student B.
- Student B says the reply aloud.
- The rest of the group guess what the question was, using reported speech.

Example

A (whispers) *What is your shoe size?*
B *Forty-two.*
C *She asked you how old your father was.*
B *No.*
D *She asked you what the number of your house was.*
B *No.*
C *She asked you what your shoe size was.*
B *Yes!*

3 Complete the gap in each sentence with the word given and up to four other words. The second sentence should have a similar meaning to the first sentence.

1 He wanted to improve his English, so he went on a summer course in York. **order**
He went on a summer course in York _____ his English.
2 Although she found it difficult at first, she studied at one of the USA's top universities. **despite**
_____ it difficult at first, she studied at one of the USA's top universities.
3 We don't mind when you come to visit us. **whenever**
You can _____ want.
4 He wrote a lot of applications and finally he got a job. **before**
He wrote a lot of applications _____ a job.
5 I saw her and immediately recognised her. **soon**
I recognised her _____ I saw her.
6 He saved all his money until he had enough to visit London. **so**
He saved all his money _____ visit London.

7 In spite of his love of Ireland and the people, he still misses Cuba. **although**
_____ Ireland and the people, he still misses Cuba.

Vocabulary

4 Do the underlined words have positive, negative or neutral connotations for you?

1 A lot of people have a stereotypical image of Australians.
2 Now the local pubs even offer spicy Cuban food.
3 There are lots of amazing animals in Australia, not just kangaroos.
4 Most languages have international words which you can understand.
5 Possums are lovely creatures about the size of a cat.
6 I was impressed – it was a very posh place.
7 I went on a really fascinating trip last year to South America.
8 One of the biggest environmental problems is drought.

5 Multi-part verbs Complete the sentences with *back, off, on* or *up.*

1 You can go – I'll catch _____ with you soon.
2 Hurry _____, or we'll be late!
3 Could you drop me _____ at the bus stop?
4 I'm tired. I'd like to go _____ home now.
5 Don't get a taxi – I'll pick you _____ at the station.
6 Don't go yet! Hang _____ a second until I get my umbrella.

Pronunciation: Difficult Words

🎧 6 Listen and repeat these words from the module.

adventurous, allergy, asylum, desirable, identification, irrational, laboriously, literary, obligatory, spontaneity, stereotypical

7 Can you say this proverb? Use the Phonetic Chart in the Mini-dictionary to help you. What does the proverb mean?

/wʌn mænz miːt ɪz ənʌðə mænz pɔɪzən/

Check Your Progress

Look back at the Module Objectives on page 105.
◉ Which activities did you enjoy most?
◉ Which activities did you have problems with?
◉ Which grammar area do you need to revise?

▸▸ Now read the story *A Horse and Two Goats*, Literature Spot 4, page 138.

10 Civilisation

In this module you will...

- **read** book extracts and a description
- **listen to** a dialogue, a TV programme and a presentation
- **talk about** history, civilisation and travel; **practise** giving a presentation
- **write** a description of a place
- **learn about** *wish*, *should have* and more verbs with *-ing* and infinitives

Warm-up

1 Look at the pictures. What do the objects tell us about the lives of the people they belonged to?

Example
The coins show the people had an organised economy.

2 Listen to two people selecting items for a 'time capsule'. Which of the Key Words do they choose?

> **KEY WORDS: Everyday Objects**
> book, cash card, CD, coffee maker, electric kettle, a football, key ring, microwave oven, (computer) mouse, mobile phone, newspaper, palmtop computer, pizza carton, radio alarm clock, TV remote, walkman (personal stereo)

3 Work in pairs. Choose ten (small) items for a time capsule. Tell the class what you chose and why.

Example
First, we'd definitely include a ...

4 Now imagine you could travel in time. Answer the questions below.

1 What period and civilisation would you choose? Give two reasons why.
2 What ten objects would you take with you? Explain the reasons for your choice.
3 What would you try to tell the people about your civilisation?

Example
I'd go back to Ancient Greece in the 4th century BC.

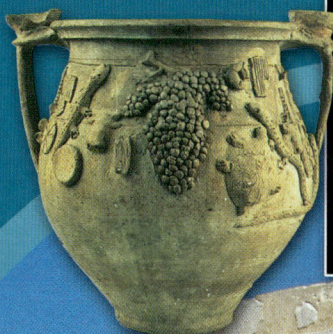

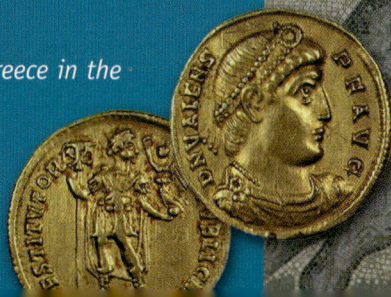

SER PENIVS

37 A Lost City

Before you start

1 Look at the photo. Describe the place and answer these questions:

1 What do you know about Machu Picchu? Would you like to visit it?

2 What other famous historical sites would you like to go to around the world?

2 **Your Culture** What are the most important historical sites in your country? Have you been to any of them? Tell the class.

3 Read the introduction about the explorer, Hiram Bingham. How do you think he felt when he found the lost city of Machu Picchu? Use the Mini-dictionary and the Key Words to help you.

KEY WORDS: Adjectives
amazed, bewildered, ecstatic, exhausted, impressed, indifferent, shocked, spellbound

Hiram Bingham (1875-1956) had an extraordinary life. He was successively a Protestant pastor, a land surveyor, a museum curator, a university professor, a World War I pilot and an American politician. However, he is best remembered as an explorer, archeologist and discoverer of lost cities. Here are some extracts from his book, 'Lost City of the Incas'.

A

'The morning 24 of July 1911 dawned in cold drizzle. Arteaga shivered and seemed inclined to stay in his hut. I offered to pay him well **1**_____ he would show me the ruins. He refused and said it was too hard a climb for such a wet day. But when he found out I was willing to pay him more, he finally agreed to go. When asked where the ruins were, he pointed straight to the **2**_____ of the mountain. No one supposed that they would be particularly interesting. And no one cared to go with me. The naturalist said that there would be "more butterflies near the river!" The surgeon said he had to wash his clothes and mend them. Anyhow, it was my job to investigate all reports of ruins and **3**_____ to find the Inca capital.

So, accompanied only by Sergeant Carrasco, we left camp at ten o'clock on July 24th. After a walk of three-quarters of an hour, Arteaga left the main road and plunged down through the jungle to the bank of the river. Here there was a primitive bridge **4**_____ crossed the roaring rapids at its narrowest part. I confess that I got down on my hands and knees and crawled across, six inches at a time. Leaving the stream, we now struggled up the bank through dense jungle and in a **5**_____ minutes reached the bottom of a very steep slope. For an hour and twenty minutes we had a hard climb. A good part of the distance we went on all fours ... The humidity was great. The heat was excessive; and I was not in training! There were no ruins of any kind in sight. I began to **6**_____ my companions had made **7**_____ right choice.'

B

*The men met some Indians who told Sergeant Carrasco that the ruins were a little further along and gave them a little boy to act as their guide. **8**_____ leaving the hut, they strolled across some open ground and went into the forest beyond.*

'Suddenly, I found myself confronted with the walls of ruined houses built of the finest quality Inca stone work. It was **9**_____ to see them because they were partly covered with trees and moss ... We scrambled along through the dense undergrowth and then ... without any warning, the boy showed me a cave, beautifully lined with the finest cut stone. Clearly, it was the work of a master artist. It all seemed **10**_____ an unbelievable dream. It fairly took my breath away. What could this place **11**_____? Why had no one given us any idea of it?'

Reading

4 **Read the Strategies.**

Reading Strategies: Word Gaps
- Read through the whole text to get an idea.
- Read the sentence with the gap and then the sentences before and after it.
- Try to work out what kind of word is missing (e.g. an article, linker, adjective etc.).
- For other words, use the general meaning of the sentence to help you work them out. (e.g. is it a positive or negative word?).
- Read the sentence again and see if it makes sense. More than one option may be possible.

5 Now read the extracts (A–C) and use the Strategies to complete the gaps.

6 Read the extracts again. Decide which of the sentences are true (T) and which are false (F).

1. ☐ Arteaga was a local guide hired by the expedition.
2. ☐ The other members of the expedition were put off by the weather.
3. ☐ The bridge looked very dangerous to Bingham.
4. ☐ They had to crawl up most of the slope.
5. ☐ Bingham was physically very fit.
6. ☐ Bingham knew immediately that he had found the lost city.
7. ☐ The two big buildings he found were Inca temples.
8. ☐ The buildings were made of large stones.
9. ☐ The sun played an important part in Inca religion.
10. ☐ Bingham took photos of the ruins.

Vocabulary: Verbs of Movement

7 **Match the verbs from the text (1–7) with the definitions (a–g).**

1	plunge (down)	a	cross on hands and knees
2	crawl (across)	b	walk in a relaxed way
3	struggle (up)	c	go up (e.g. a slope)
4	go on all fours	d	go up with difficulty
5	stroll	e	move with hands and feet
6	scramble (along)	f	go down very fast
7	climb (up)	g	go over objects using your hands to help you

How would you say these words in your language?

8 Replace the verbs in *italics* with the verbs from Exercise 7 in their correct form.

1. In the evening, I usually *walk* in the park with my elderly dog.
2. When I got to the pool, I immediately *jumped* into the deep end.
3. I *walked up* the steep hill with five or six shopping bags.
4. The entrance to the cave was small so I *went through it on my hands and knees*.
5. Last month I *went up* the Eiffel Tower without taking the lift.

Speaking

9 Work in pairs. Student A turns to page 130, Student B turns to page 131. Read the information about the Incas. Then take turns to ask and answer questions to complete the information.

10 What do you think were the most important things about the Incas?

The little boy persuaded them to climb up another steep slope.

C

'Surprise followed surprise in bewildering succession. We found ourselves standing in **12** _____ of the ruins of two of the finest and most interesting structures in ancient America. Made of beautiful white granite, the walls contained blocks higher **13** _____ a man. The sight held me spellbound. Each building had only three walls and was open on one side. The principal temple had walls twelve feet high ... The building **14** _____ not look as though it ever had a roof so the sun could be welcomed here by the priests. I could scarcely believe my senses as I examined the larger stones and estimated that they must weigh ten to fifteen tons each. Would anyone believe what I **15** _____ found? Fortunately, I had a good camera and the sun was shining.'

GRAMMAR FOCUS:

38 Landmarks

[A]

Before you start

1 Look at the photos (A–E). Where are the buildings and what are they called? Which of them would you like to visit?

[C]

[B]

[D]

[E]

2 Work in pairs. Guess the answers to the questions below.

1 How did the Bloody Tower in the Tower of London get its name?
a Henry VIII had two of his wives executed here.
b Richard III had the young Edward V and his brother murdered here.
c Ten people died here during the German bombing of London in 1940.

2 How many pairs of gladiators fought on one day in the Colosseum?
a 598   **b** 3,231   **c** 4,941   **d** 8,941

3 How far off centre is the top of the Leaning Tower of Pisa?
a 7.4 metres   **b** 5.3 metres   **c** 7.1 metres   **d** 9.7 metres

4 Which of these is <u>not</u> the name of one of the temples of the Acropolis?
a Nike   **b** Parthenon   **c** Addidas   **d** Erechtheion

5 How tall are the two towers of Notre Dame?
a 69 metres   **b** 78 metres   **c** 95 metres
d 150 metres

3 Listen to the conversation between two tourists and check your guesses.

Presentation

4 Listen again. Complete the sentences from the dialogue.

1 It's awful that I can't stay here for a whole month.
I **wish** …

2 It's a pity he wasn't there.
He **wishes** …

3 They don't make the brochures good enough.
They **should** …

4 It's a pity you didn't see the place where they executed Anne Boleyn.
You **should** …

5 It's a pity you missed Greece.
You **shouldn't** …

6 I would like to be a bit fitter.
I **wish** …

5 What time does each of the sentences (1–6) in Exercise 4 talk about: past or present?

6 Complete the table.

TIME	WISH	SHOULD(N'T)
dissatisfaction with the PRESENT	wish + _____ tense	should(n't) + _____
dissatisfaction with the PAST	wish + _____ tense	should(n't) + _____

Practice

7 Which of the options (a–d) mean the same? There may be more than one.

1 I regret I didn't learn foreign languages.
   a I wish I hadn't learnt foreign languages.
   b I wish I had learnt foreign languages.
   c I wish I learnt foreign languages.
   d I should've learnt foreign languages.
2 What a pity I went on that tour.
   a I should've gone on that tour.
   b I wish I had gone on that tour.
   c I wish I hadn't gone on that tour.
   d I shouldn't have gone on that tour.
3 I'd like to be a traveller.
   a I wish I had been a traveller.
   b I wish I was a traveller.
   c I should've been a traveller.
   d I wish I wasn't a traveller.

8 Put the verbs in brackets in the correct form. Add *not* if necessary.

Example

1 *I wish I could speak English as well as he can.*

1 John speaks English fluently. I wish I _____ (can) speak English as well as he can.
2 I can't drive. I wish I _____ (can) drive around Europe instead of hitchhiking.
3 I always buy useless things when I'm on holiday. I wish I _____(be) so careless with money.
4 He's such a bad driver. I wish he _____ (be) given a licence.
5 I didn't visit the Louvre when I was in Paris. I wish I _____ (see) the Mona Lisa.
6 We always get cheated by local taxi drivers. We wish we _____ (be) so naive.
7 I decided to go on a package tour. Now I wish I _____ (go) on my own.
8 This car is fantastic. I wish I _____ (have) a similar one.
9 Those souvenirs are so ugly. I wish I _____ (buy) them.

9 Write a few comments that the person in each picture (1–3) would make about the situation they are in. Use *wish* or *should/shouldn't*.

Example

1 *I wish it wasn't raining. I should've taken my umbrella.*

10 Re-write the sentences beginning with the words given.

1 It was a mistake not to buy a camera before our trip to Egypt.
   We should _____.
2 It's a pity we went to Berlin by plane – it was so expensive.
   I wish _____.
3 It was so silly of me to pay for the hotel in advance.
   I shouldn't _____.
4 What a pity we don't have a guidebook!
   I wish _____.
5 Why did you offer her a lift to Dublin? It was so stupid of you.
   You shouldn't _____.

11 Think about your town or area. Write notes about things that make it unattractive for tourists.

Example

Horrible fast food kiosks – hate them
Sports facilities – need more
Castle in a terrible state

12 In pairs, discuss your ideas with your partner. Use *wish* and *should/shouldn't* to express your opinions.

Example

A *I wish we didn't have all those fast food kiosks. They smell awful. I hate them.*
B *I think they aren't a big problem but there should be more restaurants with local specialities. What do you think?*

13 Personalisation Think about your last holiday and things you did/didn't do and regret now. Express your regrets using *I wish ...* and *I should/shouldn't have ...*

Example

A *I wish my family and I hadn't gone to the seaside – it was so boring.*
B *I should have spent more time with my grandparents.*
C *I shouldn't have gone to that language course in Oxford – I didn't learn anything.*

1

2

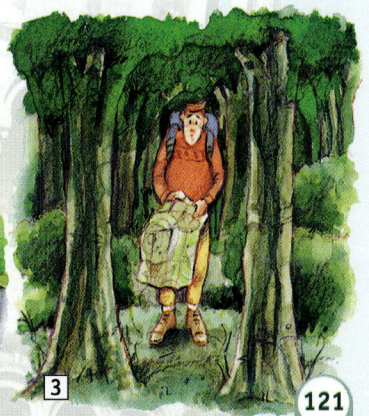

3

Module 10

SKILLS FOCUS

39 Civilised?

A

B

Before you start

1 Look at the Key Words. Classify them into these headings.

- art/culture
- technology/medicine
- agriculture

> **KEY WORDS: Civilisation**
> bronze tools, calendar, cultivation of crops, cuneiform writing, domestication of animals, gunpowder, irrigation channels, marble statues, plough, potter's wheel, surgery, telescope, wheeled carts

Now use four of the Key Words to label the pictures (A–D).

2 Which three developments in the Key Words are the most important? Tell the class.

3 What do you know about Mesopotamia? Try to complete some of the factfile.

FACTFILE

MESOPOTAMIA

- Present-day country: 1 _____
- Main rivers: 2 _____ and Euphrates
- Main cities: Ur and 3 _____
- Civilisation developed from: 4 _____ BC
- Conquered: first by the 5 _____ in 539 BC and then in 330 BC by 6 _____ the Great

Listening

🎧 **4** Listen to a TV programme. Check your guesses in Exercise 3 and complete the factfile.

🎧 **5** Listen again and answer these questions.

1 What kind of programme is it?
   a travel   **b** science documentary   **c** history documentary
2 Why was Mesopotamia probably the first place for civilisation to develop?
   a The land was fertile.   **b** They had writing.   **c** They invented the wheel.
3 Which of these things was <u>not</u> invented there?
   a bronze tools   **b** the wheel   **c** the potter's wheel
4 What was the basis of Mesopotamian writing?
   a symbols   **b** letters   **c** pictures
5 Which civilisation first developed surgery?
   a the Mesopotamians   **b** the Ancient Egyptians
   c the Ancient Greeks
6 What did they use for recording payments?
   a ropes with knots in   **b** clay tablets   **c** stone tablets

What was the most interesting piece of information that you learnt from the programme? Tell the class.

🎧 **6** Listen to another extract from the TV series. Which of the people interviewed (1–5) think we are civilised and which think we are not? Which of the reasons (a–e) do they give?

Speaker 1 _____
Speaker 2 _____
Speaker 3 _____
Speaker 4 _____
Speaker 5 _____

a war, hunger and disease
b art and architecture
c health and education
d advanced technology
e crime and violence

122

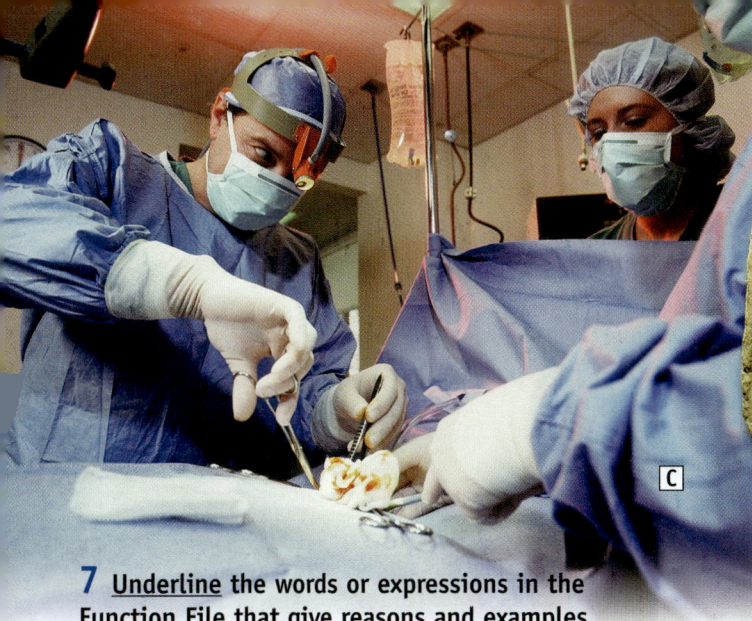

7 <u>Underline</u> the words or expressions in the Function File that give reasons and examples.

FUNCTION FILE

Opinions – Giving Reasons and Examples

1 I think we're civilised <u>because</u> we're so technologically advanced. (*reason*)
2 For example, our computers and medicine are streets ahead.
3 The reason I think so is that we've got so much poverty and war.
4 A classic example of this is the fact that millions of people in the world are hungry.
5 For that reason, we are civilised – but not as much as other cultures.
6 Take the ancient Greeks.
7 I don't think we're so civilised since we still behave so badly.
8 Look at those football hooligans.
9 I suppose we are civilised as our society tries to look after people.
10 I mean healthcare and social services are a case in point, aren't they?

8 Complete the statements below with reasons or examples.

1 'People are too materialistic nowadays. A classic example of this is _____.'
2 'We are better off than before. For example, _____.'
3 'Machines make life much easier. _____ are a case in point.'
4 'I think modern medicine is fantastic. Look at _____.'
5 'I think we are ruining the planet because we _____.'
6 'Many people in the developing world live terribly since_____.'
7 'Art and architecture is worse now than in the past. Take _____.'
8 'People haven't got any better. The reason I think so is _____.'
9 'I think women were terribly treated in the past as they _____.'
10 'Modern technology has changed our lives. For that reason, I think _____.'

Speaking

9 Which of the statements in Exercise 8 do you agree with? Work in pairs and discuss them. Use expressions from the Function File.

Example
A *I agree that people are materialistic. A classic example is the obsession we have with cars.*
B *I don't agree. Take voluntary work for example.*

Vocabulary: Multi-part Verbs (10)

10 Match the verbs below with the multi-part verbs in the sentences (1–7) from the TV programme about Mesopotamia.

produce (an idea/answer, etc.), get control, start (doing something), establish, visit, stop (doing something), become larger, discover (something)

1 The Mesopotamians *set up* a system of money.
2 Cities started to *grow up* in the area.
3 They *gave up* being nomads and *took up* farming.
4 We'll be *going around* different places in the world.
5 The Greeks *took over* in 330 BC.
6 They *worked out* how to use the wheel to make pottery.
7 We are going to try to *come up with* answers to some big questions.

11 Complete the sentences with multi-part verbs from Exercise 10 in the correct form.

1 I _____ in a small village and moved into the city when I was fifteen.
2 My mum _____ smoking last year.
3 I would like to _____ collecting Roman coins.
4 We didn't know what to do but he _____ a brilliant suggestion.
5 She's very bossy and tries to _____ the whole group.
6 The government _____ a new security system at airports around the city.
7 I just couldn't _____ how to use that new gadget.
8 I'd like to _____ South America next year.

QUOTE... UNQUOTE
'Is it progress if a cannibal uses a knife and fork?'
Stanislaw J. Lec, Polish poet (1909–1966)

40 Communication Workshops

B

Listening

Before you start

1 Look at the photos (A and B). In what ways have we made progress and in what ways have we not? Tell the class.

A Short Presentation of a Topic

Listen to a student giving a presentation about a topic.

2 Listen and complete the table.

ADVANTAGES OF PROGRESS	DISADVANTAGES OF PROGRESS
medicine	pollution

3 Listen again and complete these notes with one or more words.

1 Her topic is: Modern technology has made our lives ...
2 Medicine has improved because we can ...
3 Most people can read and write and ...
4 Nowadays nearly everybody uses ...
5 Cars and car factories cause ...
6 We have nuclear weapons that could ...
7 Scientists can't find a cure for ...
8 There are lots of people in the world without ...

4 How well did you think the girl gave her presentation? Give your reasons.

A

Speaking

Before you start

1 Classify the expressions in the Function File:

a starting/finishing
b giving examples
c correcting mistakes

FUNCTION FILE

Presenting

1 Well, *first I'd like to say* ...
2 *Sorry, I don't mean* doctors, *I mean* medicine.
3 *For example*, in medicine we can now ...
4 *Sorry, I mean* jobs.
5 It has caused problems *such as* pollution ...
6 *Like* cars, *for example*.
7 ... cancer or Aids, *things like that*.
8 So, *all things considered* ...

2 Read the Strategies.

SPEAKING STRATEGIES: A Presentation of a Topic

• Choose a topic you know something about.
• Make some notes in the form of a flowchart.

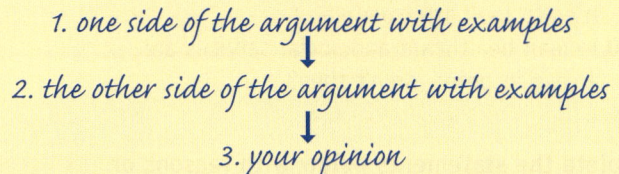

> *1. one side of the argument with examples*
> ↓
> *2. the other side of the argument with examples*
> ↓
> *3. your opinion*

• Tone of voice is important. Use your voice to show interest and try to sound convincing!
• When you make a mistake (factual or linguistic) correct yourself. Relax and remember that everyone makes mistakes!

A Presentation of a Topic

Give a short presentation on one of these topics. Follow the stages.

• Computers are a necessary part of modern life.
• More people should use public transport.
• Sports stars are overpaid.
• Young people today don't make good use of their leisure time.

Stage 1

Use the Strategies to prepare for your presentation.

Stage 2

Practise giving your presentation. Try to include expressions from the Function File.

Stage 3

Take turns to give your presentation to the class or group.

Talkback

Who do you think gave the best presentation? Why?

Writing

Before you start

1 Read the description. Match the topics (a–d) with the paragraphs (1–4).

a what to see inside   **b** conclusion
c introduction   **d** surroundings

[1] The monastery and palace of San Lorenzo del Escorial, thirty miles north-west of Madrid in central Spain is, <u>without doubt,</u> one of the most impressive places I have ever visited. It was built in the 16th century by King Philip II as a symbol of Spanish power and the scale of it is breathtaking. In fact, it has nine towers, 86 stairways, 88 fountains and 2,673 windows. You can see it from miles away and when you get closer, <u>what strikes you</u> is not only its size but also the austerity of its architecture.

[2] Inside, there is plenty to see. There is an excellent collection of tapestries and paintings, including works by Titian and El Greco. The staterooms of Philip II are magnificent, <u>full of</u> paintings of glorious victories and maps of the Spanish Empire. In contrast, Philip's own bedroom and study are tiny and extremely bare for such an important man. Other places to see are the monumental church and the beautiful library, which has over 40,000 volumes.

[3] The Escorial <u>is surrounded by</u> ornamental gardens and has views over the plains of Castille on one side and the wooded Guadarrama mountains on the other. The charming little town of San Lorenzo is also <u>well worth visiting</u> and is full of outdoor cafes and restaurants where you can recover from your trip to the monastery.

[4] I think this building <u>impressed me</u> so much because of its size, grandeur and austerity. I have always been very interested in history and I can just imagine Philip sitting in his small study administering his vast empire before going to pray.

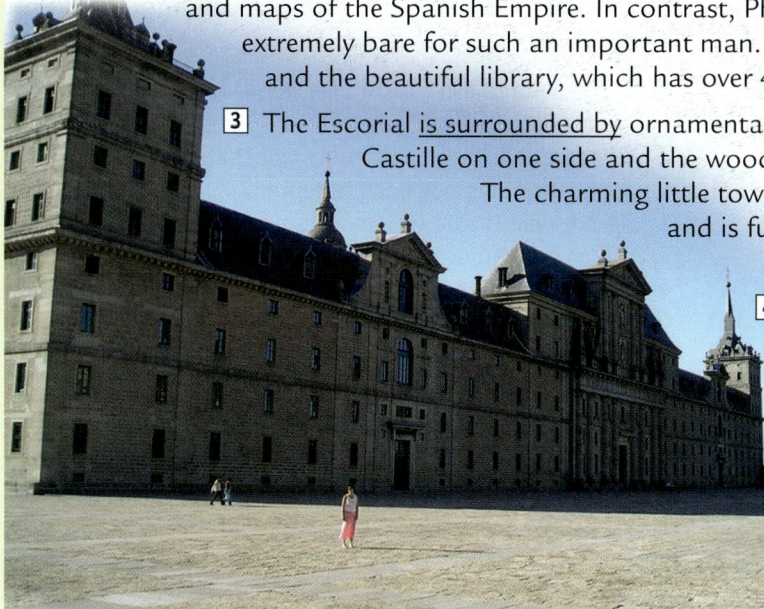

2 Match the <u>underlined</u> expressions with the meanings below.

had an effect on me, definitely, you should go there, what you notice, around it, with a lot of

3 Find the linking expressions *in fact* and *in contrast* in the text. Which adds and which compares information?

Describing a Place

Write a description of a place you have visited. Follow the stages below and refer to Writing Help 10 on page 144.

Stage 1

Decide what place you are going to write about (e.g. a historic building; a sports stadium; an art gallery). Find more information about the place and its history.

Stage 2

Write notes for four paragraphs like the description above.

- What is it/where is it/when and why was it built/what's special about it?
- What's inside?
- What are the surroundings?
- What do you think of that place?

Stage 3

Write the description and then check it for mistakes.

Talkback

In groups, read your descriptions. If you have been to the place, do you agree with the description? If not, would you like to go there? Give your reasons.

Language Problem Solving 10

1 **Match the sentences with the pictures.**

1 **Remember to visit** Notre Dame!
2 **Remember visiting** Notre Dame for the first time?

a   b

3 I've **stopped eating** sweets.
4 I've **stopped to eat** a chocolate.

a   b

5 I **regret to tell** you that all of you have failed the exam.
6 I **regret telling** them that they failed the exam.

a   b

7 It's so stuffy in here – let's **try opening** the window.
8 It's so stuffy in here – let's **try to open** the window.

a   b

9 I **forgot to buy** the milk.
10 I **forgot buying** the milk.

a   b

2 **Match the verbs in bold from Exercise 1 with these definitions.**

Example **a** = *2*

a to recall an activity that happened
b to give up something
c to make an effort to do something (see if you can do it)
d not to do something because it escaped your memory
e to feel sorry about something that happened
f to interrupt an activity in order to do something
g to do something as an experiment, to see what will happen
h to bear in mind an obligation or recommendation to do something
i to feel sorry for something you have to do
j to have no memory of something that happened

3 **Complete the sentences with the *-ing* form or *to* + infinitive of the verbs in brackets.**

1 If the soup doesn't taste very good, try _____ (add) some salt.
2 We regret _____ (inform) you that your application has not been accepted.
3 On the way to the cinema I stopped _____ (buy) the cinema guide.
4 The students couldn't help laughing when they saw I'd forgotten _____ (put) my socks on in the morning.
5 This place looks familiar, I remember _____ (come) here before.
6 You're too slow, Peter. Try _____ (run) faster or you'll never get the ball.
7 I'd like to lose some weight so I've stopped _____ (eat) sweets.
8 I've got your car keys. Have you forgotten _____ (give) them to me?
9 They regretted _____ (go) camping in May as it was cold and it rained a lot.
10 Chris never remembers _____ (turn) everything off before going out – he always leaves something on.

4 **Complete the sentences so that the dialogues make sense.**

1 **A** I think I'm ready. We can go.
   B Did you remember _____?

2 **A** I hate these cash machines! I just can't make them work!
   B Let's see. Try _____.

3 **A** How are you getting on with your new boss?
   B Oh, please, don't ask me! I regret _____.

4 **A** I feel horrible. I have headaches every day.
   B I think you have to stop _____.

5 **A** Why are you leaving so early?
   B I have to hurry back home. I think I forgot _____.

World Music

Geoffrey Oryema

1 Read the text and answer these questions.

1 When and how did World Music start to appear?
2 What different kinds of World Music are there?
3 What are the benefits of it, according to the text?
4 What styles does Geoffrey Oryema mix?

2 What World Music have you heard? Which of the music mentioned in the text would you like to listen to?

3 Listen to the song and read the lyrics.

Different kinds of music, played with different instruments and coming from different cultures have existed since prehistoric times.

However, it was not until the 1980s that the concept of 'World Music' began. Before then, virtually the only records sold in British record shops were local or American.

Suddenly, from about 1980, international sounds started appearing on the radio and African musicians like the Senegalese Youssou N'Door began to come to London to play concerts. Nowadays, it is a thriving genre, selling millions of records and helping to open the minds of many people to music from other cultures. We can now hear Zairean dance music, Mexican Mariachi bands, drummers from Burundi, traditional Australian didgeridoo players and Pakistani Quawwali singers like the great, late Nusrat Fateh Ali Khan.

However, World Music is not only traditional; it has encouraged the fusion of different styles from around the world. One example of this is the Ugandan musician, Geoffrey Oryema. Escaping death at the hands of the Ugandan dictator, Idi Amin, in 1977, Geoffrey moved to France where he started mixing his African roots with rhythms from western pop.

Nomad

The other day I looked
At myself in the mirror
Do not hide your face
Do not hide your face
From me when I feel sad.
On the day when I call you
Answer me, please answer me
And turn your shy ear towards me
No cows and no grass to graze on
Makes me feel I'm a nomad.
I'm lost and silent in the wilderness
Like an owl among the ruins
My wings lined with ashes.
Alone on the roof
I feel I'm a nomad
I feel I'm a nomad
I feel I'm a nomad
My days go up in smoke
My bones are aching
My days go up in smoke
My heart is breaking.
Good walking leaves no track behind it
Do not hide your face
Do not hide your face
From me when I feel sad

4 Answer these questions about the song.

1 Who do you think the singer is 'talking to'?
2 Why do you think he feels sad?
3 Why do you think the song is called 'nomad'?

5 Which of these things do the images from the song refer to?

• wasted time • feeling sad • African proverbs • loneliness

1 I'm a nomad/I'm lost and silent in the wilderness/like an owl among the ruins
2 my heart is breaking/my bones are aching
3 my days go up in smoke
4 no cows and no grass to graze on/good walking leaves no track behind it

6 Your Culture What traditional music from your country do you like? What modern music with traditional influences can you think of?

127

Review 10

Grammar

1 Complete these dialogues between tourists with suitable words to express their regrets.

1 A It's very crowded here. I wish there **1** _____ so many tourists.
   B Art galleries are always the same.
   A Yes, they **2** _____ sell so many tickets.
   B We should have **3** _____ to the park with Jim and Sue instead.
   A Yes, I **4** _____ we'd listened to them.

2 C I wish it **5** _____ so hot!
   D You should have **6** _____ in the shade.
   C I know one thing – we **7** _____ have come here in August!

3 E This traffic's terrible.
   F Mm. We **8** _____ have taken the train.
   E I wish I **9** _____ a book to read.
   F And I wish you **10** _____ drive!

2 Write suitable endings for these sentences.

1 I love this place. I wish I …
2 He's a lovely person. You should have …
3 She's quite shy. I wish she …
4 His room's a mess. He should …
5 My stomach hurts. I wish I …
6 He got very upset. You shouldn't have …
7 There's a lot of litter. They should …
8 That music's beautiful. I wish I …
9 You made a lot of silly mistakes in your essay. You should have …
10 She got up late for her interview. Now she wishes she …

3 Complete these sentences with the correct alternative: -ing form or to + infinitive.

1 We stopped *looking/to look* at the map because we couldn't find the museum.
2 You can stop *looking/to look* for the answer – I've found it!
3 I regret *bringing/to bring* this overcoat – I'm really hot.
4 I regret *bringing/to bring* such bad news, but you must know the truth.
5 If the light doesn't come on, try *changing/to change* the battery.
6 You must try *changing/to change* your attitude; otherwise you'll never succeed.
7 Remember *taking/to take* your mobile phone with you!
8 I remember *taking/to take* lots of photos in Florence.

Vocabulary

4 Think of animals that do these things.

Example

1 *squirrels*

1 Scramble up trees.
2 Crawl up walls.
3 Plunge into ponds.
4 Don't go on all fours.
5 Jump over fences.

5 Multi-part verbs Match the two halves of the sentences.

1 Why don't you just …
2 I really don't know what to do, …
3 This summer, a friend and I …
4 Using the instructions, …
5 I'm a bit tired of driving, …
6 I've really got to …

a give up drinking so much coffee.
b do you want to take over for a while?
c I worked out how to put up the shelves.
d are going to go around Europe together.
e grow up and act your age?
f can you come up with any suggestions?

6 Write sentences about yourself on the following:

three things you'd like to take up, one thing you'd like to give up, one thing you'd like to work out how to do, an idea or invention you'd like to come up with

Example

I'd like to come up with a machine for doing homework!

Pronunciation: Word Stress

7 Put these words into the correct column according to their stress pattern.

agriculture, architecture, calendar, ceramics, cultivation, eruption, gunpowder, irrigation, mathematics, monument, prehistoric, pyramid, religion, surgery

O o o	o o O o	o O o	O o o o
calendar			

Listen and check your answers.

8 Can you say this proverb? Use the Phonetic Chart in the Mini-dictionary to help you. What does the proverb mean?

/nəsesəti ɪz ðə mʌðə əv inˈvenʃən/

Check Your Progress

Look back at the Module Objectives on page 117.
◎ Which activities did you enjoy most?
◎ Which activities did you have problems with?
◎ Which grammar area do you need to revise?

Student Activities

Module 1 Lesson 1, Exercise 10

Read these notes about Marek Kamiński. Then answer your partner's questions.

Born: 1964, Gdansk (Poland)

Expeditions: the North and South Poles (1995); Gibson Desert, Australia (1999); the Amazon (2000), Mt Kilimanjaro, Tanzania (2001); North Pole (2004)

Greatest journeys: 1995 – the first person to go to both Poles in one year: the North Pole (23 May), the South Pole (27 December); 2004 – accompanied a disabled 15 year-old boy

Travelled: polar trips on skis (no dogs), with Wojtek Moskal to the North Pole (1995); solo to the South Pole (1995); with Janek Mela (2004) who had lost a leg and an arm two years before.

Aims of the journeys to the Poles: to be the first person to go to both Poles in the same year; to enable a disabled boy to go on an expedition to the North Pole; to collect money for charity

Other interests/activities: businessman; organises expeditions to different places in the world.

Module 3 Lesson 10 Exercise 9

Use the cues to act out dialogues.

Questions	
	• hands dirty/work in the garden
	• tanned/sunbathe
	• eyes red /cry
	• slim/work out in the gym
Answers	• fit/go swimming every night
	• angry/wait for Mary for an hour
	• tired/not sleep enough
	• spot on T-shirt/paint my room

Module 3 Lesson 11 Exercise 8

ROLEPLAY 1: AT THE TRAIN STATION

You want to buy a train ticket. Decide on:
• your destination • single or return ticket
• smoking or non-smoking compartment
You want to know the price of the ticket, the time the train leaves and from which platform.
Your partner works in the ticket office.
Act out the situation at the ticket office.
You start: *I'd like a ticket to …*

ROLEPLAY 2: AT THE AIRPORT

You work in a travel agency at the airport.
Your partner wants to buy a ticket. Ask him/her:
• when he/she wants to return
• what seat he/she would like – near the window or the aisle
You decide on the **price** of the ticket and the **gate number** the flight leaves from.
Act out the situation in the airport.
Your partner starts.

Module 5 Lesson 17 Exercise 8

Read the advert. Then answer your partner's questions.

Module 7, Lesson 28 Speaking Workshop

1 You are the secretary of this school. Read the information.

Gleeson Language Academy *Dublin, Ireland*

Small school in the historic city centre of the capital. • Two-week courses. Maximum class size 14. • Four lessons per day. • Computer room and self-study centre. • Coffee bar. Accommodation with families or single room flats near the school.
Cultural visits: tour of Dublin + trips to historic places in Ireland. Social events organised, e.g. parties.
Unfortunately, we are a small school and unable to offer sports.
Cost: €900, including fees, accommodation and trips.

Your partner phones you to ask for information about the school. You begin by answering the phone.

2 Now change roles. You want to study English in a summer school in the USA. Your partner is the secretary of a school in Florida. Phone the school and ask for information. Your partner begins.

Module 9 Culture Corner 9 Exercise 2

Read the factfile. Ask your partner questions to complete it. Also, answer your partner's questions. Your partner starts.

FACTFILE

AUSTRALIA

Area: 7,682,300 sq km

Population: _____ million

Capital: Canberra

Official language: _____

Political structure: Independent constitutional monarchy

Head of State: Elizabeth II of Great Britain

HISTORY:

_____ : Aborigines arrive in Australia

16th century: Portuguese and Dutch sailors explore the Australian coast

1770: Captain _____ lands in New South Wales and claims the continent for Britain

1788: first prison colony established near Sydney in New South Wales

1820s: free settlers begin to arrive

_____ : gold discovered. Aborigines pushed off tribal lands by white settlers

1901: Australia becomes independent

2nd World War: Australia fights on the side of the allies against _____ and Germany

2000: Olympic Games held in Sydney

Module 10 Lesson 37 Exercise 9
Read the information about the Incas. Then ask and answer questions to complete it.

History:

Originally the Incas were a small group of Indians living around
1_____ (where?). In the fifteenth century, they established a huge empire including present day countries like Peru and Bolivia. In
2_____ (when?), Spanish invaders under Pizarro arrived. They captured 3_____ (who?) and later killed him and took control.

Government/Society:

The Inca capital was Cuzco – a city with huge buildings covered with
4_____ (what?). The supreme ruler was the Inca. Under the Inca was a class of nobles and below them a large number of peasants. The Incas had a system of 15000 km of roads for communication with their empire. They communicated 5_____ (how?). The Incas did not have the wheel and used llamas for transport. The main crops were
6_____ (what?) and meat was a luxury.

Art and culture:

The Incas did not have writing but used 7_____ (what) to store mathematical information. They made lovely gold and silver jewellery and were great architects. They built many temples and palaces. These were made from huge 8_____ (what?) that fitted together perfectly.

Questionnaire scores
Module 5 Lesson 19, Exercise 2

1 a) 3 points b) 2 points c) 0 points
2 a) 0 points b) 1 point c) 3 points
3 a) 0 points b) 1 point c) 3 points
4 a) 3 points b) 1 point c) 0 points
5 a) 3 points b) 1 point c) 0 point
6 a) 3 points b) 1 point c) 0 points
7 a) 3 points b) 1 point c) 0 points
8 a) 2 points b) 1 point c) 0 points

Results

0–5 points: You are a bad consumer. You need to work harder to get value for your money!

6–11 points: You are quite good. But you need to pay more attention to your rights.

12–23 points: You are an excellent consumer. Well done!

Module 1 Lesson 1, Exercise 10.
Read these notes about Helen Thayer. Then answer your partner's questions.

Born: 1938, New Zealand.
Expeditions: the North Pole (1988), the Amazon jungle (1995), New Zealand (1995), the Sahara desert (1996)
Greatest journey: 1988 – first woman to travel solo (alone) to the North Pole (she was fifty years old!).
Travelled: to the North Pole on skis, with her dog, Charlie.
Aims of the journey: to get to the North Pole; to write a book about it ('Polar Dream', a bestseller)
Other interests/activities: writes travel books; gives talks to schools; collects information and photos for educational books.

Module 3 Lesson 10 Exercise 9

Questions	fit/cycle a lot
	angry/argue with someone
	tired/work too hard
	spot on T-shirt/cook
Answers	hands dirty/repair bike
	tanned/use the sunbed in my club
	eyes red/sleep badly in the last few days
	slim/not eat any sweets

Module 3 Lesson 11 Exercise 8

ROLEPLAY 1: AT THE TRAIN STATION
You work in the ticket office at the train station.
Your partner wants to buy a ticket. Ask him/her about:
• single or return ticket • smoking or non-smoking compartment
You decide on the **price** of the ticket, what **time** the train leaves and from which **platform**.
Act out the situation at the ticket office.
Your partner starts.

ROLEPLAY 2: AT THE AIRPORT
You are at the airport. You want to buy a ticket. Decide on:
• your destination • the date of your return journey
• the seat you would like – near the window or the aisle
You want to know the **price** of the ticket and the **gate number** the flight leaves from.
Your partner works in a travel agency at the airport. Act out the situation at the airport.
You start: *Good afternoon. Are there any seats for the 14.30 flight to …?*

Module 5 Lesson 17 Exercise 8
Read the advert. Then answer your partner's questions.

MUSICMAN

Now at only €750!!!

The NEW COOL way of listening to music – Musicman digital personal stereo.

♪ a digital music player plus earphones
♪ battery-operated
♪ has Internet connection
♪ can store 10,000 songs!
♪ cool modern design

You can build your own library of favourite music. You can even download music from the Net. Just sit back and listen to it when and where you want!!!!

Module 7, Lesson 28 Speaking Workshop

1 You want to study English in Ireland next summer. Your partner is the secretary of a school in Dublin. Phone the school and ask for information. Your partner begins.
2 Now change roles. You are the secretary of this school. Read the information.

The Hemingway Language Academy — Key West, Florida

Small town with fantastic beaches and water sports.

Warm climate all year.

Three-week courses. Maximum class size 20. Fifteen lessons per week.

Swimming pool. Tennis courts. Coffee bar. Discotheque.

Accommodation in holiday flats; all rooms with own bathroom and air-conditioning.

We organise water sports (diving, sailing, windsurfing) and fishing boats.

Excursions to Disneyworld, the Everglades National Park and Miami. Regular beach barbecues and discotheques.

Cost: $850 (only includes classes and accommodation)

Your partner phones you to ask for information about the school. You begin by answering the phone.

Module 9 Culture Corner 9 Exercise 2

Read the factfile. Ask your partner questions to complete it. Also, answer your partner's questions. You ask the first question.
Example What is the area of Australia?

AUSTRALIA

FACTFILE

Area: _____ sq km
Population: 18 million
Capital: _____
Official language: English
Political structure: Independent constitutional monarchy
Head of State: _____
HISTORY:
48,000 BC.: Aborigines arrive in Australia
_____ : Portuguese and Dutch sailors explore the Australian coast
1770: Captain James Cook lands in New South Wales and claims the continent for Britain
1788: first prison colony established near _____ in New South Wales
1820s: free settlers begin to arrive
1850s: gold discovered. Aborigines pushed off tribal lands by white settlers
_____ : Australia becomes independent
2nd World War: Australia fights on the side of the allies against Japan and Germany
2000: Olympic Games held in Sydney

Module 10 Lesson 37 Exercise 9

Read the information about The Incas. Then ask and answer questions to complete it.

History:
Originally the Incas were a small group of Indians living around Cuzco in the Andes mountains. In the 1_____ (when?), they established a huge empire including present day countries like 2_____ (what countries?). In 1523, Spanish invaders under Pizarro arrived. They captured the emperor Atahualpa and later killed him and took control.

Government/Society:
The Inca capital was Cuzco – a city with huge buildings covered with gold. The supreme ruler was 3_____ (who?). Under the Inca was a class of nobles and below them a large number of peasants. The Incas had a system of 4_____ (how many km?) of roads for communication with their empire. They communicated by a system of runners. The Incas did not have the wheel and used 5_____ (what?) for transport. The main crops were maize and potatoes and 6_____ (what?) was a luxury.

Art and culture:
The Incas did not have writing but used knots in ropes to store mathematical information. They made lovely 7_____ jewellery (of what metals?) and were great architects. They built many 8_____ (what?). These were made from huge stone blocks that fitted together perfectly.

Answers

Module 8 Lesson 30 Exercise 2

This data is taken from the US Bureau of Labor Statistics, and so only refers to jobs in the USA. Jobs in the Key Words box which are not in this table, did not appear in the list of statistics.

Job	Relative Risk*	Most common cause of death
fishermen	21.3	drowning
forestry workers	20.6	falling objects
pilots	19.9	crashes
taxi drivers	9.5	murder
construction workers	8.1	falls; accidents in vehicles
lorry drivers	5.3	road accidents
farm workers	5.1	accidents in vehicles
police officers	3.4	murder; road accidents
electricians	3.2	electrocution
cashiers	0.9	murder

* Relative Risk Rate is the fatality rate for a group of workers divided by the fatality rate for all workers. A rate of 2.0 means the worker is twice as likely as the average worker to die at work.

Frankenstein

Mary Shelley

Mary Shelley was born in 1797 in London. In 1814, Mary met and fell in love with Percy Shelley, the poet. Mary travelled around Europe with Percy Shelley and another poet, Lord Byron. One night, while they were staying in a villa in Geneva, Byron announced: 'We will each write a ghost story.' Percy Shelley began a story but didn't finish it; Byron wrote a story about a vampire; and Mary began to write *Frankenstein*. The sad life story told by the monster has often been ignored in film productions of the book.

Before you start

1 Read the background to the story. Why did Mary Shelley write the story?

Reading and Listening

2 Read and listen to the story. Are these sentences true (T) or false (F)?

1 ☐ Victor was interested in science.
2 ☐ Victor was pleased with his creation.
3 ☐ The monster killed the servant girl, Justine.
4 ☐ The monster hated people.
5 ☐ Victor created the female monster.
6 ☐ The police accused Victor of murdering Henry.
7 ☐ Victor decided to wait for the monster and kill it on his wedding night.
8 ☐ The monster killed Victor's wife and then escaped.
9 ☐ In the end, the ship's captain killed the monster.

3 The story is told by three people. Order the five parts of the story.

a Conclusion: Captain Walton
b Development of story: Victor Frankenstein
c The monster's story
d Introduction: Captain Walton
e Background to the story: Victor Frankenstein

4 Complete the sentences with a word formed from the words in brackets.

1 My grandparents have had a long and happy _____. (marry)
2 At first, I didn't realise the importance of my _____. (discover)
3 I had never felt so _____ and sad. (misery)
4 I was frightened when I saw my _____. (creator)
5 I had made a _____ monster. (horror)
6 I wanted to _____ it. (destruction)

Talkback

5 In groups, or with the whole class, discuss the following.

1 Why didn't Victor tell anyone what he had done?
2 Did you feel sorry for the monster? Why or why not?
3 Did you feel sorry for Victor? Why or why not?
4 What is the moral of the story?

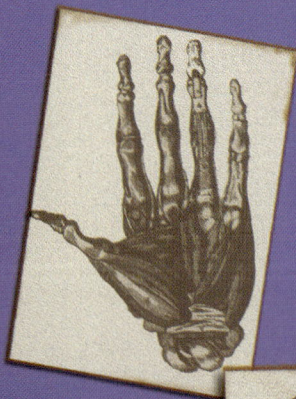
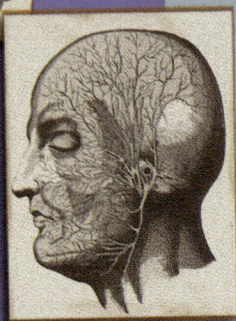
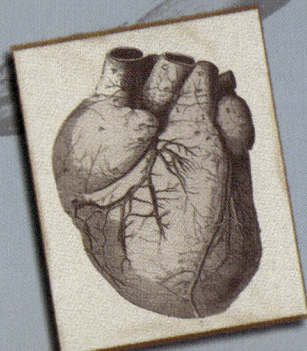
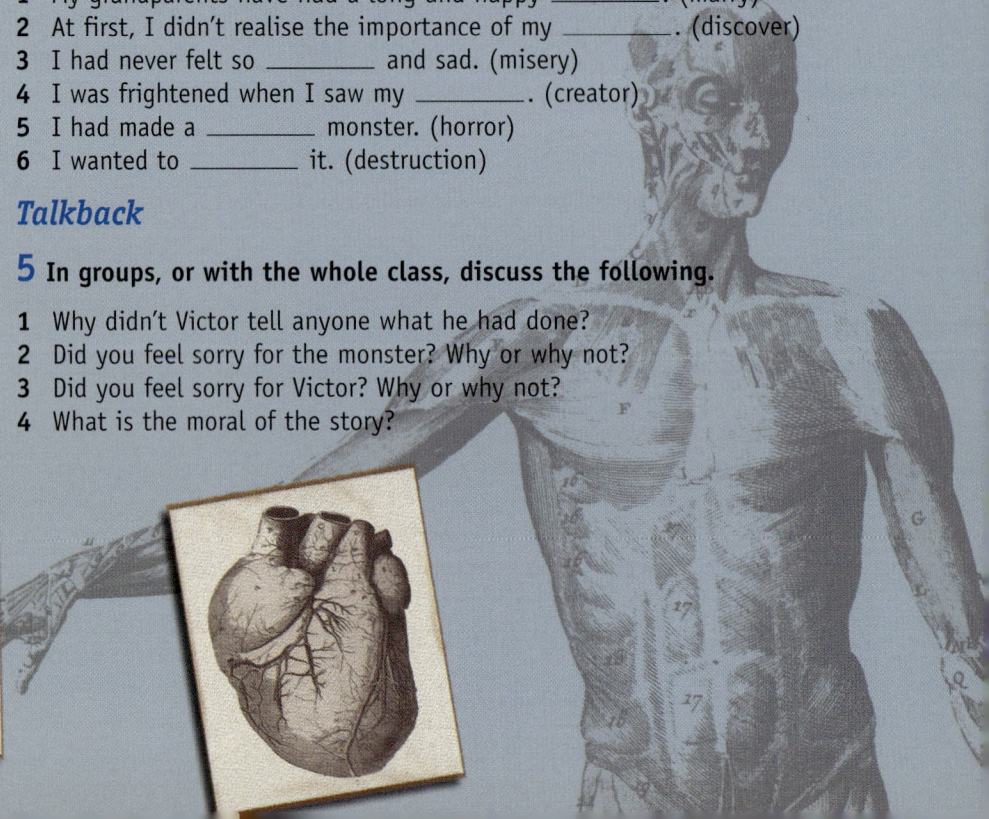

My name is Captain Walton. My ship was exploring the Arctic when we found a man on a piece of floating ice. He was called Victor Frankenstein. One night, he
5 told me a strange tale.

'My dear captain, how shall I begin? I grew up near Geneva. I was a happy child. My parents had two other sons, Ernest and William, and they took in an orphan, Elizabeth. When I was seventeen, I went to the
10 University of Ingolstadt. A professor there inspired me to study chemistry. This changed my life as I became obsessed with the search for the secret of life. I worked day and night for two years and, finally, I found the secret. To test my discovery, I decided to create a new
15 life in the laboratory.

I collected parts of bodies and, after two years, I was ready to bring my creature to life. But when I saw the monster I had created, I felt horror and disgust. How can I describe the monster? You could see the muscles
20 under his thin, yellow skin. His hair was long and black, his teeth were pearly white, but his eyes were watery and his lips black.

When my friend Henry Clerval arrived, I said nothing about the monster, which by now had left my house.
25 Henry brought news of my family. They were well and had taken in a servant called Justine. Imagine my shock when a letter arrived from my father – my young brother William had been murdered!

I went to my parents' house. Just before I got there,
30 I saw the monster running through the trees. I realised the monster I had created killed my brother! When I got to the house, I was horrified to discover that Justine, who had been found near the scene of the crime, was accused of the murder. I knew she was
35 innocent but could say nothing. She was hanged.

Soon afterwards, while I was spending some time alone in the mountains, I met my evil creation again. The monster begged me to listen to his story. This is what he said:

40 "When I left your house, I came across a cottage and lived secretly in the barn watching an old, blind man and his children. I learned how to speak and I realised how miserable I was. I had no family, no memories, no childhood. One day,
45 I decided to speak to the old man. He was kind and couldn't see my ugly body. But as soon as his children returned, they screamed and hit me with sticks. I ran away. On one occasion, I saved a girl from drowning in a river but when her
50 friend saw me, he fired a gun at me. This was the reward of kindness. I promised eternal hatred and revenge on mankind. My first victim was your young brother. But now I want nothing more than a companion. I want you to make
55 me a female companion and we will live together far away from all humans, I promise."

I agreed to his demand, though the idea was terrible to me. When I returned home, my father mentioned his wish for me to marry Elizabeth, whom I loved dearly.
60 But before the marriage, I needed to go to England to complete my work.

Henry came with me to England and, eventually, I completed my second creation. As I was bringing her to life, I began to have serious doubts about what I was
65 doing. But suddenly, my monster arrived. He said: "You are my creator but I am your master!" In my confusion, I broke the body into pieces. The monster left, saying: "I will be with you on your wedding night!"

The next day the police arrested me. I was accused of the
70 murder of a young man. They showed me the body - it was my friend Henry! My monster had claimed his third victim. They put me in prison but, in the end, I was proved innocent.

I was haunted by what the monster had said about my
75 wedding night and I wanted to destroy him. On our wedding night, I was checking for the monster outside when I heard screams. I ran upstairs, only to find Elizabeth dead! The monster was at the window. He laughed before he ran off into the night.

80 The destruction of the monster was now my only aim. I followed him all over the Earth – the Mediterranean, the Black Sea, Russia – but he always escaped. He went north. I followed him to the frozen wastes of the Arctic but he was one step ahead. I was drifting on a piece of
85 broken ice when, dear captain, you found me. I am dying. Please believe my tale and promise me you will do all you can to kill this monster.'

Those were his last words. He died in my cabin. I went out and then I heard strange noises. When
90 I returned to my cabin, I saw the monster, a horrible creature, kneeling next to Frankenstein and crying. He told me how miserable he had been and how guilty he felt. He wanted to die and assured me he would destroy himself. Then, he jumped out of the
95 cabin window onto the ice and was taken away by the waves into the darkness.

THE THIRD MAN

Before You Start

1 Read the background about Graham Greene and answer these questions.

1 What different jobs did he do?
2 What places did he travel to?
3 Why are his books both serious and entertaining?

Graham Greene

Background

After leaving Oxford University, Graham Greene (1904–1991) became a journalist and started writing novels. His first big success was the thriller, *Orient Express* (1932). In the 1930s, Greene travelled widely. In 1938, he visited Mexico and wrote *The Power and the Glory* (1939). During the Second World War, Greene worked for the British secret service in Sierra Leone, which became the setting for *Heart of the Matter* (1948). After the war, he worked as a journalist and many of his novels were set abroad: *The Quiet American* (1955) in Vietnam; *The Comedians* (1966) in Haiti; *The Honorary Consul* (1973) in Paraguay. Greene never won the Nobel prize for literature but was perhaps the greatest British novelist of his generation. His novels are full of adventure and suspense but at the same time deal with serious moral issues. *The Third Man* is one of three screenplays that he wrote.

Reading and Listening

2 Read and listen to the story. Put the following events in the order they happen in the story.

a Harry Lime escaped into the sewers but Holly killed him.
b Holly Martins arrived in Vienna and went to Harry's funeral.
c Holly escaped after the lecture and went to see Calloway.
d Holly realised that there was something strange about Harry's death.
e Calloway told Holly that his friend was a criminal.
f Holly and Harry met on the great wheel.
g Holly found out about a mysterious 'third man' at Harry's death.
h Holly went to Harry's real funeral.

3 Read the story again and answer these questions.

1 Why did Holly go to Vienna?
2 How had Harry 'died'?
3 Why did he agree to give the lecture?
4 Why did he think that Harry's death was not an accident?
5 Why did he have to escape from the porter's house and the lecture hall?
6 Why did he finally believe Calloway about Harry?
7 Why did he agree to help to catch Harry Lime?
8 Why did Holly shoot his friend?

4 Which of the characters can be described as

a good-looking and loyal? b dishonest and evil? c stubborn but honest?

Talkback

5 Work in pairs. Discuss these questions.

1 Do you think Holly was right to help to arrest his friend? Why or why not?
2 What would you do in this sort of situation?
3 What other good thrillers have you seen or read?
4 What happened in them?

Holly Martins, an American writer of bad cowboy stories, arrived in Vienna one very cold February morning, It was soon after the Second World War; Vienna was in ruins and was occupied by the Americans, Russians, British and French. Holly Martins had been invited to Vienna by an old friend, Harry Lime, and so he was surprised that Harry was not there to meet him. When Holly went to Harry's flat, he found out that his friend had been killed by a truck as he was crossing the street outside his flat.

Harry Lime hiding from the police, in the sewer.

In fact, the funeral was taking place that afternoon so Holly went straight to the cemetery. There were very few people there. A beautiful dark-haired woman was the only person among them who looked upset. After the funeral, Major Calloway, a British military policeman, told Holly that his friend Harry had been a criminal but Holly did not believe him. Back at his hotel, Holly met a man who mistook him for a famous American novelist and asked him to give a lecture. Holly accepted, as this would give him a chance to stay in Vienna for a few days and find out what had happened to Harry.

The next day, Holly began his search. He first met an Austrian friend of Harry's called Kurtz. Kurtz described how he and another man, Popescu, had carried Harry's body to a square after the accident. Before he died, Harry had asked Kurtz to look after Holly. This surprised Holly because Calloway had told him that Harry's death had been very sudden. Holly asked Kurtz about the woman at the cemetery. She was Harry's girlfriend, Anna Schmidt, an actress.

That evening, Holly met Anna and she told him more about the accident. Harry's doctor, Dr Winkel, had been passing and had certified the death. The driver of the truck had been Harry's own driver. In fact, there had been no strangers there at all. Holly began to think that it might not have been an accident. The porter of Harry's flat then gave Anna and Holly another version. Harry had died immediately and *three* men had carried the body. So who was this mysterious 'third man'?

When they got back to Anna's flat, Calloway was there and arrested Anna because her papers were forged. Holly told Calloway what he had learnt about Harry's death but Calloway told him to 'leave death to the professionals' and go home. However, Holly was determined to find out the truth. He talked to Dr Winkel and to Popescu, Harry's Rumanian friend. Popescu denied that there had been a 'third man'.

When Holly went back to the scene of the accident, the porter said, 'I'd like to tell you something ... tonight.' But when he and Anna went to see the porter that night, they found that he had been murdered. The porter's son accused Holly of being the murderer. Anna and Holly had to escape and hide in a cinema. Holly finally got back to his hotel to find a taxi waiting to take him to his Wednesday evening lecture.

Holly's lecture was so terrible that most people walked out but Popescu was there. He asked Holly questions about his new 'novel'. Holly said it was a 'murder story', it was 'based on fact' and was called 'The Third Man'. There were two other men with Popescu so after the lecture, Holly ran out of the room. He managed to escape a second time and went to police headquarters. Calloway told Holly in detail about his friend Harry's crimes. He had sold diluted penicillin that had caused the deaths of thousands of innocent victims, especially children. Holly was finally convinced and decided to leave Vienna.

He went to see Anna to say goodbye and saw a man standing in a door on the other side of the street. It was Harry Lime! He called out but Harry mysteriously disappeared. Holly rang Calloway and they realised that Harry had escaped underground into Vienna's sewers. Holly spoke to Kurtz and Winkel and told them to organise a meeting with Harry. The two friends met at last on the big wheel in the Prater amusement park. Harry showed no regrets for the crimes he had committed and even threatened to kill Holly. After that, Holly agreed to help Calloway catch Harry.

Holly arranged to meet Harry in a café which Calloway and his men had surrounded. Anna came in and tried to warn Harry but it was too late. Harry pulled out his gun to kill Holly but the police came in. Harry escaped and disappeared underground. Calloway, his men and Holly followed him into the sewers where there were shots. Cornered like a rat and badly wounded, Harry tried to go up a ladder out of the sewer. Holly saw his friend and went after him. Calloway shouted: 'Martins. If you see him, shoot.' Harry looked at his friend and nodded. Holly pressed the trigger.

Before he left Vienna, Holly went to his friend's second funeral. There were even fewer people than at the first funeral. Afterwards, Holly tried to talk to Anna but she ignored him and walked away.

Holly meets his friend Harry.

Thomas Edison's Shaggy Dog

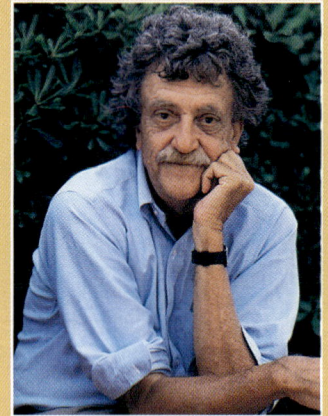

Kurt Vonnegut

Before you start

1 Read the background about Kurt Vonnegut. Answer the questions below.

1 What event affected his life and writing?
2 What kind of writer is he?
3 What does he think of modern society?

Reading and Listening

2 Read and listen to the story. Match the characters (1–4) with the actions (a–h).

1 Bullard   2 the stranger   3 Thomas Edison   4 Sparky the dog

a   bored everyone he met
b   went into Thomas Edison's laboratory
c   tried out his machine on the boy
d   suggested testing the dog's intelligence
e   came out as incredibly intelligent on the test
f   planned to tell the world about the discovery
g   told Edison how to make a light bulb
h   got angry and didn't believe the story

3 Read the story again. Answer these questions.

1 What kind of personalities have the characters got (Bullard, the stranger, Edison)?
2 Why did Edison invent the 'intelligence analyser'?
3 What result did the boy have in the test?
4 What did Edison think when he saw the dog's result?
5 How did they realise that the dog was really smart?
6 How did Edison show that he was a really great scientist?
7 What agreement did they all come to?
8 Why was Sparky killed by the other dogs?
9 Why did the stranger give Bullard's dog his garters?

Vocabulary

4 Match the expressions (1–6) with the meanings (a–f).

1 bet he was sore
2 let sleeping dogs lie
3 hold on
4 hogwash (AmEng old-fashioned)
5 you have my (solemn) word
6 a small token of esteem

a   wait
b   I promise
c   he must have been angry
d   don't disturb things
e   a present to show my respect
f   rubbish

Which of the expressions above do you think is an English proverb?

Talkback

5 Work in pairs. Discuss these questions.

1 What parts of the story did you find unbelievable?
2 Is there a moral to the story, and, if so, what is it?
3 What do you think would happen if we had an intelligence analyser and dogs were more intelligent than us?

Background

Kurt Vonnegut was born in 1922 in Indianapolis, USA, to a middle-class family of German origin. After leaving school, he studied chemistry at Cornell University and then joined the army in 1943. He was captured by the Germans and was a prisoner of war in Dresden when it was virtually destroyed by Allied bombing. This experience, which made him a lifelong pacifist, was later to provide the basis for his best-known novel, *Slaughterhouse-Five* (1969). Vonnegut published his first novel, *Piano Player*, in 1952, and has been writing for over fifty years. Amongst his novels are *Cat's Cradle* (1963), *Breakfast of Champions* (1973), *Jailbird* (1979), *Galápagos* (1985) and *Timequake* (1997). Vonnegut has often been classified as a science fiction writer. In fact Vonnegut is much more; he is a satirist, social critic and moralist. His work constantly returns, with dark humour, to the theme of human decency and morals in a mad, bad world.

Two old men were sitting on a park bench in Florida. One of them, Bullard, spent every day in the park with his Labrador dog, boring everyone he came across. The other man tried to escape Bullard and his dog, who kept trying to chew the garters for his socks. The stranger went to another bench but Bullard followed him. Bullard asked the stranger about his line of business.

'My line?' said the stranger crisply, laying down his book. 'Sorry – I've never had a line. I've been a drifter since the age of nine, since Edison set up his laboratory next to my home and showed me the intelligence analyser.'

'Edison?' said Bullard. 'Thomas Edison, the inventor?'

'If you want to call him that, go ahead,' said the stranger.

'If I want to call him that?' – Bullard guffawed – 'I guess I just will. Father of the light bulb and I don't know what all.'

'If you think he invented the light bulb, go ahead. No harm in it.' The stranger resumed his reading.

'Say, what is this?' said Bullard, suspiciously. 'You're pulling my leg? What's this about an intelligence analyser? I've never heard of that.'

'Of course you haven't,' said the stranger. 'Mr Edison and I promised to keep it a secret' …

Bullard was entranced. 'Uh, this intelligence analyser,' he said. 'It analysed intelligence, did it?' …

'It was back in the fall of eighteen seventy-nine,' said the stranger at last, softly. 'Back in the village of Menlo Park, New Jersey. I was a boy of nine. A young man we all thought was a wizard had set up a laboratory next door to my home …

I didn't get to know Edison right off, but his dog Sparky and I got to be steady pals. A dog a whole lot like yours, Sparky was … Well, one day, Sparky and I were wrestling around and we wrestled right up to the door of the laboratory. The next thing I knew, Sparky had pushed me in through the door and Bam! I was sitting on the laboratory floor, looking up at Mr Edison himself.'

'Bet he was sore,' said Bullard, delighted.

'You can bet I was scared,' said the stranger. 'I thought I was face to face with Satan himself. Edison had wires hooked to his ears running down to a little black box in his lap! I started to scoot but he caught me by the collar and made me sit down.'

' "For over a year, my boy," Edison said to me, "I've been trying to find a filament that will last in an incandescent lamp … So while I was trying to think of something … I put this together," he said, showing me the little black box. "I thought maybe intelligence was just a certain kind of electricity, so I made this intelligence analyser here. It works! You're the first one to know about it, my boy" … And it did work … I let him try it on me and the needle just lay where it was and trembled. But dumb as I was, then is when I made my one and only contribution in the world …'

'Whadja do?' said Bullard eagerly.

'I said, "Mr Edison, sir, let's try it on the dog". … And would you believe it, that needle sailed clear across the dial, way past a little red pencil mark on the dial face!'

' "Mr Edison, sir," I said. "What's that red mark mean?"

"My boy," said Edison, "it means the instrument is broken, because the red mark is me." '

'I'll say it was broken,' said Bullard.

The stranger replied gravely, 'But it wasn't broken. No sir. Edison checked the whole thing … When Edison told me that, it was then that Sparky, crazy to get out, gave himself away … We really had him locked in, see? There were three locks on the door … That dog stood up … and had the knob in his teeth when Edison stopped him.'

'No!' said Bullard.

'Yes!' said the stranger, his eyes shining. 'And that is when Edison showed me what a great scientist he was. He was willing to face the truth, no matter how unpleasant it might be.

"So!" said Edison to Sparky. "Man's best friend, huh? Dumb animal, huh? … Pretty soft, isn't it, Sparky?" said Edison. "Let somebody else worry about getting food, building shelters and keeping warm while you sleep in front of a fire or go chasing after the girls or raise hell with the boys. No mortgages, no politics, no war, no work, no worry. Just wag the old tail or lick a hand and you're all taken care of."

"Mr Edison," I said, "do you mean to tell me that dogs are smarter than people?"

"Smarter? I'll tell the world!" said Edison. And what have I been doing for the past year? Slaving to work out a light bulb so dogs can play at night!"

"Look, Mr Edison," said Sparky, "Why not –" '

'Hold on!' roared Bullard.

'Silence!' shouted the stranger, triumphantly. ' "Look, Mr Edison," said Sparky, "why not keep quiet about this? It's been working out to everybody's satisfaction for hundreds of years. Let sleeping dogs lie. You forget about it, destroy the intelligence analyser, and I'll tell you what to use for a lamp filament." '

'Hogwash,' said Bullard, his face purple.

The stranger stood. 'You have my solemn word as a gentleman. That dog rewarded me for my silence with a stock market tip that made me independently wealthy for the rest of my days. And the last words that Sparky ever spoke were to Thomas Edison. "Try a piece of carbonised cotton thread," he said. Later, he was torn to pieces by a pack of dogs that had gathered outside the door, listening.'

The stranger removed his garters and handed them to Bullard's dog. 'A small token of esteem, sir, for an ancestor of yours who talked himself to death. Good day.'

He tucked his book under his arm and walked away.

A Horse and Two Goats

Before you start

1 Read the background information. List the places in the world that have produced major writers in English in the last fifty years.

R.K. Narayan

Reading and Listening

2 Read and listen to the story. Match the characters with the sentences.
(**M**) Muni, the shepherd, (**T**) the American tourist, (**B**) both the characters

1 He was very poor.
2 He wanted to fill up with petrol.
3 He thought the statue was beautiful.
4 He was afraid of the other man at first.
5 He couldn't understand the other man's language.
6 He thought the other man was the owner of the statue.
7 He liked the sound of the other man's language.
8 He explained the meaning of the statue.
9 He offered to pay the other man money.
10 He was happy with the business deal.
11 When he got home, his wife was angry with him.

3 Read the story again and answer these questions.

1 What did the American want from the shepherd?
2 Who did the shepherd think the American was at the beginning of the conversation?
3 Why was the American surprised that the shepherd couldn't speak English?
4 Why was the horse important to Muni and the other villagers?
5 What was the American talking about while Muni spoke about stories of Hindu gods?
6 Why did Muni think the American wanted to buy his goats?
7 Why did Muni disappear quickly?

Background

In the second half of the twentieth century, many important writers in English have come from outside Britain and the USA. These include writers from English-speaking countries like Australia (Patrick White, Peter Carey), South Africa (Nadine Gordimer) and Canada (Robertson Davies). There are also major writers in English who have different cultural roots, e.g. the poet Derek Walcott and the novelist V.S. Naipaul from the Caribbean; African novelists like Chinua Achebe and Ben Okri; Indian writers such as Arundhati Roy, Vikram Seth and Salman Rushdie. R.K. Narayan was born in Madras in the south of India. He has written several important novels such as *Swami and Friends* (1935) and *The Painter of Signs* (1977). He has also written three collections of short stories as well as collections of essays.

Talkback

4 Work in pairs. Discuss this question:
How does the story show the differences between the two men's cultures? Think about their attitudes to these things:

time, the past and the future, money and possessions

5 Have you ever been in a situation in which you did not understand the other person? How did you feel? What happened in the end? Tell the class.

Muni was a very poor shepherd. He lived in a small village in the south of India and he only had two goats. Every day, he took them outside the village to the edge of the main road. He would sit underneath a statue of a horse and a warrior, watching the buses and lorries go past.

One day, Muni was sitting under the statue when a large yellow car stopped near him. A red-faced man got out.

'Excuse me? Is there a gas station near here?' Then the man suddenly saw the statue of the horse and cried, 'Marvellous!'

Muni was afraid. Maybe this man was a police officer.

'Marvellous!' the man said again, looking at the statue. Then he smiled. 'How do you do?'

Muni used the only expressions he knew in English. 'Yes, no.' Then he began to speak in Tamil. 'My name is Muni.'

The red-faced man offered him a cigarette. Muni accepted. The man said, 'I come from New York.' He took out his card and presented it to Muni. Muni was worried. Maybe this man was trying to arrest him.

'Before God, sir, I know nothing about any dead body,' he replied in Tamil.

'Please, please. I will speak slowly,' said the red man. 'Can't you speak a word of English? Everyone in this country seems to know some English.'

Muni made some sounds and shook his head. The other man continued, saying every syllable very slowly and carefully. 'Isn't this statue yours? Why don't you sell it to me?' Muni understood the reference to the horse.

'I was very young when my grandfather explained to me about the horse and the ...'

The other man interrupted him, 'I will offer you a good price for the horse.' He had decided that Muni was the owner of the horse.

Muni continued with his memories about the horse and his grandfather. The foreigner listened with fascination.

'I wish I had my tape-recorder here. Your language sounds wonderful. But you don't have to waste time with sales talk.'

Muni went on, 'I never went to school. So I don't know the language you speak.'

The foreigner looked at the statue. 'These colours are lovely.'

'This horse is our guardian, it means death to our enemies. At the end of the world, the horse Kalki will come and kill all bad men.'

'I promise you that the statue will have the best home in the USA. I'll put the statue right in the middle of the living room.'

Muni continued talking about the end of the world, 'Do you know what's going to happen?' he asked.

The foreigner understood that this was a question.

'How am I going to carry it? Well, I can put it in the back.'

Muni continued with his memories. 'When we were young, we used to act out the stories of the Hindu gods.'

'Will you accept a hundred rupees for the horse?'

'We also played Ramayana. Do you know the story of Ramayana?'

'We must talk business. Give me a hand with the horse.'

At this stage the confusion was complete. Muni carried on. 'You are a good man. I normally have nobody to talk to. How many children have you?'

Realising that a question was being asked, the red man replied, 'I said a hundred rupees.'

'How many of your children are boys and how many girls?' The red man put his hand into his pocket and took out a hundred rupee note.

The old man looked at the note. He had never seen a note so big in his life. He thought the man was asking for change.

'Go and ask the village headman. He's always got money. He doesn't like me because he says my goats eat his vegetables.' He pointed to the goats.

The foreigner decided to show attention to the old man's pets and stroked their backs. Suddenly, Muni realised what was happening. The man wanted to buy his goats! The red man shook his hand and put one hundred rupees in tens into his hand.

'Are you taking them away in that?' said Muni, pointing to the car.

'Yes, of course,' said the foreigner.

'This will be their first time in a car. Wait for me to go or they will only follow me.' Soon Muni was out of sight.

The red man stopped the first truck that came past. The men helped him take the statue of the horse and put it in his car. He then drove off.

Muni went back home and showed the cash to his wife. 'I have sold our goats to a red man.'

Just at that moment, the goats appeared at the door.

'Where is that man? Why did you come back?' he asked the goats.

His wife was angry. 'If you have stolen something, the police will come and break your bones. Don't involve me. I will go away to my parents ...'

Writing Help

1 A Personal Letter (1) (page 17)
Layout

Your address
The date

Greeting
Hi Tania!/Dear Tommy,

1 Introductory questions
How are you? Have you decided where to go on holiday? Did your mum pass her driving test?

2 Describe where you are (the place/the weather)
Anyway, we're camping in the Isle of Skye. It has rained every single day ...

3 Say what you are doing
We're very busy. We go walking every day and ...

4 Mention the people in the group
Our news: Predictably, ...

5 Ending. Make up an excuse to stop writing.
Well, I must finish. It's my turn to cook tonight. Write back soon.

Say goodbye and sign your name.
All the best,/Lots of love,
Janet.

Useful Vocabulary
Weather: *changeable, cloudy, cold, freezing, hot, rainy, sunny*
Accommodation: *cabin, campsite, farm, guest house, hotel, rented cottage, tent, youth hostel*
Locations: *in a forest, in the middle of nowhere, in the mountains, on the coast, near a river, near a town*
Activities: *canoeing, diving, horseriding, parachuting, rafting, sailing, skiing, snowboarding, trekking, windsurfing*

Informal style
Involve the reader with questions: *How are you?/Can you believe it?/That skiing break sounds the best, doesn't it?*
Refer to the reader: *I hope the summer job is going well/Here's some news for you/So you can imagine what he's like/Tell me all your news!*

Linking
Begin sentences with informal linkers: *Anyway, we're .../Luckily, we didn't .../Actually, there isn't .../Unbelievably, .../Predictably, .../But then we're .../And Tom has .../Well, I must finish ...*

Checking
Style: Have you used informal linkers, words and expressions?
Grammar: Check your letter for verb tenses.

2 An Adventure Story (page 29)
Layout

1 Set the scene
Write a few sentences to set the scene and introduce the characters.
It was a beautiful day in spring and the sun was shining*. The night before, my cousin Sam, my boyfriend, Tom, and I had decided** to go canoeing down the river. We had arranged** to meet up at eight o'clock. When I arrived, Sam was waiting*.

* To set the scene or say what was happening at a particular time, use the Past Continuous.
** To say what had happened before, use the Past Perfect.

2 Say what happened to start with
Begin narrating the main action. Include some dialogue. Use speech marks and reporting verbs (*say, shout,* etc.)
Suddenly, it started to rain heavily. Sam shouted, 'Look over there! It's Tom's helmet!'

3 Develop the story
Write what happened next.
We got out of our canoes and walked back up the rapids looking for Tom ...

4 Write the ending
Write a suitable conclusion to your story.
In the end, our parents came to collect us ... but we all felt very happy to be back home.

Useful Vocabulary
Weather: *cloudy, foggy, freezing, rainy, sunny, wet, windy*
Places: *castle, forest, mountains, old house, park, river, valley, woods*
Verbs: *argue, crash, escape, fall, find, get back, get lost, hunt, hurt, meet, realise, recognise*
Adjectives: *afraid, amazing, awful, beautiful, exciting, frightening, strange, terrifying*

Linking
After I had arrived, we started to get ready.
By the time I got to the bus stop, the bus had gone.
Before leaving, I had breakfast.
When we saw him, we rang the emergency services.
While we were having lunch, it started to snow.
My sister had an accident in the kitchen. Immediately, I rang for an ambulance. (very quickly)
I was sleeping. Suddenly, I heard a scream. (a surprise)
I arrived at school late and was coming through the door. Just then, I bumped into the head teacher. (at that moment)
I waited for him for hours. At last he came. (after a long time)
He had a lot of problems getting his driving licence. In the end, he passed the test. (finally)
I missed the bus yesterday. Luckily, Pat gave me a lift. (fortunately)
I was really tired after the first few kilometres of the walk. Somehow, I managed to finish it. (with difficulty)

Checking
Grammar: Have you included examples of all the past tenses?
Linking: Have you included a few linking words and expressions?

3 A Report (page 41)

Layout

<blockquote>

Heading
To: From: Date:
Subject:

</blockquote>

<blockquote>

1 General Description
Introduce the report with your aim and a general description of the place.
Beverley is a small town in the east of England. The aim of this report is to ...

</blockquote>

<blockquote>

2 List of good points
Give a list of things that you think are good about the place.
There are several things tourists will find attractive ...
a It has got ...
b In addition, there is ...

</blockquote>

<blockquote>

3 List of bad points
Give a list of your criticisms of the place.
On the other hand, tourists might find some things disappointing.
a There are not enough ...
b Another thing is the ...

</blockquote>

<blockquote>

4 Conclusion
Finish the report with a brief summary of the main points and make suggestions.
To sum up, ...
The council need to do something to ... They should ...

</blockquote>

Useful Vocabulary
Positive adjectives: *cheap, clean, easy, excellent, free, frequent, punctual, safe*
Negative adjectives: *damaged, dangerous, dirty, expensive, inefficient, polluted, unsafe*
Nouns: *accident, museum, old buildings, pedestrians, pollution, public transport, shopping centre, traffic jam, train service*

Linking
To list ideas:
The old buildings are dirty <u>and</u> damaged.
The old buildings are dirty. Some of them are damaged, <u>too</u>.
The old buildings are dirty. Some of them are <u>also</u> damaged.
The old buildings are dirty. <u>In addition</u>, some of them are damaged.
The old buildings suffer from dirt <u>plus</u> damage.
To contrast ideas:
The buses are cheap <u>but</u> not very frequent.
<u>Although</u> the buses are cheap, they are not very frequent.
The buses are cheap. <u>However</u>, they are not very frequent.
<u>On the one hand</u>, the buses are cheap. <u>On the other hand</u>, they are not very frequent.

Checking
Layout: Have you followed the layout above? Has your report got clear paragraphs?
Linking: Have you used the linking words in the list above?
Spelling: Use the Mini-dictionary to check spelling of words you are not sure about.

4 A Review of a film or TV drama (page 52)

Layout

<blockquote>

1 Introduction
Give basic information about the film or programme. Say where and when it is set and give some background.
This episode of the historical drama 'Clifton Heights' was on Friday night at 7 pm on Channel Four. It is set in Bristol in the 19th century and is about the people who live in a beautiful square.

</blockquote>

<blockquote>

2 The plot
Briefly mention some of the main events – don't go into details. Use present tenses.
In this episode, Polly's daughter Charlotte gets lost when they are out shopping in the town centre. Luckily, Sebastian is there to save the day and takes her back.

</blockquote>

<blockquote>

3 The actors, characters and dialogue
Evaluate the performance of the main characters. Comment on the script and dialogue if you wish.
Gemma Harvey (Polly) is convincing as the absent-minded housewife with a secret fantasy life as an actress. However, the performance of Robert Martin (Sebastian), the local police officer is not so good.

</blockquote>

<blockquote>

4 Location, scenes, costumes
Evaluate the filming, locations, costumes. Mention one specific scene if you wish.
The old locations are very realistic, and the costumes are excellent.

</blockquote>

<blockquote>

5 Conclusion
Finish with a brief comment and make a recommendation.
To sum up, this episode was another example of a historical drama with fantastic locations and costumes but a rather dull plot. I certainly would not recommend you to watch it.

</blockquote>

Useful Vocabulary
plot: *locations exciting/gripping; predictable/boring; too much action/sex/violence; not enough dialogue/action*
dialogues: *realistic/funny; unnatural/tedious/dull*
acting: *a strong/outstanding/convincing performance a weak/uninspired/unconvincing performance*
filming: *imaginative/unimaginative*
costumes: *beautiful/realistic/unrealistic*
locations: *spectacular/unspectacular/beautiful*

Linking
To contrast ideas:
<u>Although</u> the acting was good, the filming was poor.
The acting was good. <u>However</u>, the filming was poor.
The acting was good. <u>Nevertheless</u>, the filming was poor.
The film was good <u>in spite of</u> the poor filming.
<u>Despite</u> the poor filming, the film was good

Checking
Layout: Have you followed the layout above? Has your review got clear paragraphs?
Vocabulary: Look at the adjectives you have used. Can you be more descriptive? Use the Useful Vocabulary and the Mini-dictionary to help you.
Mistakes: Check through your review for mistakes of grammar and spelling.

5 A Written Enquiry (page 65)

Layout

To: the name of the person or the company
From: your name and email address
Subject: specify the subject in one or two words

1 Introduction
Give your reason for writing and say where you saw the advert.
I am writing to ... which I recently saw ...

2 Initial questions
First, it says that ... Does that mean ... ? The advert also ... What exactly does that mean?

3 More questions
Another question I have is about ... I am also a bit worried about ...

4 Final questions
Finally, I am not sure what you mean by ... Could you tell me how ... ?

5 Ending
I look forward to hearing from you.
Yours, (Your name)

Useful Vocabulary
size/length/height/weight/speed/power/clarity
how big/long/high/heavy/fast/powerful/clear?
easy to use/understand, difficult to carry/use
fully guaranteed, the guarantee covers accidents/loss/theft

Linking
To list ideas:
First, it says ...; The advert also mentions ...; Another question is ...; I am a bit worried about ..., too ; Finally, I am ...
To express result:
It's so heavy that you can't carry it. (so + adj + *that* + clause)
It's such a fast computer that you can use the Internet easily. (such a(n) + adj + noun + *that* + clause)
It is not big enough to type with. (not + adj + *enough* + infinitive)
It is too big to put in my school bag. (too + adj + infinitive)

Checking
Style: Have you used formal language? (e.g. no contractions, no informal expressions)
Linking: Have you included some of the linking words and expressions above?

6 Describing a Person (page 77)

Layout

Paragraph 1
Introduce the person and give a bit of background, e.g. where he/she was born, where he/she lives now, his/her job, his/her dislikes.
I'm going to write about my grandfather. He's called Dennis and he lives on his own in a little cottage in the country. He used to work as an engineer but now he is retired though he still does some consultancy work.

Paragraph 2
Describe the person's physical appearance (but not too many details), personality and character.
Dennis has not got very much hair and what he has is white. He's got a large nose and a very round red face. He's a rather eccentric man and likes being on his own. He can be irritable especially in the early morning but he is a very generous person.

Paragrah 3
Give some examples of the person's behaviour or relationships with other people.
He's very well-known in the village where he lives because he is often out walking his dog, an old labrador called Einstein. He gets on with most people but is very impatient with children, particularly when they come and knock on his door at Halloween.

Useful Vocabulary
Hair: long/short/shoulder-length, black/blond/brown/dark/fair/grey/red/white, curly/straight/wavy, pony tail, plaits
Age: in his/her (early/mid/late) teens, twenties, thirties, elderly, middle-aged, young
Face: beard, chin, eyebrows, freckles, lips, moustache, wrinkles
shape: long/narrow/round/thin/wide
General: good-looking, overweight, short, slim, tall, well-built
Personality: bad-tempered, cheerful, creative, disorganised, dynamic, generous, hard-working, helpful, honest, insensitive, kind, lazy, materialistic, mean, moody, nervous, outgoing, relaxed, reliable, selfish, shy, sociable, strong, stubborn, sympathetic, tolerant, weak
Likes/Dislikes: animals, chess, collecting things, computers, playing/listening to music, playing/watching sport, reading, travelling, watching videos

Linking
To give examples:
She loves animals, especially dogs.
She hates junk food, such as hamburgers.
She is helpful. For example, she often baby-sits for people in her street.
They often argue, particularly about politics.

Checking
Spelling: Use the Mini-dictionary to check your spelling (especially adjectives).
Style: Check that the description is quite informal (e.g. with contractions) but make sure there are no very informal words or expressions.

7 A 'For and Against' Essay (page 89)

Layout

> **Introduction**
> Introduce the essay. Begin with either some **personal information** or some general **social** or **historical background** related to the topic.
> *Every year, thousands of students take important exams which can decide their future.*

> **Arguments 'for' the title**
> List one or two arguments that agree with the title and give examples if you can.
> *On the one hand, exams seem fair. The questions are the same for all students. Also, ...*

> **Arguments 'against' the title**
> Now list arguments that disagree with the title and give examples if you can.
> *On the other hand, there are some drawbacks with exams. Despite some students ...*

> **Your conclusion**
> Summarise the arguments very briefly and then give your personal opinion.
> *To sum up, exams are not the ideal way of testing students ... In my opinion, the best system would be ...*

Useful Vocabulary

Subjects: traditional subjects: *foreign language, geography, history, information technology, literature, maths, science;* alternative subjects: *cooking, do-it-yourself, driving lessons, self-defence;* after-school activities: *chess club, choir, drama club, photography club*
School holidays: *free time, school trips, summer job, work experience*
Discipline: *code of conduct, monitors, punishments, rules, vandalism, warnings*

Linking

To list ideas (addition):
Students <u>also</u> need more time to study.
<u>Furthermore</u>/<u>In addition</u>/<u>Moreover</u>, students need more time to study.
Students need more time to study, <u>too</u>.
To contrast ideas:
<u>On the one hand</u>, students are prepared for university. <u>On the other hand</u>, students are not prepared for work.
Students are prepared for university <u>but</u> they are not prepared for work.
Students are prepared for university. <u>However</u>, they are not prepared for work.
To give examples:
Exams are important – <u>for example</u>, university exams.
Exams, <u>such as</u> university exams, are important.
Conclusion
<u>To sum up</u>, exams are not the ideal way of testing.
<u>In my opinion</u>, a student's work during the term should count.

Checking

Introduction: Does this get the interest of the reader?
Layout: Have you organised paragraphs according to the plan?
Linking: Have you included linking words?
Punctuation: Check your writing for capital letters, commas and full stops.

8 A Letter of Application (page 100)

Layout

> Your address
> The date

> Name and address of the company

> **Greeting**
> *Dear Mr/Mrs/Ms ...,* (if you know their name)
> *Dear Sir/Madam,* (if you don't know their name)

> **Paragraph 1**
> Simply state your reasons for writing.
> *I am writing to you with reference to ...*
> *I am interested in applying for the job/position of ...*
> *I enclose a copy of my CV.*

> **Paragraph 2**
> Explain why you are interested in the job.
> *I would like to work for you because I am very interested in ...*
> *I would also like to learn about ...*
> *I feel that ... is extremely important.*

> **Paragraph 3**
> Give examples to show your qualities.
> *I think I am a ... person. For example, I have ...*
> *I also feel that I can ..., Last year I ..., Finally, I am familiar with ...*

> **Paragraph 4**
> Write about your qualifications and practical skills.
> *I think I would be a good ... due to my ...*
> *I am fluent in spoken and written ...*

> **Formal ending**
> *I look forward to hearing from you soon.*
> *Yours sincerely,* (when you know the person's name)
> *Yours faithfully,* (when you don't)
> *Signature* (+ print your name clearly)

Useful Vocabulary

Reasons: *get experience, learn about, find out about, interested in*
Personal qualities: *committed, hard-working, reliable, determined, enthusiastic, creative*
Experience: *voluntary work, holiday jobs, participation in activities*
Qualifications: *hold a certificate in ..., passed exams in ..., completed a course in ...*
Practical skills: *fluent in (language), driving licence, cooking, carpentry, first aid*

Linking

To give reasons:
I would like to work for you mainly <u>because</u> I am very interested in environmental and development issues, but also <u>due to</u> my interest in the problems caused by flooding.
I am familiar with problems of flood control, <u>since</u> I have lived all my life in a farm on Holland below sea level! I have a clean driving licence. I am a capable mechanic, <u>as</u> I have completed a three-year course of evening classes.

Checking

Style: Make sure you use formal words or expressions. Don't use contractions.
Grammar: Check your letter for grammar mistakes.

9 A Personal Letter (2) (page 113)

Layout

Greeting
Dear ...

Paragraph 1
Say hello, ask a few personal questions and/or make a few chatty comments.
How are you? Did you pass the exam? I hope so. The weather here is really bad at the moment. Last week, I went to ...

Paragraph 2
This is your main reason for writing. Answer questions your partner asked.
Anyway, I'm writing to ...

Paragraph 3
Talk about some of your plans for your exchange partner's visit to your country.
We'll probably visit ...

Paragraph 4
Finish the letter with an excuse to stop writing.
Well, I have to go now because ...

Say goodbye and write your name
See you soon/Write back soon/Lots of love

Useful Vocabulary

Presents: *book about Britain, box of chocolates, CD of traditional music, ornament, perfume*
Music: *classical, folk, heavy metal, jazz, rock, techno*
Clothes: *gloves, jeans, jumper, raincoat, shorts, suit, swimming costume, trainers*
Places to go: *art gallery, cinema, club, football match, gym, museum, park, party, restaurant*

Linking

To give more information:
You can go <u>wherever</u> you like.
We can go and see <u>whoever</u> we want.
You can buy <u>whatever</u> you like.
You can make a cup of tea <u>whenever</u> you like.

Checking

Layout: Have you organised your letter correctly?
Punctuation: Check your letter for full stops, capital letters and apostrophes in contractions.
Spelling: Check your spelling – use your dictionary.
Content: Have you answered the questions?

10 A Description (page 125)

Layout

Paragraph 1
Introduce the place and give a bit of background, e.g. what it is (e.g. castle/football stadium/a place of natural interest); where it is; when it was built (or set up); its size and what it looks like
Niagara Falls is without doubt one of the most impressive places I have ever been to. It was developed as a tourist resort in ...

Paragraph 2
Describe what there is to see and do in the place.
There is plenty to do in Niagara on both the American and Canadian sides of the border. The views of the falls are absolutely fantastic and as well as that, ...

Paragraph 3
Describe the surroundings and what to do there.
Around the town there are lots of places to visit. There are several theme parks in the area plus museums which show ...

Paragraph 4
Sum up why you like the place.
I think Niagara impressed me so much because of the scale of the falls themselves and the number of activities round them.

Useful Vocabulary

Opinion adjectives: *austere, beautiful, breathtaking, charming, dramatic, grand, historic, impressive, magnificent, monumental, spectacular*
Descriptive adjectives: *bare, glass, granite, huge, stone, tiny, ornamental, wooded*
Buildings: *entrance, dome, facade (front), fountain, roof, ruins, stairway, tower*
Nature: *forest, glacier, hill, lake, pond, waterfall, wood*
Expressions: *Without doubt, it is the most important ...,*
What strikes you (about it) is the ..., ... is well worth visiting,
... is surrounded by ..., ... impressed me so much because of ...

Linking

To list ideas:
It is extremely large. <u>In fact</u>, it is the biggest church in Spain.
To compare ideas:
It is very crowded in August. <u>In contrast</u>, in February there is hardly anyone ...

Checking

Style: Have you followed the paragraph plans?
Vocabulary: How many opinion or descriptive adjectives have you used? Can you add more?
Spelling: Use the Mini-dictionary to check the spelling of the words you are not sure about.